OVER THE BRIDGE

THE AUTHOR IN LATER LIFE

OVER THE BRIDGE

An Essay in Autobiography

BY

RICHARD CHURCH

WILLIAM HEINEMANN LTD
MELBOURNE :: LONDON :: TORONTO

FIRST PUBLISHED 1955
REPRINTED 1955 (twice)

PRINTED IN GREAT BRITAIN
AT THE WINDMILL PRESS
KINGSWOOD, SURREY

Contents

The frontispiece, *The Author in later life*, is reproduced from a drawing by Robert Austin, R.A.

"I have left it so that among our passions, among the human problems which we desire to master, to express, to solve, there might always remain one room devoted to the most intense self-recollection. And I truly hope that it is in that room that we shall die."

(Patrice de la Tour du Pin. From *The Correspondence of Laurent de Cayeux*.)

The Aquarium

IT WAS THE FIRST OF JANUARY, 1900: New Year's Day; New Century's Day. But that portentous fact was of no interest to two little boys walking with extreme care and anxiety across Battersea Bridge at half-past three in the afternoon.

Their concern was immediate, for the elder brother, a small fellow of eleven, with a large nose, brown eyes, and a sallow skin that gave him a Spanish cast, was carrying an aquarium.

This task so occupied him that his follower, the brother who shadowed his life, and for whom he usually felt solemnly responsible, was for the moment forgotten.

This did not disturb the junior, for he too was as anxious, and as signally concentrated, as his brother. Though only seven years old, he carried the burden of life with gravity. His nose was smaller than his brother's, and it was somewhat pinched, the nostrils white and enlarged. This made the red cheeks all the more noticeable: and it may have added to the fiery light of his eyes, which were also brown.

Rather short of breath, from excitement and not from haste, he trotted along close to his brother, from time to time putting out a worried hand and grasping the elder's coat-tail, only to be shrugged off with a muttered exclamation of "Stop it! You'll make me drop it!"

He appeared to understand this abruptness, for his brother, always sardonic even in affection, was inclined to be sharply irritable in moments of stress.

And how tense, how critical, was this particular moment! It marked a stage, a peak-point, in their lives. Both had longed, through childhood's infinity of time, for a goldfish. Their father, however, was so boyishly concerned with his own enthusiasms that he had ignored this longing. Their mother was by experience and temperament so generally apprehensive that she hesitated before committing herself, or her children, to the caring for livestock. There was already a cat in the house, and she had made this excuse for banning the buying of a gold-fish. She said that the cat would hook it out of the bowl and eat it, thus adding to the general redness and toothiness of nature, under whose menace she was convinced that her two boys were doomed to fulfil their fragile destinies.

This timid philosophy, however, had been shaken by a touch of kindness; and kindness from a humble quarter. One of the father's many colleagues in the South-West District Post Office had been prematurely pensioned after having his wits perma-nently addled by a blow on the head from the lid of a post-van. The poor man, semi-speechless and existing in a mental vacuum, fortunately possessed a sensible wife who happened to be handsome in a pre-Raphaelite way. She got a job as caretaker in the house of the American artist Abbey, in Tite Street, Chelsea, where she lived in the spacious basement with her little daughter and her now wholly innocent husband.

The boys' father still befriended this man, for he had a strong *esprit de corps* (a characteristic which will be explained later), and appeared to be personally intimate with several hundred of his fellow mail-sorters in the red-brick building behind Victoria Street, adjoining the site where the Byzantine cathedral of Westminster was at that time being built.

Regular visits were paid to the retired comrade in the com-fortable basement in Tite Street, and on occasion the two boys were taken along too, the father having a sentimental pride in his youngsters.

So it was that the craving for a goldfish became known to the wife of the stricken man. She may have spoken to her employer about it, for a message at Christmas had said that if the boys came over the river to Tite Street one afternoon, she would have a surprise for them.

That younger ' other being myself, I can now recall, with envy, the shudder of excitement with which I crossed the river that day, chattering to my silent brother, who even at that time was something of an enigma, and an oracle, to me. My attitude was not unusual, for a child's world, while being time-less and spaceless, is also closely hedged-in by fear, brevity of attention, lack of association of ideas and experience, and all the rest of the unattempted potentials of the infant conscious-ness.

My universe was still centred in my mother's fragrant person: her lap, her caress, her hair and eyes so curiously the same nut-brown colour, warm and glowing. The garments she took off —the apron, the dropped handkerchief—shone for a while with her light, and I would touch them with rapture, beside myself with love. She and these detachable attributes were like the sun and his flakes of fire. The further I got from her, the colder and darker fell my living days and nights. And the fall was rapid: so small was my own supply of vitality, the confidence of flesh and bone.

Thus my realisation of the outside world was confined to a few streets around our little semi-detached house in the marshes of Battersea, between the famous park and the old parish church that stood out on a curve in the river. I seldom ventured as far as the park or the church; they were shadowy, foreign. A vague obscurity closed about me much nearer home. I doubt if, at that age of seven years, my world was more than a quarter of a mile in radius, though I was frequently carried beyond that small area of light by my parents, the outer dim-ness being penetrated during such excursions by the all-powerful light-beams of their divine authority.

A lesser power, but wholly trustworthy, was my brother Jack, whose taciturnity I took for granted, never questioning the odd-ness that made this lad of eleven so different from both our parents. They were happy people; my father a perpetual boy He seemed to be a creature released, like a colt from a stable, and he galloped about the paddock of life with a thunder of hoofs and a flashing of nostrils, drinking the very air and intoxicating himself on it.

My mother, the fountain of Father's confidence and hilarity, was demonstrative, passionate, and subject to storms of jealousy. But her mind was cool, and her moral courage

infinite. It was she, therefore, who made the home and held
the world in place. In spite of this Atlas-burden and responsibility, she was capable of gaiety, moods that suffused her brown
eyes, parted her lips, and revealed her faintly prominent teeth,
so that she became sylvan, a woodland creature, with just
that small reservation of autumnal reminder that woodland
creatures can never wholly discard.

Just as my brother's eyes were of a darker brown than my
mother's, so what was in her nature merely a reservation, a
reminder, became in his a background of melancholy. He
appeared to have been born against it, and he remained there
all his life. It cast a slight shadow before him, so that in spite
of his *absolute* nature, his air of distinction and authority,
he appeared to be always in retreat, elusive, deprecatory.

So we set out on that New Year's Day, with our characteristic
definition, in a timeless world symbolically reflected in the wayward course with which my memory returns to it half a century
later.

My brother walked as if he were concentrating upon walking,
distrustful of his ability, or perhaps of the ground in front of
him. This made his replies to my chatter somewhat delayed
and perfunctory. But I did not mind; I was used to his temperament, and accepted it as I accepted the leaves on the trees.

My brother refused to quicken his pace, though, as I knew,
he was as eager as myself: more so, indeed, for to him the goldfish was only one factor in a large prospect; large and constructive. For, as I was to learn, his aim was to establish a *real*
aquarium, with fresh water-scape scenery of strange, sodden
greens, coralline grottoes, mosses, rondures, recesses, mournful
weeds, sandy beds, pitted with glints of mica, animated with
caddis-worms and mollusc; the silk-tinted water peopled not
with *one* goldfish, but a number ranging in size, form, colour as
various as a flight of Titania's fairies.

My brother was one who looked ahead, and liked things to
be in proportion and complete. That may be why he walked
with such grave attention to his footsteps, head bent and
deliberate of mien.

Finally, our measured procedure brought us across the river

to Chelsea, where at once we were in so foreign a land that I shrank closer to the side of my familiar Virgil, even daring to grasp his hand and cling to it, as we turned a little way along the Embankment, passing what seemed to me at that time the vast mansions whose inhabitants were beings so fabulous that my mind did not attempt to envisage them. I did not even think of them as rich, or high-born, for those categories had not yet reached me.

But I was not intimidated; merely nervous at the remoteness, the *difference* of this tall and silent district from the cosy, working-class streets of houses so far away across the river, my native land. Indeed, I felt some half-sense of recognition, as though a self beyond myself welcomed these huge doorways, these noble windows, recalling them as familiar to a way of life impossible to a Battersea-born child, but which I must have known.

I was half-conscious of this while we made our way to Tite Street, I still clinging to my brother's hand, though my fears were assuaged by this other sensation; dim enough, but before the afternoon ended, to be unforgettably brought forward to the front of my mind, and kept there for deeper cogitation when, later on, life brought some possible evidence to explain its genesis.

We were met at the area door by Mrs. Langton, the care-taker. Going down a flight of stone stairs off the street level was interesting to me, though I had made this adventure several times before. I knew what I should find: the wide spaces, the low ceilings in the great kitchen with its dresser armoured with copper pots and pans and silver-plate. I knew that I should find Mr. Langton sitting in a wooden arm-chair to the left of the vast cooking range (as big as our whole kitchen at home across the river), with a shawl over his knees. He would be staring patiently out of the window at the white-washed wall and the door to the cellars under the pavement: staring without seeing, sometimes nodding his head gravely and saying "Yes! Yes!" with an eagerness that only his patient wife could comprehend. For though she usually took no notice of these void ejaculations, there would sometimes be such an added emphasis in her husband's other-world assents that she would smile at him, and murmur soothingly, "There, duck! There now!" in tones so gentle that he would give her a fleeting but hopeful glance, then subside again into his Trappist rumination.

All this my brother and I found, as expected, on that New Century's Day. We also found Gracie, the Langtons' daughter, a year or two older than myself, and even more sedate. She was red-haired, like her father, and her temperament seemed to be conditioned by the fate that had overtaken him, for she had about her an air of the Sleeping Princess, an almost inhumanly quiet simplicity, that made her an apt companion to her father. Mrs. Langton seemed to understand her also, and to be content to live with, and minister to, a husband and daughter dedicated to silence, or near-silence, and comparative inanition.

Maybe Mrs. Langton was glad, from time to time, to escape from this cloistral company, and to release a flood of pent-up conversation, rich with endearments, that bewildered my brother and me, while warming us to her as a kind soul who made the outside world almost as comprehensible, and as trustworthy, as our own home.

We greeted her shyly, and Mr. Langton and Gracie still more shyly. We were not afraid of them. We were not even fully conscious that they were 'different'. We merely took them at face value; and it was a blank face. Mr. Langton gave us his usual swift glance that just failed to carry a smile of recognition. Then he returned to that interior retreat which he had inhabited since his accident. What kind of man he had been before that sudden climacteric, we were too young to ask. It was in the past; and when one is seven years old, or even eleven, the past is of no account, unless it be lighted by a myth, and even then its scenery is fitful and murky. We were not concerned to speculate about the strangeness of a man's whole nature being obliterated by a single blow on the head, and his small daughter too being removed from normal social conduct by the same event.

Gracie smiled at us, and showed us the new doll which had been her Christmas present from Mr. Abbey, the artist upstairs

who was so different from people of our kind that he needed
this great house to live in alone. We did not ask how he
managed to do so; how he paid for it all, and the servants that
looked after it and waited on him during his infrequent visits
there. For we never saw him. He remained a legend, a god-
like figure, spoken of as something absolute, unaccountable.
He must have been kind, and he must have been rich. We
could appreciate and gauge the former attribute. The latter
was still outside our field of consciousness, for in our home
money was not discussed, it was merely saved, or apportioned
out, there being no question of *making* money, of increasing by
even one penny the salary of something under £150 earned by
our father as a minor Civil Servant, or the £100 a year paid to
our harassed, overworked but happy mother as a teacher in
one of the London Board Schools, in the Battersea Park Road,
rougher even than the one we attended in a side-street called
Surrey Lane.

So we admired Gracie's doll, and I did not disguise my un-
boyish interest in its eyes that opened and closed with a bland
innocence, and a loud click. Then we were each given a piece
of iced cake, a luxury never known at home, this being preface
to an invitation to be 'taken upstairs' to see the studio and
drawing-room.

I followed my brother, who followed Mrs. Langton, Gracie
being left contentedly to play with her doll and to keep
company with her father, the one with orbs that could ogle
in a mechanical way, the other with eyes comparatively
expressionless.

We walked along the basement passage, past several closed
doors, and one that stood open upon a boiler-room where I
could see a faint glow round the door of the furnace. The oilcloth, with a plain blue border (so different from the Greek key-
pattern of the stair-covering at home), was continued up the
flight of dark stairs which led to a landing, facing a door
covered in green baize.

Mrs. Langton pushed open this door, and ushered us on
under her outstretched arm. We entered another world, like
Gulliver entering the land of the giants. A vast hall soared

above us, with a correspondingly vast front door at the end of
it. I drew in my breath sharply. I must have given a gasp that
Mrs. Langton misconstrued as fear, for she bent down and
kissed me, and took me by the hand, leaving my silent brother
to follow us.

She approached a tall, wide door on the left, opened it by
turning first the key and then the china knob, and led us into
the studio.

Here was something still more gargantuan. I stopped, and
Mrs. Langton was forced to stop with me, so forceful was my
reaction. Jack trod on my heel, and impatiently pushed me in
the back. But I did not move. I stared. I stared up, into the
vault, a height such as I had never seen before. I stared at the
huge north-light, that sloped over part of the vaulting and then
came down straight almost to floor level. A black blind was
drawn *up* from the floor to about the height of my head, but a
tear in it revealed the glass behind.

The sun shone on a naked tree outside, with a golden light
that struck back into the studio; but it did not warm the great
space, or fill the emptiness. Yet I was neither chilled nor
repelled by this austerity. Looking up into the shadowy height,
I felt that I was *returning* to something just right, a place where
I could breathe and move without restraint.

"Oh!" I cried, in a hollow, round voice; and I flung up my
arm in a gesture of magnificence that made Mrs. Langton study
me with surprise and amusement. She gave me a playful hug.

"What? You like it?" she said. "This bare old place; dusty,
and cold as charity?"

I didn't know what she meant by 'cold as charity', but I
could see the dust, a pallid mantle on the tops of stacks of
picture-frames turned to the wall; on a huge easel on four
wheels; on odd chairs and stools; on a piano loaded with piles
of papers, books, portfolios; on a long sofa at the other end of
the studio, raised on a dais. The only object free from this
indoor frost was a life-size lay-figure in a velvet robe, with a
cape of brown paper pinned round the shoulders.

Mrs. Langton saw me studying this.

"Sharp eyes! Sharp eyes!" she said, and squeezed my small

body again. "They don't miss much, I'll lay! But I have to keep her clean. It wouldn't seem right!"

I knew what she meant, for I lived in a home where scrubbing and dusting were a daily routine in which my brother and I had to play our parts. We never questioned these duties, any more than we questioned the round of meal-times, or the ritual of going to bed.

"Well, that's where he does his painting," said Mrs. Langton. "Shabby old barn: but he won't have anything touched."

It wasn't shabby to my eyes; and I had never seen a barn, so I could not compare it. I saw a noble chamber that was just right; much more acceptable and liveable-in than the cosy little rooms at home, over-crowded with furniture, and ferns.

No doubt in recalling those distant scenes I am translating them into the language and concepts of adult life; but the only original I have to work on is what the child saw, and felt. One of the most vivid of these tributaries is that unaccountable moment of recognition, that sense of returning to a place whose *dimensions* were more familiar, more fitting, than those of my home; and that home one where all was secure in confidence and unrestrained love. "You'll catch your death, and Mother won't thank me for that," said Mrs. Langton, shepherding us back to the hall, and leading the way to the drawing-room.

Here again I was joyously puzzled by the sense of space, though I missed the great height of the studio, and the soaring window whose lifted lights had carried me up to that moment of something near delirium, making me want to sing, or burst into tears, though I had been too timid to do either.

This great room slumbered in semi-darkness, for venetian blinds were drawn down, with slats half-closed, so that we saw shapes of sheeted furniture, striped with shadow. My memory of this is equally vague, but I recall some statuary, and a carved fireplace flanked by two vases taller than myself. These great pots were understandably recognised, for in our parlour at home we had two vases, on a smaller scale, that stood exactly thus, one on each side of the fireplace, like two of the oil-jars in the story of Ali Baba. I used to peer into these, imagining strange contents conjured by the faint musty smell that hovered

B

over those circular mouths, as a whiff of smoke hangs over a sleeping volcano.

We did not remain long, staring at this twilight splendour under a shroud. Taking Mrs. Langton's "Well now!" as a signal, we followed her down to the basement, where we ceremoniously said good-bye to Mr. Langton and Gracie (rather a one-sided ritual) and were led by our hostess to the area door. On a shelf beside it, where tradesmen left their goods, stood the surprise which had been promised us; the aquarium.

What puzzles me now is that instantly we knew what it was; for we had never seen goldfish in anything but small glass bowls, in the window of a shop at a cross-roads called The Latchmere, a sinister junction that always filled me with dread, perhaps because one of the radiations from it led past a candle factory, where Mr. Price made his world-famous night-lights. The ugly building with its ranks of inhuman windows, and the rancid smell that sank from them over the pavements, so that they appeared to be permanently greasy and cold, like dirty plates after a dinner of mutton, must have been offensive to my virgin eyes and nostrils. I shuddered whenever I approached The Latchmere and sniffed that dull, rank odour.

We stood spellbound by the area door. Neither of us dared believe in our hope, for gifts from the outside world seldom came our way. Indeed, nothing of much account came our way from beyond the four walls of home. We were a close community of four, on guard against some invisible peril, so that all our family happiness (and it was a constant feast) had something of the Syracusan banquet at which Damocles sat beneath a naked sword suspended by a single horsehair.

Somebody had to make a move, however. It was my brother who broke the spell. His taciturnity for once gave way under pressure of this long-nurtured passion. His dark, full eyes flashed, the long lashes flickered, and he spoke.

"It's an aquarium," he whispered. And he repeated it; teaching me something.

"Is it any use to you?" asked Mrs. Langton. Her question had the intended rhetorical effect, for my brother put on his cap, and I dragged on my tasselled tam-o'-shanter, while Mrs.

Langton opened the door. "Now go steady," she said, and gave me a final hug as I followed my brother, who had seized the aquarium in his bare hands, and was groping his way up the area steps, stubbing his toes on the risers because his attention was wholly concentrated upon the precious burden, the almost holy burden.

Once he stumbled and might have fallen backwards to disaster, but was saved by his own powerful infatuation, which gave him a sixth sense, and a superhuman authority over the laws of nature, especially that of gravity.

I was also there to steady him from beneath. Thus, an uneasy tandem, we reached street level, and did not even turn to wave good-bye to Mrs. Langton, who had cried out in alarm at the near-disaster on the steps. We did not realise that we had failed to thank her, an omission that haunted us later when we got home, and Mother inquired, "And what did Mrs. Langton say when you thanked her?" It was always her habit to want to know what people said, and to be given verbatim the whole of a conversation in which she had not taken part because of her absence from that particular drama.

Now began the balanced pursuit of the journey home. have described how we ordered it, with Jack leading the way, like a priest of one of the more austere brotherhoods carrying the Host, or a casket of reliquary bones; I, a nervous acolyte, grasping his coat-tails.

Tite Street and Chelsea Embankment were empty, and the day was dying under a shroud of frost. Through this fawn-grey world we made our way, moving with spasmodic slowness, the spasms due to bursts of eager excitement, our desire to get home safely with the aquarium, tempered by fear of dropping it.

At the back of my mind lurked a greater fear. I knew that, once across the bridge, we were likely to encounter school-fellows, bands of marauding freebooters of the Battersea gutters, ripe for any action, so long as it was destructive. I knew that the sight of a large glass aquarium in the arms of a boy somewhat more warmly dressed than themselves would rouse their hunting gusto.

For a moment, however, I was sufficiently concerned with

the immediate cares. I saw the signs of strain on my brother's face. His huge nose was blue, his eyes even more cavernous than usual. He had forgotten, in his excitement, to put on his gloves before leaving, and now was unable to do so, the idea of committing the aquarium to my hands, even for a moment, being quite unrealistic.

Within five minutes of our setting out, his hands were lifeless with cold. I watched them, my attention rigid with sympathy. For even at eleven years of age my brother was fastidious about his hands; kept them clean, as though they were objects of *vertu* exterior to his person. This odd habit, as I discovered later, was an unconscious precursor of other remarkable characteristics soon to develop. Already, however, not only my attention but that of many adults had been drawn to the exquisite shapeliness of my brother's hands; their sensitive veins, their slimness, the proportion of the long fingers, the almond-shaped nails which our mother proudly trimmed once a fortnight and smoothed round with pumice-stone. I too had to submit to this minor torture, which caused us both to set our teeth, in order to prevent ourselves from dribbling, as a sort of reflex action.

To see Jack's hands clasping the cold metal and glass, and growing stiff in nervous tension and clay-like under the insidious caress of the falling night-frost, filled me with foreboding. I could have shed a few tears; but I dared not. It was as much as I could do to keep up with his wolf-like flight. For he too was apprehensive of a thousand dangers. The air was full of swords, and treachery waited at every street corner. I watched those hands, studied the signs of numbness, the dead-white of the knuckles, the earthy pallor of the finger-nails as the blood fled from the combined attack of frost without and morbid concentration within.

So intent were we both that neither remarked on the splendour in which that first day of a new century was closing. Safely reaching Battersea Bridge, we waited for a horse-bus to clatter past, the sound of the hooves dropping a half-tone as they struck hollow on the bridge. Then we crossed to the up-river pavement; an instinctive move, because that was also the home-side. Thus, over the parapet, which was just about at my eye-level, we saw the river as a long stream of troubled fire. The tide must have been up and on the turn, for the waters were weltering like a den of snakes, breaking and scattering the reflection of the sunset, in a contusion of angry browns, reds and purples, shot with sparks and needles of white-hot steel.

Both colours and sounds affected me and I remember still how I struggled with the conflict of emotions while we crossed the bridge: fear for the worshipped brother, terror of the almost certain ambush that would bring destruction to our treasure, rapture before the glory of sky and water; and behind all these sharp and immediate sensations a remote, racial dread at the fall of the winter day.

So we crossed the bridge; and at every passing of a horse-bus, or a brewers' dray, the pavement trembled, the aquarium trembled, and we trembled.

After that, all went well, a fortunate diversion saving us from the attention of the Battersea gangs. My brother thought it safer to keep to the main road, where there was likely to be more adult life, and even a policeman or two on their beat. We had to turn right at the 'Rising Sun', a public-house standing at the corner of Surrey Lane, near two old country cottages set amid trees in gardens large enough to give a rustic touch to this stony suburb.

We were now in our home country, or at least on its outskirts, and my small-radius instincts came to life again: with that life, alas, the certainty of trouble ahead. For our local streets, thickly populated by lower middle class, artisan, and labouring folk, were prolific in children who ignored these three social barriers, and swarmed together like wild bees, buzzing about the neighbourhood in search of the honey of adventure. And by a miracle of ingenuity and ruthlessness, they found it.

The social mixture, the range and variety of talent and background were remarkable. Political theorists, especially Left-wing theorists, are apt to write of the great class-groups as though they are homogeneous; but in reality they are subject to a constant, osmotic infiltration, each into the other, under the leakage of chance, and the pressure or degeneration of individual character. I recall that in our little side-street, shopless and wholly residential, consisting perhaps of not more than fifty houses, each a family home, there were Irish, Scottish, Cockney, provincial stocks; some poor, rough and brutal, others comfortable, scrupulous in religious and social observance. Sometimes this disparity existed between adjoining households; usually, birds of a feather flocked together street by street, or even street-ends. Our own street, for example, consisted mainly of the families of skilled artisans, minor Civil Servants, white-collar workers of the more servile kind, wage-slaves because of their low mental equipment and submissive temperaments: salt of the earth; and like grains of salt, not especially distinguishable from each other, except in the intimacy and temporary safety of their own homes.

Almost opposite us lived an Aberdeen family named Ritchie, consisting, like us, of the parents and two sons, half a generation senior to us. The father was a lift-maker. So was his elder son, but this young man's spare-time occupation was the making of violins, a hobby which has since brought him a unique and particular fame in the technical room of the house of music.

A few doors from the Ritchies lived a bluff, square-bearded old man who came to our house whenever a window-pane needed to be replaced. His name was Froude, and one day when I was watching, entranced by the scratch of the diamond glass-cutter, he told me that he came from Devonshire, and had not done too well by the migration to London, for his home had been a grand old hall by the River Dart, "smaller and swifter than Father Thames" he said. And his brother was a historian, and had made himself widely known. This name stuck in my magpie memory, unassociated until many years later.

Still on that same side of the street, which to me at seven years of age was the beginning of the foreign world, and therefore slightly suspect, lived an ex-soldier, his wife and daughter. How he got a living I am not sure, but I believe that he was some sort of door-keeper, or commissionaire. He was a fine figure of a man, bolt upright, and he marched off every morning at the same time as we were running to school. His front door slammed as he jerked it, then came the clang of the iron gate by the palings, and left-right, left-right, he was up the street and gone, looking neither to right nor left. His name was Macdonald, and his brother General Hector Macdonald was a current hero during these days of the Boer War. This general's square face figured on the little celluloid portrait buttons which we collected and pinned on our coats or jerseys: of General Roberts, Buller, White, or Baden-Powell somewhat different because he wore a strange hat since become familiar in the Boy Scout gear.

Here, then, were two examples of the upward and downward interplay between the social and functional classes; confusing to the theorists, and those politicians who are anxious to standardise peoples, the better to control them, and ride on top.

My brother and I, meanwhile, have been left fugitive through the dusk of the back streets of Battersea, still not out of danger. We were made aware of this as we passed the end of the lane where our school stood, a three-storey building with cold, expressionless windows, and a faintly Germanic character that must have been a defiltration, down through the whole of English society, from the good intention of the Prince Consort, that apostle of efficient administration.

A boy hailed us; a big boy whom I did not know. My brother tried to quicken his steps, but by this time he was near exhaustion. The aquarium had become a monster. I could see Jack's arms trembling, and I could feel how the pain had made him set his lips more grimly than usual.

Again the boy hailed us, his voice brawny and powerful with that general-public indifference which in the end is more penetrating than true curiosity. "What-yer got there?" he yelled. The shadows deepened, and the menace gathered. We again tried to hurry, and I struggled to come alongside my brother, to bring a flanking protection to the aquarium.

Our furtiveness was noticed, however. It was obvious that we had something to hide, and therefore it must be valuable. This Francis Drake of the back streets thereupon gave a brain-piercing whistle, to summon other buccaneers, who must have been lurking in Surrey Lane and the streets that turned off at regular intervals, each the length of two houses and two back-yards.

In twos and threes they gathered, with an eleventh-hour reluctance more dreadful than the most eager blood-lust. They came from yards and doorways where they had dispersed, about to go under cover for the night. Darkness had not com-pletely come down over the streets, their 'steep Atlantick', and there was enough twilight for a last adventure. My brother and I, vaguely known to them, never wholly of their brotherhood, were fair game. And at that moment, with our precious cargo exposed in such brittleness, we might have been likened to a fat Spanish galleon sneaking up the Trade Winds, heavy with ingots.

The familiar sinking feeling in my stomach assailed me. Nausea soured my mouth and I wanted to be sick; but an antidote of dull anger kept me going. Jack was now gliding along under the power of a self-hypnosis, the aquarium still safe, still borne aloft with religious awe.

Cries of excitement approached, and the pursuers began to run after us.

We had only two more streets to pass before reaching our own; and our home lay half-way along that. Not many yards, but we were handicapped by terror, and for all the progress we appeared to make, we might have been running backwards, or working a treadmill.

"Come on!" breathed my brother, without a glance to right or left. "Take no notice!"

It was a command, not advice. I braced myself, and released my hold of his coat, thus intending to throw myself to the wolves, in the hope of giving him a momentary advantage.

This act of heroism, however, came to nothing, for as we passed the top of the first of the two remaining streets, the hunted and the pursuers were divided by another drama. I saw my brother look swiftly down the street at a second gang of urchins. It was following a navvy, a hatless figure with features flaming and eyes distorted by drink and fear. He was running, and gasping as he ran. One trouser-leg was gartered below the knee, the other had burst the garter, and this gave his flight a clumsy lopsided character that added to the effect of panic.

He turned the corner as we reached it, almost knocking us down. Jack fortunately was a yard ahead, and I spurted to avoid the crash. I heard the man whimpering for breath; and I smelled sweat and beer. I heard too the chorus of jeers and yells from the juvenile furies that followed. But between him and them was the real cause of his flight. It was a woman, ragged and shameful, her hair torn down, her blouse gaping, and one eye laid open and bleeding on her cheek. She was mad with fury and screaming with pain, plunging blindly to right and left, but striving by sheer power of rage to follow her man who had thus ill-treated her. The mob was at her skirts, urging her on, making an Elizabethan sport of this horror.

It was a lucky intervention. Our own pursuers at once joined this larger hunt, and in a moment we were alone, with the uproar dying away along Surrey Lane, in the direction from which we had fled. We did not pause or look back. I had seen everything in that woman's face: the eyeball hanging on her cheek, and the blood flowing; the degradation of her cries as she cursed her man, and at the same time appealed to him. Such a complication of extremes was beyond my understanding. The worry of it, and the horror at the sight of blood coming after the mixed excitements which had stormed round me so extravagantly since Jack and I left home after the midday meal, now sent me running ahead, crying with hysteria. Jack followed, still master of himself, and still responsible for me. But he was concerned, at the same time, to bring the treasure home safely, and he hardly altered his pace. Our mother, who had grown anxious as darkness began to fall, was at the gate, and I collapsed, shouting incoherently, into her arms, and was instantly sick over the front step.

CHAPTER TWO

Delayed Reaction

IN THE CLOSED WORLD OF HOME, I quickly recovered, for no
horrors were entertained there for long. I took this assurance
for granted. Now I look back, I see how miraculous was the
achievement of my parents, who created it. The most static
institution human society has ever known must surely be the
lower-middle-class household, consisting of a small family, at
the slow end of the Victorian era in England. Below that level,
the economy, promiscuity and often dire poverty made a close,
safe corporation impossible. Above that level, parents were,
usually, kept somewhat more at arm's-length from their children
by the intervention of a servant, or servants, and some degree of
intellectual and cultural preoccupation in their own lives.

But that relatively small group, the lower middle class, a
purgation group between the vast and still increasing masses,
and the true middle class of professional administrative, employ-
ing folk, is one which has never been fully explored. A few
novelists, Gissing, Wells, Bennett, Swinnerton, have drawn the
plush curtain aside, but even these masters of fiction have
tended to over-dramatise that odd, quiet, mezzanine floor of
the house of man.

I see it, in retrospect, as a phase, a pocket of civilisation
utterly quiet and self-sufficient. But I speak out of the limited
knowledge characteristic in a child of that little world. Latter-
day publicists, the economists, the politicians, proclaim that it
is a world which has disappeared; those, that is, who have
noticed its existence. And they gloat over the fact, because to
them it is a dark, obstinate hedgehog in the human menagerie.
They say that with their Trade Unions, their Adult Education
Movements, their reformed school methods and academic

18

avenues, they have smoked out this unco-operative anti-social group.

But I distrust generalisations, and I will return to the particular, that small citadel once the solid core of the universe, but now vanished with all that it represented; if indeed it represented anything but its own odd, isolated self. Sometimes, in a different world, the world of today, I am tempted to recall that household of my childhood, and to see it again in a modern *ménage* here and there, in the suburbs, and in provincial towns, where, after giving a public lecture, or a reading to a literary society, I make a contact (now as a foreigner, or a Rip Van Winkle) with some individual in the audience, or an officer of the organisation, and am invited 'home'. In recognising that home, I am tempted to wonder if two world wars, the decay of Christianity as a moulder of society, the inquisitive penetration of radio and television into domestic privacy, and all the mechanical revolutions produced by applied science have yet dislodged the lower middle class, the human hedgehogs, and filled in their holes.

Neither Jack nor I had a coherent story to tell our mother, and she, alarmed by my behaviour on the threshold, asked no questions. I was carried in, washed, and put to bed, with a hot flat-iron wrapped in a piece of blanket at my feet. A cup of sweet tea reduced my hysteria; and the familiar comfort of bed, the touch and mere proximity of Mother, her hand on my forehead, her voice a golden command, gradually closed the abyss.

She left me, having turned down the fish-tail flame of gaslight to a tiny spearhead. The bedroom was at the back of the house, overlooking the yard and out-houses. I saw a sickle-moon, banana-coloured in the frosty night; but it added to the faint glow within the room, so that I need fear no more.

I lay there at peace, mouse-like in my snugness. I could not sleep, however, for I heard Jack and Mother talking in the kitchen below. I was quite happy; everything forgotten. The moon was kind, shining through my own window, on one of whose panes I had only recently scratched a letter 'D' under

Mr. Froude's supervision, with his glass-cutter. The bed was our bed, with the knitted square black-and-red quilt made by Mother, and the sheet turned down over it when she ran her fingers through my hair and leaned over me so that I smelled the deep comfort of her. My brother's pillow, with his flannel night-shirt folded on it, waited beside me, reassuring.

Yet suddenly I began to cry again. I cried silently at first, acting a part because I was left out of the low, murmuring conversation downstairs. But this was ineffectual. I sat up, and saw the sinking moon now blood-red. I lost all restraint, and knew the menace was upon me. I called, but not loud enough. I stopped crying, to listen. The voices were far away. Something lay between them and me; waiting. I could not see it: but that made it only the more terrible. I did not see the poor woman who ran bleeding and screaming through the street, or the man with face distorted by fear of what he had done. Indeed I saw nothing but the dim furniture in the room, the bead of gaslight reflected in the further brass knob of the bedstead, the crescent of moon falling back into the smoky night, jagged and blood-red.

Then the voices downstairs stopped, and I was utterly alone. The nothingness which had made me begin to cry took on a shape, and I saw it as a misgiving, a betrayal, a form, but not material. I was also conscious that I was *using* it as a means toward some purpose that made me feel guilty, a cheat. But I *had* to be comforted. I could not bear this burden alone. And I was in pain too, a familiar pain that seized me from time to time, gripping me with tongs in the small of the back, and twisting the tongs until they drew all my stomach into a knot of writhing agony.

I almost welcomed this visitation that night, for here was something recognisable, a part of my regular life to which I was accustomed, could even be proud of, since it never failed to make me the centre of attention and sympathy. I seized on it now with gratitude, and called louder, with an edge of urgency in the cry.

I heard the kitchen door open, then an exclamation; the stairs creaked, the door opened, and I was lost in my mother,

her arms round me, her voice dangerous with emotion, murmuring with lips touching my ear, my eyes, my cheeks, "What
is it: what is it then? Tell me, tell me now."

But I could not tell her: my mind was confused in this
bewilderment of horrors, these primeval threats. I could only
cling to her, moaning, twining my fingers in her soft hair and
rapidly making little curls of one strand, then another, and
whispering the name "Nancy! Nancy!" which I had invented
for her, and which she had accepted as but another sign of my
oddity. I too, for I was already an observer of myself, and
marvelled at these unaccountable manifestations.

I could not tell her of the hideous street scene because it had
already sunk through my conscious mind, into depths from
which it has only now emerged, more than half a century
later. Where has the image lain all that time, under the
accumulating husks of later experiences, through boyhood,
youth, the long years of marriage, parenthood, professional life,
combat with circumstance and fate? What has kept it intact,
as firm as a beaker found in an Egyptian tomb, or a finger-ring
in a Saxon grave, with only the jewel blind? So too is this
image of that moment in the Battersea side-street faintly
dimmed as it comes up out of my buried self; but its form is
perfect still, with colours, sounds, gestures almost as vivid as
they were during that fugitive second on New Year's Day, 1900.
If that image has thus survived through all the physical renova-
tion that has changed, again and again, every material cell in
my body and brain, might it not have existed before its immediate apparition in that dreadful moment: and may it not
survive when the tired machinery of my life shall have come to
a standstill?

The bouts of pain were always accompanied by vomiting, a
process which made me feel degraded and outcast. I was sick
now, and comforted only by my mother's nearness and help.
Shivering after this bout, and shaken by the assault of the
friendly old enemy in my swollen stomach, I clung to Mother
and would not let her go. But Jack was hovering behind her,
dour and anxious, and he was despatched to heat up another
flat-iron, and to bring the bottle of eau-de-Cologne from the

dressing-table in the parental bedroom at the front of the house.

Awaiting these aids, Mother sat on the bed and talked to me, while she tried to conjure the pain away by massage. Jack had turned up the gaslight, so I could see Mother's head silhouetted against the triangular yellow flame, her face in soft shadow, her hair a halo round it. Her gold-rimmed spectacles gleamed in front of her eyes, half-veiling them. I saw the moisture on her lips, which moved in sympathy as her hands communicated with the pain in her child's body.

Such a scene, such an almost sensual relationship, is incredible, and will probably be indecent to latter-day parents and children. It belongs rather to the Middle Ages, the centuries of superstition. It also serves to show how different are the family relationships, how much closer and fiercer the intimacies, in the lower-middle-class homes, from those in the classes above, where servants, boarding schools, wider intellectual interests, came between parents and children, to make their affections more formal and restrained.

Social critics, especially the theorists basing their science on economics and politics, tend to overlook the result of the close, hugger-mugger home atmosphere in the child-life of the great masses. It is that which makes them over-emotional, unadventurous, matriarch-ridden. It makes them gullible too, thin-skinned and hostile, yet at the same time almost embarrassingly kind.

When a boy from such a home meets a public-school boy, or when as a man he meets that antagonist further case-hardened by the university, he draws in his horns like a snail. He is intimidated by the hardness, the arrogance of manner, the accent of superiority in the man's voice; the ease, the knowledge with which he commands the situation. The difference is in the age at which the emotional weaning takes place. With the English middle-class child it is usually too soon, so that his sensibility is permanently blunted by the shock. With the child from the small home, the weaning comes too late, or never. But I am writing of things as they were half a century ago. The structure of the whole of English society has been broken down since then, into new shapes and oddities. But I believe that relics of the past survive, like pockets of snow during a general thaw; and they can cause many an ideologist to lose his footing.

With another hot flat-iron at my back, and my soiled and sweaty face freshed with eau-de-Cologne, I settled down into the bed, the horror exorcised. Mother lingered, and I drowsed, lulled by the hypnotising effect of the pain as it receded. Mother was gone. No, she was still there, for her hand drew the bed-clothes up as I stirred. Then I heard the front door slam, and Jack talking with Father, who had just come home from work. Jack must have told him that I was having one of my bouts, for he came upstairs and into the bedroom. Out of my pretended sleep, I could see him. He put his arm round Mother, kissed her, then came to the bedside and peered at me. But I kept my eyes closed.

"He's all right," he said in a hearty whisper, and embraced Mother again, jockeying her out of the room, and turning the gas down as he passed the bracket.

A few minutes later Jack crept in.

"Silly!" he said. "That man was only drunk." I found the explanation satisfying, and fell asleep, safely home at last.

Hours later, in another lifetime, Jack came up to bed, and I woke with the pain gone, and only a numbness in my back and stomach, as though I were weighted inside with stones.

"Dad's seen the aquarium," he said, "and has promised us a bag of silver sand. He knows a man in the office who goes rowing on the river every Sunday, and will bring us some water-weeds."

He undressed by the dim light, under orders, no doubt, not to disturb me: but, as always, his mind was active, and here was one of those rare occasions when he could no longer contain himself within his habit of taciturnity. At such times his slow but passionate enthusiasm, that refused to be defeated by the worst odds, drew me to him like a needle to a magnet. I sat up and watched him struggling into his biscuit-coloured flannel night-shirt, his head coming through like that of an eagle, the great beak gleaming in the gaslight under his silky hair. He might have been a hundred years old, rather than eleven, so

serious, so responsible was he, planning ahead, nothing forgotten or neglected.

I listened, a silent lieutenant, proud and adoring. But I was
also detached, and half-ashamed of the fact that I was wonder-
ing how he could be so completely given up to these intense
preoccupations with things: the aquarium, or the building of
an engine, or the making of a sailing boat. I thought him a
magician: but I did not want to imitate him. I was not patient
enough to use my hands as he used his; there was always some
further impulse disturbing me, wasting the hours of the day and
peopling the night with a sense of purposes and frustrations.

"We can set it up in the bay window in the kitchen, and the
light will shine on it from three sides," he whispered. He told
me how he had read in *The Boys' Own Paper* of a device for
keeping the water agitated with bubbles of air so that it should
not grow stale and stifle the fish. He intended to 'save up' to
buy glass tubing and miniature rubber hose, to make this
apparatus. He was always 'saving up' for some long-term
project, denying himself the normal boyhood day-to-day
pleasures.

I listened entranced, but totally uninterested in the technical
details. It was his intense concentration that held me, a willing,
indeed eager, little rabbit. This response to the spoken word
became a habit of which I have never been able to rid myself.
When I ask the way in a strange place, the person addressed
no sooner begins to tell me than the timbre of his or her voice,
the gesture accompanying it, the character sounding through
it, hold me spellbound, completely unreceptive of the needed
information. I often see, in the eye of the stranger, a quizzical
look, which suggests that I am suspected of being mentally
deficient. It is probably a right suspicion, for a person who
puts the cart before the horse cannot be quite sane.

"Were your hands *very* cold?" I asked, at the end of this
discourse from the neighbouring pillow.

"What d'you mean?" he said, angry at my imbecility; and
he ordered me to go to sleep. It may be that my reactions
of this kind, so irrelevant to any conversation in hand, yet
with a remote sense of earlier problems and their consequences,

must have been in my brother's mind when he described me to Mother as "an old-fashioned boy"; a phrase suggesting that my peculiarity was perhaps an unconscious imitation of his example.

CHAPTER THREE

Some Years Earlier

NEITHER MY BROTHER NOR I was born in this cosy little house which my parents were struggling so tenaciously to buy, with the aid of the Temperance Permanent Building Society. In those wombful years of our arrival, our parents had been living in flats (or rooms in other people's houses) in one or other of the quiet roads near the bridge end and the gates of Battersea Park. That park, still to me a place of forbidding jungle, vast forests, terrifying stretches of veldt, might well be saluted by me as 'my most kindly nurse', for it was there that I first became aware of a living and changing world, something other than bricks, slates, mortar, chimney-pots and kerbstones. The early gropings of consciousness have little interest to anyone other than the person recalling them. Back they go, more and more intermittent as they recede into the dawn twilight of babyhood. I can see, for example, a four-sided cot in which I lay against a wall, sideways-on to the double bed of my parents: a brown picture above me, of a scantily-clad man under a tree, pushing a swing to which clung a scantily-clad maiden wreathed in flowers. I can see myself disturbed from sleep, surprised by a light in the room, and voices of visitors, and of my own voice loudly demanding, "Please lift me out of my cot," a request coming so surprisingly from an apparently sleeping innocent that it provoked a burst of muffled laughter from the several ladies who had retreated there at Mother's invitation.

I can also recall odd moments, scenes, moods, quite dissociated, incidental to visits to the park in a wicker mail-cart pushed by Mother. I hear the iron-shod wheels grating on the grit of the suburban roads and the gravel paths in the park.

26

I smell the grass, the green leaves, the damp earth, and am again intoxicated, a little animal recognising the sources of its own life, with eager nostrils and darting eyes. I remember the mail-cart being halted, and Mother lifting me down and settling herself on a seat under a gigantic tree-trunk, to bring out her crochet, and jerk away at it with those long, work-worn fingers so exactly like those of my brother Jack, but whiter, and with blue veins running up the backs of the hands in a pronunciation of delicacy.

We were never so much alone together as on those occasional expeditions to the park; not even during the wonderful Sunday morning hour when I crept into bed beside her, to fondle her there, to murmur to her in a kind of Garden of Eden bliss, and to feel her gentle response so acutely that I could hardly bear the joyous pain of it, and had to turn away. For on these occasions Father was lying on the other side of her, and probably Jack would be there too, all four of us squeezed into the great six-foot bed, indulgent and relaxed at the beginning of the Day of Rest.

Mother and I, alone in the park, gave ourselves up to ourselves, in a world of leaves, and dusty sparrows twittering and pecking round us, and pigeons startling us with clap and whirring of wings.

She sat, with medallions of sun-gold on her figure, arrows of foliage-filtered light flashing on her glasses, the love-brown eyes behind the lenses observing me from time to time, protective, the deep instinct latent in them, watchful of danger.

I, assured of all this, and aglow with it, played near the seat, squatting behind it on the border of the loose soil of the horse-riding track, lost in my pleasure at being able to scoop up this element of earth in my hands, and to let it trickle away, grain by grain, here and there an atom of it sparkling, so that I crowed with delight and crooked my fingers like a miser round the treasure.

Repeated visits to the park piled experience upon experience, adding to my wisdom, making me more resourceful in exploiting the wonders. I would pluck leaves from bushes, and the branches of trees so wide and laden that they reached to the

ground. I would read those leaves like a book, seeing hiero-
glyphics where my finger-nails had bruised the surface into
darker green lines and shapes: wordless words in chlorophyll.
I hoarded twigs and small sticks, pebbles and feathers, intuition
telling me that this was to some purpose of lasting importance;
so necessary, so significant, that I was worried and feverish
with excitement, and prone to another sudden bout of the pain
that brought me up short, as though old Satan were laughing
at my foolish intensity, my blind faith that these moments of
recognition, of mental groping, must mean something that one
day I should be able to piece together, and make myself master
of.

One afternoon in early spring, Mother and I trundled along
to our favourite seat, to find that the horse-track had been
refreshed with a layer of peat. It smelled of leather, and it
looked russet-warm in the light of the sun. I was beside myself
with pleasure. I chattered and sang, and filled my bucket with
peat, only to find it obstinate stuff, so dry and elastic that it
sprang out of the bucket, and rustled through my fingers. Sadly
defeated, I climbed on to the seat beside Mother, and glowered
so angrily at the world that two ladies, wheeling bicycles which
they had been riding round the park, handed the machines to
a groom, and stopped to inquire about my over-adult mood.
Mother answered them shyly, looking them up and down with
some severity, for they were wearing bloomers. I, too, at the
age of four or five, was shocked; but not on moral grounds. I
was merely puzzled, that grown-ups could have separate legs
like men, yet retain piled-up hair, veils, and sweet voices.

I remember being attracted by those two voices, for they
were so much louder and more distinctive than the voice of
my mother, or those of any other of the few women who came
to our house: aunts, or wives of my father's Post Office
colleagues. Stooping to look into my face, the two ladies spoke
so that each word had a clear beginning and end. This I
instantly noticed, though the ladies' faces were dimmed by
veils that covered their straw hats and were tied under their
chins.

"How happy you must be," said one of them, as they moved

off after wishing Mother and me good afternoon. I was impressed by the gravity and courtesy of this departure; but I could see from the heightened colour on Mother's thin cheeks, and the fire in her eyes, that she took this last remark as an impertinence. We watched them walk away under the plane trees, until an empty landau overtook them, and stopped for them to get into it, another groom jumping down from beside the coachman, to put a rug over their pseudo-masculine legs.

"Nice ones to say that to one of us!" said Mother, thinking aloud rather than addressing me. I failed to understand, though her words lodged in my memory because my mind was actively working at that moment, puzzling over the contrast between the shapes of the words moulded by her lips and those much more boldly sculptured syllables produced by the two ladies who had taken a passing interest in my sulky mood, which was instantly dispelled by the satisfying sound of their voices.

But Mother remained less enchanted than I, and as the carriage drove away, her eyes followed it with a critical severity which again I could not understand. She seemed even to include in her condemnation the first groom who was walking away after the carriage, wheeling the two bicycles. Nor did she appear to be reconciled to the rest of the bloomered and knickerbockered cyclists, figures in a parade which appeared every week-day afternoon in Battersea Park during the spring and early summer of those years round about the turn of the century.

The resentment which I observed in Mother's eyes that day must have had a deeper cause than the temporary disapproval of the patronising remark about her happiness, or of the unfeminine garments worn by the two ladies, imperilling the mystery of their sex.

All the way home that day Mother was out of humour, and I sat in my mail-cart feeling lonely and bewildered, with a touch of remorse at my disloyalty in having been so infatuated by the roundness and beauty of the words blossoming on the lips of those two strangers whose friendliness had been unwanted by my mother.

Father was home when we got back to tea, and Mother instantly busied herself getting the meal. I went out to the back garden, looking for the cat, and found Father and Jack (the latter home from afternoon school) busy on an upturned bicycle, the pride of Father's heart. With greasy rags and an odd-shaped brush, they were polishing the gun-metal hubs and the rims of the wheels, selecting each spoke for separate attention, so that the little nuts and nipples joining the spokes to the rims shone like jewels.

It was impossible to separate our idea of Father from the ancillary one of bicycles. Here was his real interest in life, dominating even his sentimental love for his wife and two boys. He was always trying to associate the two emotional pulls, and the home atmosphere was full of projects for getting us all mounted, so that the whole family could take the road.

The road! There, perhaps, even more than for the vehicles, was his worship. He was never quite at ease within doors. I was to discover later, when at last he had succeeded in his relentless purpose of putting us all on wheels, that he had a Macaulayesque memory for the roads of England. His eyes, pale grey and unshadowed by perplexity, appeared to register, for ever, each main road from London, and all by-roads between John o' Groats and Land's End. Even remote lanes winding among the mountains of Wales, or over the Yorkshire dales, were as familiar to him as the veins in his hand, so that he could offer a detailed direction to any would-be tourist, telling him how, on reaching a certain cross-road in the Cotswolds, or the Trossachs, he should follow the left-hand or right-hand highway until he came to a wood, or a milestone beside a five-bar gate, where he would find an unmetalled lane which was to be ignored, the further turning, by a signpost saying 'seven miles to X', being the road to take.

Our home was littered with early road-maps, whose covers carried advertisements of tourists in tiny caps and baggy knickerbockers, riding penny-farthing machines, or solid-tyred 'safeties' such as this expensive beauty now being so lovingly cleaned in front of the wooden cycle-shed, a double-doored house standing on legs about nine inches from the ground, and occupying at least a third of the whole backyard. It was large enough to house the wheels of a complete touring club.

I was to learn, within the year, the reason for Father's foresight.

The interior of this high hut, and the walls of the outside water closet, were covered with pen-and-ink drawings, the illustrations cut out of a weekly magazine called *Cycling*. Long before I learned to read, I used to study these highly-skilled representations of English landscape, buildings in town and village, most of the drawings contriving to include one or more 'knights of the wheel' with the road before them, all time theirs to command. Here was pictured a way of life that, for my father, was the utmost mankind could ever attain.

Failing to find the cat, I stood looking on, too intimidated by the solemnity of the ritual to interfere, though I would dearly have liked to pick up, and play with, the spanners, bits of chain, odd nuts and bolts, and the oil-can, all displayed on a greasy duster.

When Mother appeared at the back door to summon us to tea, she was still moody. This was so unusual that I instantly noticed it, and was reminded of her sharp words in the park, and the incident that provoked them. The recollection caused me to experiment, by repeating her summons to tea in accents imitating the rich, modulated voices that had so incensed Mother. Father and Jack looked at each other, then at me, and suspended work.

"What's the matter with you?" said my brother, as though suspecting an indecency. I retreated, crestfallen, to the kitchen. A few minutes later, the others followed me indoors, and were busy in the scullery, scrubbing their hands with 'Monkey Brand' soap, while I sat at the table, waiting, and listening to the kettle on the 'Larbert' range, and the ticking of the German clock on the high mantelpiece.

Suddenly I heard Mother's voice, with an edge of anger and bitterness, say to Father, "What right have they to talk to us of our happiness? We don't owe it to them. For all people of their class care, you would have been left to starve with your mother."

I was terrified. I did not recognise Mother, the gentle, the patient, the all-understanding figure who could absorb our troubles, spinning round Father, Jack and myself a golden cocoon of solicitude in which we lived secluded from the harshness of the world. I stared at her as she snatched a second kettle from the stove and carried it out to them. She had returned to the kitchen before Father could find words to reply.

"That'll do, old girl," he said, evasively. "That'll do. We don't want any of that."

Mother drew a deep breath that ended in a sob, burst into tears, cried out, "It's you I'm thinking of; nothing else," and fled upstairs.

Father came into the kitchen, looking shy, even furtive. He was obviously out of his depth.

"Here, Jack," he said plaintively, "get on with your tea. Look after Dick. I'll take Mother a cup."

He was gone some time, during which Jack and I sat opposite each other, chewing bread and butter and jam that refused to go down. I tried to distract myself by watching the double-arc of light reflected from the gas-jet on the surface of the tea in my cup. But I was desperately worried, and so was Jack, though we were too infantile to be conscious of that worry; and still less could we understand what the storm was about.

At last Father came down, his pale grey eyes even more expressionless than usual. I was lost in sympathy for him: his handsome face was so woebegone.

I got down from my chair and clambered up on his knee, remaining there for the rest of the meal-time, playing with his gold watch-chain. Jack's face was dark with thought, but he said nothing, as usual.

When tea was over, Father sighed, put me down, and said to both of us, "Mother's got a bad headache. So we'll wash up for her." But at that moment she reappeared, her dear self again; and our home sprang to life instantly. The fire shone brighter through the bars of the grate. Father's black hair regained its lustre, and he twirled his moustache, before giving Mother a kiss, and bundling Jack and myself out of the scullery, where we were to help him wash up the tea-things, so that Mother could have a few quiet moments after her 'headache'.

CHAPTER FOUR

Ancestral Voices

THAT PERIOD OF WARM AFTERNOONS in the park with Mother must have been an interlude due to illness. I know that after my birth during violent weather at four o'clock on the morning of 26th March, 1893, Mother's health had greatly deteriorated though she was still a young woman in her thirty-first year, my father being five years younger.

My arrival was characteristically impetuous, preceded by Mother's pains which caused Father to set off in the tempest to fetch the midwife, who lived in some other part of London. He went, of course, on his bicycle, breaking his flight to rouse Mr. Brown, a Battersea man who owned a four-wheeler cab and made his living by driving it himself.

Father rode on through the storm, urged by the picture of his wife left alone with her birth-pangs, except ior the four-year-old Jack asleep in the next room.

Turning a corner sharply, Father was caught in a buffet of wind and rain, which caused him to skid against a kerbstone and threw him off his bicycle. He cut his knee, and was badly shaken. But the occasion was desperate, and he was a man totally fearless in physical matters. He remounted and rode on, not even stopping to bind up the bleeding knee-cap. Thus he reached the midwife's house in a sad state, bedraggled and rain-sodden, his trousers torn and blood-stained, and his leg rapidly stiffening.

Fortunately, further haste was useless, for the midwife had to await the arrival of Mr. Brown with his growler. She spent the time in giving first aid to my father, and sewing up the leg of his trousers. Further, she insisted that he should leave his un-damaged bicycle to be reclaimed later, and go back with her in the cab.

Meanwhile, I was born, Mother having got up in the process to call the woman from downstairs. The storm still raged when Mr. Brown's cab jingled up to the house, and Father and the midwife took over the later stages of the ceremony, by the light of a wild March morning.

Both man and wife being wage-earners, and Mother especially being ambitious to get a more substantial home together, with a house of her own, the young couple could not allow this alarming adventure to discompose them. Within a few weeks Mother was back to her teaching in an elementary school in the Horseferry Road, Westminster. How she travelled to and fro at that time, I have no idea; but the fatigue of this journey four times a day (for she had to come home to feed me), plus the task of handling some sixty slum urchins from the wilderness of Pimlico, must have taxed her vitality.

To make this way of life possible, and to ensure the care o my brother Jack, a young woman named Harriet was hired. She came from a large family in a neighbouring street, and knew how to deal with children, having practised lifelong on her younger brothers and sisters.

To help her in looking after us while Mother was at school each day, Harriet brought her mandolin adorned with a dozen multi-coloured ribbons that folded round the instrument like a shroud when it lay in its black case. Harriet was a dry, sardonic Cockney, with no false sentiment, and a brusque hand that would jerk us back, when we erred, into the path of good behaviour. I was her favourite, but she did not like my brother. Perhaps they were rival philosophers, two Diogenes in the same tub. This prejudice caused him some suffering, and exaggerated his native melancholy.

Mother had, in addition to her school-teaching, to do the planning and take the responsibility for the family economy, Father being boyishly confident in her in all such matters. In his eyes she could never make a mistake, either as lover, mother or chancellor. He was content to leave all to her. His own wants were simple: the freedom of the open road, a gallant steed in the form of the latest bicycle, and the promise of his near and dear ones sharing these delights with him when

Mother was strong again, and Jack and I old enough to be taught to ride. Ways and means would be found, by Mother's ingenuity, to provide the mounts for us.

Father, jubilant over my birth, could not contain himself within the usual routine. Three weeks after my arrival, he set off on his solid-tyred bicycle for a ride to Aberdeen and back, staying there for a night or two with some people who welcomed him so warmly that when he got home he insisted on my being christened with the name of Richard, after a young man there who later visited us, on his way out to take part in the Boer War, and to be killed at Ladysmith.

This spontaneous friendliness was an endearing quality in my father's nature. It made Mother, perhaps, a little protective toward him, and sometimes inclined to outbursts of a jealousy that could become dramatic. Certainly he was always subdued when they occurred, and he added to his devotion to her an ingratiating deference that at first fanned the flames, but brought the flare-up to a quicker conclusion, so that once more Mother submitted to his charm, and loved him with an ardour that filled the home with warmth, and drew her two children into its certainty and comfort.

Nothing could depress Father for long, or subdue his simple confidence in life, in himself, or in the perfection with which he surrounded himself. This included his wife and sons, of whom he was unreservedly proud. Indeed, he was reserved about nothing, except one subject, that of his own origin. In more than usually expansive moods, he would tell us that he was descended from Boadicea. One day he even took Jack and me to see the Celtic Queen standing in effigy in her bronze chariot at the corner of Westminster Bridge.

His energy, his *joie de vivre* were astonishing. They filled me with wonder, and they also gave me a very early sense of estrangement, because I had not inherited this physical exuberance. Later in life, I found myself critical of him because he did not carry it further, beyond his passion for exploring the roads and by-lanes of Great Britain, and put it to some purpose in the countries of the mind.

I have always wondered who bequeathed to him this

abundant physique, the perfectly proportioned figure, the handsome head, so well poised, the fine black hair and grey eyes, the firmly-sculptured nose with its defined bridge, the shapely hands, sun-tanned even in winter because no week-end passed without his going off for a ride.

I was to learn, from hints dropped in the family when on rare occasions Mother's sisters (to whom she was hostile) visited us, that Grandfather Church was only acquired after my father's birth, and that he had married his encumbered cousin Hannah Swain, when he returned from Malta, where he had been stationed in the Garrison Artillery.

This old man was another Homeric character, quite incapable of leading an adult and responsible life once he was withdrawn from the shelter of the army. But he was gay company for Jack and me whenever we went up to Hampstead to stay a while with Grandmother, while our parents were off on one of the cycle trips that Mother so distinctly dreaded.

He was a giant, and had been a regimental champion with the sabre. As we knew him, he had been somewhat reduced by age, and the bewildering environment of civil life. His jobs were promiscuous, and his wages made negligible by frequent visits to the public-houses on the borders of Hampstead Heath. He and Grandmother inhabited three squalid rooms near the heath, with a daughter who was withdrawn at an early age by tuberculosis, so that my recollection of her is of a silent young woman in a stiff and grubby garment of black, sitting on a chair against the wall of their front room, and being apparently incapable of speech. I saw her thus only on few occasions before she disappeared.

Grandmother too was a person of humble mien and few words. I sometimes doubt if she was quite intellectually capable, for she did nothing and said nothing, except to chide her husband when, in his cups, he blasphemed against Jesus Christ and offered to change jobs with Him. She was still of Baptist persuasion, despite the vagaries of her life, and the break made from her strict family at the time of my father's birth on the 10th August, 1866, in the Bedfordshire town of Leighton Buzzard, whither she had retreated from

Woburn to be sheltered by one or other more lenient member of her family.

I remember her as a woman still handsome in a saturnine way, with hair jet-black when she died at the age of eighty-two in the year 1912. By that time she was witchlike, her coal-black eyes screwed up wickedly as she gazed out of the window and pointed out 'her Blessed Saviour' walking up the hill to prepare a place for her where she would at last be at rest.

I was not aware that she had ever been in any other condition than that of rest, for I never knew her to lift a finger to do any domestic work. I remember, too, how my mother would have to harbour the old couple in our home during periods of Grandfather's unemployment, and how Mother would hurry home from school at midday to cook a meal for them, and to scrub the kitchen floor, while Grandmother sat meekly, her hands folded in her lap, and her glittering eyes maliciously hooded as she brooded over far-off wrongs and ancient humiliations which served, however, only to increase her certainty of rehabilitation in the Baptist Heaven toward which she was so complacently resigned.

It has taken me many years to piece together the story of her downfall, and even now it remains discontinuous and veiled in mists of innuendo and shame. All this will be quite unintelligible to present-day readers, who will not remember the rigid orthodoxy of most lower-middle-class folk in the nineteenth century, when the influence of Wesleyanism was still a major social force, especially in the Midlands.

My grandmother's family was yeoman stock, on the Duke of Bedford's estate of Woburn: grim puritans descended from members of Cromwell's image-breaking army. What Hannah Swain did with her life up to the age of thirty-six, when my father was born to her shame, I have never been able to find out; but from reluctant hints prised out here and there from relatives (but never from my father, whose mind was cauterised after his suffering as a consequence of these matters) I believe that she was employed at Woburn Abbey. She would have been a handsome woman in those early years, probably less submissive and stunned-seeming than she afterwards became.

What in old age was a sullen and sly glitter in those dark eyes shone as a provocative challenge half a century earlier. I think she must always have been simple-minded, even submissive.

Whatever advantage was taken of her, she would not have had enough worldly intelligence to make the most of it, and to fight back, as she might well have done. For in those decades of the mid-century even the aristocracy had been considerably affected by the Wesleyan code of morals, and the renewed hedging round of sex by an odd blend of chivalry and family sanctity. The old *droit de seigneur* attitude had been frowned on by Victoria's Court.

This was not altogether beneficial to the community. Formerly, the nobility and squirearchy, in their feudal freedom, had openly taken their women from amongst the daughters of tenants, and kept a healthy paternal interest in the children born on the wrong side of the blanket. But when these lords of the manor, large and small, were expected to conform to the domestic morals of the majority of the people, their old habits, where indulged, became furtive and shamefaced.

I may, however, be generalising from a particular case, and I suspect that human nature never conforms easily to monogamy, with either sex. Neither religious teaching, social demands, love for children, nor indeed the love between man and wife, can wholly canalise the creative instinct, or attaint its overflow as evil.

So Hannah Swain, as a result of one of these outbreaks to which she had submitted, I fear, with docility rather than ardour, found herself sheltering in an ancient cottage in Friday Street, Leighton Buzzard, cared for by a relative who had come from the village of Wardington in Oxfordshire.

My father sometimes referred to this cottage, and its vast open fireplace, before which he spent the first few years of his life. From time to time there would be a knock on the door, and Grandmother would dutifully present herself to the man on a horse who had summoned her with the handle of his riding-whip. "How is the boy?" he would inquire, without dismounting; and on being assured of the infant's well-being, he would ride away.

This cavalier, about that time, married a Frenchwoman by whom he subsequently had four sons and two daughters. Maybe it was she who suggested a less insular and Victorian attitude toward Hannah Swain. Or other persuasions may have urged that cavalier to dismount from his horse. Some ladies of the Digby family appear to have played a part in getting Grandmother and the child removed from the scene of her downfall, and installed in London, where she could be lost, and put out of mind by her reproving family.

She was set up in a little house in Markham Square, Chelsea, and a marriage arranged for her with her cousin John Church, who undertook to father the child.

He did so, to the best of his ability: but it was a brutal one, with a technique learned from the army of those days, when soldiers were regarded, Chinese fashion, as the dregs of society, the misfits, the runaways, the ne'er-do-wells.

Under this military patronage, so primitive and macedonian, the *ménage* deteriorated. Though my father continued to be watched and kindly treated by the Digby ladies, who saw that he learned his Catechism and attended St. Luke's Church, whose vicar at that time was Gerald Blunt, brother of the poet Wilfred Scawen Blunt, he was driven by his stepfather's old army belt-buckle out to work at the age of nine.

The house in Markham Square was soon given up, the small family moving into rooms in the less respectable quarters of Chelsea. During those dark and unrecorded years of my father's boyhood, he was knocked into shape by the rudiments of schooling, and the experience of the streets. His mother failed to protect him from the brunt of this continuous assault. Even when he was knocked down and had his right arm broken, she hardly noticed the incident.

The arm was never set properly, and this lack of surgical attention caused the muscles of the hand to wither later in life.

But the boy never lost his capacity for enjoying the passing moment. One such occurred at that time when he was ranging the streets. He was carrying home a basin of pickled onions, and he had made a detour along the Embankment by Cheyne Row, with one or two other urchins. Their attention was drawn to a fierce old man in a black hat with a wide brim. He wore a cloak, and carried a blackthorn stick, stalking along with deliberate tread and muttering to himself. The tall crown of that hat, and the obvious irascibility of the old eccentric, offered too great a temptation to the urchins. They pelted him with pickled onions until the bowl was empty. During the fusillade he retaliated by roaring at them and menacing them with upraised stick. When the engagement broke off, Thomas Carlyle turned into Cheyne Walk, and the attackers dispersed.

This appears to have been my father's only contact with the world of letters during his formative years. He learned to read, however, and his handwriting was so well guided that it remained copperplate for the rest of his long life.

Passing from one casual job to another in the neighbourhood of the King's Road shops, my father managed to survive the brutality of his stepfather and the incompetence of his mother. The Digby ladies continued to show an interest in him, keeping him attached to the life of St. Luke's Church, a field where his native generosity and good-will blossomed, and where he learned that life did not consist wholly of blows, drudgery and domestic squalor. He sang in the choir, growing into such an attractive and presentable youth that efforts were made by his good fairies, with the help of the vicar Gerald Blunt, to find him a more promising employment, in the Government service. This consummation followed a precedent started by Royal practice a century or two earlier, one which was to come to an end with the innovations brought by Mr. Gladstone into the structure of the Civil Service and the recruitment of its members.

The near-nepotism exercised in my father's favour, however, did not amount to much. He became a postman, and continued in that employment until he met my mother.

During those years spent in delivering and collecting mail, he laid the foundation of that remarkable knowledge of local geography which he never lost, even when senility crumbled his memory in all other matters.

It was at a Christmas party given for church folk by the Digby ladies, at a house in Cheyne Walk, exactly opposite Mr.

D

Carlyle's, that my father and mother met. And they met on the doorstep, in a downpour of rain. My mother had driven up in a hansom cab, fellow-guest of a Chelsea friend with whom she was staying. The two young women, struggling under the oppression of bustles and mantles, were dealing with the cabby and trying to hold an umbrella over their party clothes, when a young man approached, took the umbrella from my mother, and looked into her eyes.

He saw that they were brown, shaded and troubled. He saw a thin face, with exquisitely moulded cheek-bones touched with warm colour. He saw how her hair clustered softly over a pale forehead, whose serenity belied the trouble in the eyes below.

As for my mother, she saw a stranger who had approached with such calm leisureliness that he had been unnoticed until he took the umbrella from her hand. She told me, years later during one of our confidential evocations of the past, that she was instantly attracted by the young man's grey eyes, black moustache and striking personal cleanliness. She said that he stood firmly before her, as though possessing the earth below his feet. This physical confidence, the sign of health and courage, was therefore a quality that showed itself early in my father's development. It served him well, for it must have been his support during the humiliations of his childhood, the squalor, neglect and brutality. It may have kept the Digby ladies faithful to their original purpose of making up in some way for the unhappy beginnings of his life and the irresponsible paternal attitude.

Finally, it won him the love of a woman whose character, intelligence and education were to lift him up to an enlargement of life such as he had never known, and for which, in his own odd way, he was ever grateful and filled with wonder.

Mother's maiden name was Orton, and her father's family were Staffordshire yeomen, with members of it in the towns of Leek and Teen. Her father was to become a townsman, for, a servant of the Midland Railway, he settled in London, being made Goods Manager at St. Pancras.

I remember Benjamin Orton as a holy terror, a perfect

example of the Victorian domestic tyrant. He drove his son to half-failure in life, and his three daughters to marriages only one of which found his arrogant approval. It was not my mother's.

But even before my father appeared, Grandfather Orton and his eldest daughter joined battle. It was over an early indiscretion which had nearly driven Mother from the savagely conducted home. She had escaped, however, by going to a teachers' training college, called The Home and Colonial, in north London, near their Highgate home. Happily it was a boarding establishment where she could be screened somewhat from the Old Testament wrath.

In another of her evocations of early life, she described to me how her mother and the four children were expected to be at home and waiting when Grandfather returned from his day's work at St. Pancras. The ritual was always the same. There would be a loud, single blow on the front-door knocker. Either Grandmother or my uncle, as the heir, would then open the door and wait at the threshold. Grandfather would enter, thrust his umbrella into the stand, and pass his hat to the attendant member of his family. It was a tall black hat, of dull felt. Then he was helped off with his overcoat. Having inspected his daughters, to ensure that they were still safe and virginal in his bosom, he was ready for supper, which everyone secretly prayed would be to his liking.

On one occasion it had not been so. He picked up the offending viand on his fork, examined it, looked angrily at his wife, and said, "What is this; an *attenuated* mutton chop?" And he flung it into the grate.

On another occasion, also at the meal-table, he had so savagely harangued his son in front of the girls that the youth lost control of his own temper, snatched up the carving-knife, and would have committed parricide, had not my mother seized him by the wrist, persuaded the now weeping boy from the room, and returned, with the knife in her hand, to pass it to her father and openly to declare war.

From that day onwards the tyrant changed his tactics, becoming less oriental in his attitude to wife and family. He continued, however, to anoint his feet with olive oil every evening, and to expect his wife to stand by, towel in hand during the ceremony.

He never again dominated his eldest daughter, and she went her own way, by sheer emphasis of character and originality, breaking down the patriarchal control, so that the rest of the family enjoyed some degree of freedom, with only a grumbling Zeus in the background, still dangerous, but latent.

She was not thanked for this. Indeed, her sisters and brother were jealous of the courage and temper which had won them at least a promise of release. When my mother's impulsive heart nearly betrayed her into an early disaster that threatened to reimpose the old tyranny in the home, they let her bear the brunt alone, and were derisive when she side-tracked by going off to the training college.

The years she spent there followed by a decade those when the country was convulsed by the Tichborne Case, in which an impostor named Orton claimed the wealthy estates of Sir Roger Tichborne, who had gone off long before to foreign parts (there still being such fabulous regions in those days).

The missing baronet's own mother was imposed on by the false claimant, and the nation took sides in the ruinous lawsuit that followed.

My mother was nicknamed Roger Tichborne throughout the two or three years spent at the college.

As a trained elementary school-teacher, she was able to maintain some degree of independence at home. This was an unusual freedom for young women in the eighteen-eighties, and Lavinia Orton made the most of it, and of the hospitality offered by friends amongst her fellow-teachers. For years she lived half-estranged from her father, sisters and brother, and would have left home had not her love for her mother held her.

It was a love well merited, and fully returned. Ann Sanders was a Warwickshire woman, from the village of Meriden. Her father was agent at Packington Hall, seat of the Earls of Aylesford, between Coventry and Birmingham, and in his house on the estate he showed some singularity by knocking the ceiling out of his wife's parlour and installing a pipe-organ which rose majestically to the roof.

His cousin Robert Evans, father of the novelist George Eliot, was agent at Arbury in the same county. My mother's family were not proud of this literary connection. For them, Marian Evans's brazen unconventionality over her domestic affairs far outweighed her merits and fame as a writer. I doubt, indeed, if she would have been thought much of by her relations even had she been a model of Victorian propriety; for it seems to be almost a rule that whenever a middle-class, bourgeois family throws off a sport, in whatever walk of life, there is disapproval, sometimes veiled, sometimes open. It is as though the solid, respectable mediocrity is a standard jealously preserved, and that a member who soars to fame, or drops to notoriety, is breaking the humble tradition.

Marian Evans broke away in both directions, and the family reacted only to her disgraceful conduct in living openly with G. H. Lewes, another woman's husband. The literary genius that made George Eliot one of the most influential women in Victorian England was ignored by her family. That again is in the tradition of all good burgess and yeoman folk, for people of this solid stock seem to be unconscious of æsthetic values. They are suspicious of the arts, just as they are suspicious of gypsies.

Marian's only brother Isaac refused to communicate with her until, in the last months of her life, at the age of sixty-one, she married a man of forty, John Walter Cross. As Gerald Bullett records in his biography of the novelist, "Marian's brother was placated at last. Breaking his long silence of disapproval, he sent her 'kind words of sympathy', and doubtless thanked his dreary god that someone at last had made an honest woman of Isaac Evans's sister. The stain on an illustrious family was all but rubbed out." I believe it is probable, however, that Isaac Evans did not regard his family as illustrious, and that part of his disapproval of his sister was because she had made it so.

When in 1869 the young Mr. Cross first met George Eliot in Rome, he noted "the low, earnest, deep musical tones of her voice . . . the fine brows, with the abundant auburn-brown hair framing them . . . and the finely-formed, thin, transparent hands".

That description might accurately be applied to my mother, Marian's distant kinswoman. The only difference is that the novelist had blue eyes. My mother's were a warm brown, the same colour as her hair; but they too were lightened "always with a very loving, almost deprecating look".

My mother had a light contralto singing voice, which she exercised upon the tuneful, sentimental ballads popular in those days before home-made music was displaced by radio and gramophone. The piano pieces which she delighted to play with those "thin, transparent hands" were of a similar kind to the ballads. She always opened one of her sessions at the pianoforte with a bravura piece called 'Tarantella', by Sidney Smith. I have never heard that key-rattling solo performed elsewhere. Her copy of it, published by Mr. Boosey with lavish engraving of trumpets, viols, and vine leaves on the title-page, was so tattered that it disintegrated early in my life. But I recall still that the solo opened with so definite a statement of the main theme that our solid English instrument, made by Broadwood-White (a dubious trade signature which again I have not met elsewhere), would rumble like a husky bull, or a distant explosion of fire-damp in a coal-mine.

Miss Orton sang at that Christmas party in Cheyne Walk, and thus furthered her conquest of the presentable young man whom she had met at the front door. For he too was musically inclined, and had been taught to sing in St. Luke's choir.

The courtship flourished in spite of Mother being five years senior to him, and of her father forbidding 'Postman Church' to enter his house. Mother was undeterred, and set about to checkmate the second drawback. As often as possible she met Father when he came off duty at a branch of the South-West District Office, which was at that time in the Buckingham Palace Road opposite the Royal Stables. The lovers would then stroll up and down the Birdcage Walk and the Mall, while she coached him in arithmetic, grammar, and the other elements required from candidates for the Civil Service examination for Post Office sorters.

The collaboration was successful and Father won the grudging consent of Benjamin Orton. The couple were married in

1888, and set up home in the rooms where my brother was born in the summer of the following year. My father, long conditioned to bullying, refused to be intimidated by his father-in-law, and the two men came to a friendly understanding. Grandfather was so softened that one Sunday, when the young family were visiting the Highgate home, he took my brother, aged three, between his knees, tweaked the infant's long nose, frowned at my father, and growled, "This child is not unlike you, Tom Church!" Mother, additionally emotional because at that time she was carrying me, was so moved by this unexpected overture from her father that she wept, and was finally reconciled to him.

Father took the occasion more coolly, for his early experiences had given him a distrust of violence and violent people. All his life, as I knew him, he would avoid conflict. This may have been partly an inheritance from his mother. It kept him unadult, an avoider of responsibility. It also made him a lenient father. Never once during our childhood did he raise a hand to punish me or my brother; and I never heard him swear. Our home was, in consequence, serene and equable in its domestic atmosphere. It might have been merely negative, but for Mother's rich personality, her fearless ambitions, and her quick, intuitive intelligence.

Less than two years after my birth, our home was seated in the house where I was to spend the next ten years of my life. Mother having returned to school-teaching as soon as her health permitted, she saved enough of her salary and so shrewdly controlled my father's that they were able to start buying the comfortable little semi-detached house, with its front and back yards soundly concreted, except for a small flower-bed running along the fence and a little tile-edged parcel of soil by the french windows, where a large white jasmine grew so freely that it formed a green tunnel every summer along the narrow way beside the house, joining the front and back yards; a green tunnel fragrant with white blossoms, beneath which I lay in my pram, alone but contented with this star-studded ceiling, or serenaded by Harriet's beribboned mandolin.

CHAPTER FIVE

The Age of Bliss

IT IS DIFFICULT TO DESCRIBE HAPPINESS, and impossible to dramatise it. Nobody will listen to an account of other people's bliss. For a hundred people who read the 'Inferno' and 'Purgatorio' of Dante's *Divine Comedy*, there is surely but one who penetrates to, and sustains a passage through, the 'Paradiso'.

I cannot hope, therefore, to re-create the scene and atmosphere of the first five joyous years of my life, spent so peacefully among the labyrinthine streets covering the Battersea marsh, between the park and the old village that jutted out into a curve of the Thames, with the church standing so conspicuously on the promontory.

My range of physical consciousness, at first limited to the cot and the mail-cart, gradually widened, enriching me with a house full of light, colours, shadows, shapes. They became significant. They related themselves to each other: the furniture, the windows; a still vague background beyond the windows that came forward, to be day, and retreated, to be night, almost with a slow, tick-tock surety, through which my personality headed its way, asleep, awake, gathering momentum.

Mother and Father disappeared during the day, and after my first year or two Jack also vanished each week-day, Harriet and I escorting him to and from the infants' school in Surrey Lane, some ten minutes' walk from home.

Thus my earliest years were spent much in the company of Harriet, the caustic Cockney girl, who took me out in the mail-cart, sometimes calling in at her own home, where I was welcomed into a teeming mass of live creatures, seemingly dozens of brothers and sisters, and a tiny yard at the back, whitewashed throughout, and furnished with tiers of rabbit cages, peopled by lovely pink-eyed, lavishly be-furred pets who paused from their lettuce-chewing to stare at me with milky pupils dilated by alarm. I too was alarmed, by the very abundance of vitality in this working-class home, its noise, restlessness, inconsequent good humour, and occasional outbreaks of storm.

There was nowhere to put down a thing. My rattle, my woolly ball, my cape and gloves, instantly vanished in the seething flood of animal life, and had to be searched for with loud hue and cry when Harriet declared that we must be getting back to prepare tea for 'Jacky and the Missus'.

The father's employment must have been casual, for he was often found at home in the afternoons, sitting in the kitchen, or out in the yard before the rabbit hutches, with a last between his knees, hammering crudely-cut leather on to innumerable pairs of boots, of all sizes and all degrees of dilapidation.

My first introduction to class barriers, and the way snobbery works, was made during these regular visits to Harriet's home. Gradually I grew aware that I was given special consideration among those swarming infants and elders. Rabbits were brought out from hutches for me to stroke. My mislaid toys and garments were searched for with anxiety and recrimination. I was fawned on and flattered.

This was not a personal matter. It was because I represented a higher social layer. My parents were in regular employment, and permanent employment: privileged, enviable. A schoolteacher carried a certain authority of magic: less than a doctor (doctors were really more than human) or a clergyman; but a magic nevertheless, and unquestioned.

Here, in action, was the pedal articulation of the machine of snobbery, which maintains the shape and movement of human society. I saw it at its best and purest, for these folk in the slums of Battersea had little to look down upon and everything to look up to. Their impulse of snobbery was wholly positive. They acknowledged qualities, circumstances, endowments, which they never aspired to possess, except when they were drunk with politics or angered by the injustice that springs from the negative workings of snobbery, that makes one class look down upon another, to despise it and deny its dignity.

My daily outings with Harriet did not take us far. She found the park to be 'lonely'. Her preference was the high-road junctions, such as The Latchmere, where four roads met, and horse-trams and buses clanged and clop-clopped ceaselessly past the shops, and ground their way round the junction by the Victorian drapery store of Messrs. Hunt and Cole, where little aerial railways carried the customers' money in wooden containers to the cashier's desk set high like a pulpit.

Harriet had a distaste for solitude and silence. When she was not banging dust out of the carpets and saddle-bag chairs, or clashing pots and pans like cymbals in the scullery, she was singing to me or strumming on her mandolin.

Even during her restful moments, when she worked at a huge rag-mat intended for her 'bottom drawer', her bright eyes and sharp nose were alert for the smallest sign of anything that might become festive and communal.

It may have been the slightly oppressive effect of her personality that made me, at an early age, content to be alone, and even eager to be surrounded by silence and a revealing nothingness. Yet I was devoted to her, and even enjoyed her brusque kindness, which took the form of a slap and a shake as medicine for my tears when I fell down, or was frightened by a dog or a policeman, or broke a toy.

In that little world (which comprises at least nine-tenths of the human race) the policeman was always to be feared. Even to have a policeman pause on his beat, to stand outside the house while he looked to right and left and hitched his trousers, caused us to suspend our normal life, and to feel guilty. What would the neighbours think, was the subconscious question. No policeman ever called at our house, but we had seen such disgrace occur further down the street, at the *wrong* end. We never learned the reason for that call, and would not have dared to ask. Mother and Father had a gift for ignoring life's solecisms. No comment was made, for example, when Jack told Mother about that frightening incident during the journey home with the aquarium. "You should have told me before," was all she said: and we forgot it.

In the same way we overlooked the existence of the policeman, police stations, prisons and crime. This family timidity explains perhaps, why I have always been unable to read thrillers and detective stories. I suspect that they are the diversion of a more comfortable and professional middle class, to whom the policeman is a servant and never a bully. When I hear today of university dons and other intellectuals using crime-stories as bed-time soporifics, I think grimly of the small margin of safety which my parents struggled to maintain between their respectable little home and the hungry ocean of violence whose thunder never left our ears; the violence of the street, the crass mob, the ever-rising waters of the indifferent masses.

Much of the timidity, the furtiveness, the humility, of the anonymous folk, the majority of society, is due to the fear of being submerged in this welter. 'Keep yourself to yourself' is the motto made from this universal suspicion which is only broken down in moments of crisis, and only between individuals when 'trouble, need, sickness', have increased that perennial social fear, making it bold with desperation, so that it breaks into compassion and the momentary recklessness of charity.

The Battersea that I explored was not so red in tooth and claw as I have suggested. Generally, it was a slumbrous suburb, largely peopled with artisan folk, clerks and minor Civil Servants such as my father, whose surface uniformity was deceptive.

The little streets had a character that made me think of sailors rather than industrial workers. This may have been caused by the tidal waters of the Thames that ebbed and flowed round the parish, giving it a strand of mud enlivened with washed pebbles, and salt-breasted gulls that screamed as though a herring-fleet were coming in.

The streets, too, aided the illusion, for most of the householders maintained the practice of lime-washing their yards, front and back, and even the lower courses of the house-walls, to preserve the health of their copious livestock: rabbits, poultry, pigeons, and even goats. The effect of this was to give the impression of sailors ashore; of holystone and white-scrubbed decks, of painted masts, of furled sails and gleaming port-holes.

Pigeon-flying was a weekly sport, especially among the tattooed men in the poorer quarters of the parish, costers with flat black caps and hoarse voices, chokers instead of collars and ties, and Sunday boots of a ginger-yellow.

These men, scrubbed and shaved, red-faced and blue-lipped, would rattle off on Sunday mornings in their coster-carts behind ponies and donkeys, or on the newly-favoured bicycles, anxiously guarding long wicker baskets out of which floated the soft sub-chorus of pigeon voices, and the fidget of crowded feathers.

Toward tea-time on these Sunday afternoons, after the muffin-man had made his round of the streets, his tray covered by green baize and carried on a round pad on his head, his right hand ringing a bell at arm's-length, stiffly because of the balancing act required to keep the tray steady, the pigeon-flyers would come trundling home with empty wickers, their faces mantled from red to purple, and their eyes glazed, all still very serious under the stress of this grave occupation. The murky sky above streets that now covered the Battersea marshes would grow wild and lyrical with homing wings before the day's sport subsided, the carrier birds returning without error to the cotes, to be content with captivity for another week.

All this world beyond the house and yard, however, remained largely foreign, and frightening to me during those puling years while I was tied to Harriet's mandolin strings and streamers. I spent eternities in the backyard, especially on summer days when tall plants flashed their blossoms at me from the restricted and tile-edged flower-bed, and the dark alley roofed with jasmine all the way to the side gate offered me shelter from the hot concrete, and a fragrance that filled my nostrils with a rapture that almost reached my nursling intelligence.

Beside the outsize cycle-shed stood a solidified sack of cement long since denuded of its fabric. It stood under a sycamore tree which was the proudest growth within a radius of several streets. My brother and I learned to expect, every spring, the coral-tinted flowerets, and in the autumn the winged seeds that could be thrown into the air, to come helicoptering down, though in those days we could not so describe that enchanting movement, for the word had still to be coined to describe an invention yet undreamed of.

The lump of concrete became Dick Whittington's Milestone, and it played many parts in our make-believe, an activity in which I followed my brother, whose creative genius was already pronounced before I had learned to talk. I could not reasonably object to his fantasies, therefore, except by going off in a sulk, or collapsing into tears; and these methods were usually prohibited by his affectionate explanations of his vivid imaginings, his plans and his careful allowance for the share I was to take in these adventures. I seldom rebelled, because the games were always inspired. I blundered my way through them, pinafore-clad, and worked myself up into frenzies of excited half-comprehension that sent me to bed with flushed face and burning eyes, worrying Mother, who feared I was sickening. Harriet, anxious to get away home as soon as Jack and I were bestowed for the night, would reassure Mother by saying laconically, "It's his disposition," and trying to wipe the flush from my cheeks with a slap of the face-flannel.

So the days and nights passed. They cannot be of interest to anyone else, for babyhood is much the same everywhere, propelled on those 'trailing clouds of glory', in a protective nimbus of animal innocence, demanding few things, but much of those few, only gradually multiplying the demands, diffusing them through a widening experience, thus growing simultaneously richer and richer, and poorer and poorer.

Those first years are recalled through odd and incoherent memories, seen larger than life, vague and shadowy, by the myopic infant eye. The pains are mostly forgotten, the outstanding joys remain. Thus, I can see now the gloomy Battersea Park Road, newly set with electric arc-lamps, tall, futurist standards, that began to hiss and splutter at dusk, and needed no kindling by a man with a pole, as did the homely gas-lamps in our side-streets.

The lamp-lighter was a half-fairy figure, always followed by a number of children who danced about him and shouted with glee when he stopped at a lamp, flipped open a little glass trap-door at the bottom of the lantern, pushed his brass-topped pole into it, and kindled a fish-tail flame that flashed into life with a pop like a bursting balsam-seed. Then the magician, with his chorus of urchins, went on to the next lamp-post, the flame inside the brass head of his caduceus flickering, but never quite expiring.

One of those Victorian gas-lamps stood outside our house, and its feeble fish-tail flame threw a light that gentled its way into my parents' bedroom, streaking the ceiling with elongated patterns of the two windows, shapes which I studied as I lay in my cot, too young and unscientific to be able to trace their origin. But they comforted many moods of terror following monstrous dreams, when I awoke prepared to scream in fear. There above me shone the familiar shapes, warm as firelight to my frozen nerves.

How different was the light from those experimental electric standards in the Battersea Park Road. It had a kind of darkness in its very centre, changing the street scene into something comparable to a photographic negative, the familiar objects melting away and the recognisable distorted into despairing shapes that could nudge the imagination of the most matter-of-fact citizen, inducing gloom and foreboding of dreadful events, and desperate innovations.

I was too seldom out after dark to be so affected. What attracted my attention to these arc-lamps was the fact that they frequently spluttered and spat, relapsing into darkness, and throwing out sticks of carbon, several inches in length, smooth and brittle. This substance, strange and unearthly to child-eyes, was precious because of its very uselessness. I collected these fragments as a rajah collects rubies, and I hoarded them in the certainty that sooner or later they would be a currency of great value, so dead-cold were they, so elemental and unchanging.

Another recollection of those preparatory years, still drowsy from the womb, is that of seeing Queen Victoria on the day of

her Diamond Jubilee in 1897, when I was four years old. Father,
Mother, Jack and I stood in the Mall, not far from Buckingham
Palace, on the north side facing St. James's Park. A single iron
rail and posts ran alongside the roadway in those days, and
we were stationed behind this rail, so close to the policemen
and soldiers lining the route that I could see the grains of pipe-
clay on the soldiers' belts, and the texture of their red tunics.

The crowd was thick about us, and when the Royal procession approached from the Admiralty end of the Mall, the
cheering swept along with it, like the roar accompanying a
prairie fire.

I began to shiver, for even at that early age I was intensely
alert to sound. Time has not subdued that alertness, and my
life has needed a constant discipline to keep this physical
responsiveness in check, so that I might concentrate on whatever matter was in hand, and prevent my attention from being
lured away by a whiff of street music, the twittering of a
sparrow above my window, the ticking of a grandfather clock,
or the tremulous whisper of falling rain. No matter how deeply
I may be involved in some drama of love, or death, or
threatened security, a snatch of chords on a pianoforte, wafting
from the wings of the theatre of daily life, can distract me at
once, so that I fumble, lose my lines, and go dancing away after
the Pied Piper towards the fatal door in the mountain, heed-
less of the surprise, consternation and even anger of those near
and dear to me, or fellow committee-men with whom I was, a
moment since, in responsible conference.

So at that moment as the Royal carriage approached
followed by the jack-in-the-box Life Guards, I was unable
instantly to collect my wits. But the cheering swept over me,
and I was still standing there behind the pipe-clayed belts,
the scarlet coats, and the wind-stroked busbies. Father thrust
me under the rail, and a policeman smiled and put his hand
on my shoulder, steering me slightly forward.

I was too dazed to be frightened by this dreadful proximity,
and there I stood, as it were under arrest, staring at the open
chaise, and at the little huddled figure in bonnet and shawl,
bobbing forward and up, forward and up, in a rhythm set by

the jolting of the carriage and the response of the spring cushion on which she sat. I even saw the Queen's feet on a little stool, peeping out below the rug tucked round her.

My second experience of a Royal procession was at the time of the old Queen's funeral ceremonies, when she was brought from Osborne. Once again we attended, but by chance, for the family was on its way from Battersea to Highgate to visit the grandparents. We were caught near Victoria station, and took our stand on a step, in the private doorway of a shop at the corner of Buckingham Palace Road. This time, Father sat me on his shoulder, though I was then nearly eight years old and a hardened schoolboy.

We saw the coffin on a gun-carriage, followed by the princes of the blood, and the strange new King, on dark horses. I remember most clearly the Kaiser, because he rode a white horse, a nonconformity which caused the crowd to murmur with astonishment and dismay. I was troubled because my mother was crying, as were most other women around us. I can see flowers and swords and reversed rifles carried stiffly by sailors marching with bent heads. I can hear a low sighing from the crowd, a wind touching and passing a forest, bringing down a few leaves here and there.

But these are public events, familiar to several generations, two of which still survive into the middle of the twentieth century, after a surfeit of street scenes, many too horrible to recall.

As for the recollections of more personal events, they come creeping in like stragglers from a fishing-fleet, as I gaze out over the ocean of the past. What is so astonishing is the vast fullness of the hours during those first five years of life, when the universe has just begun to spin, with a child's eye watching it in rapt astonishment.

At five years of age, I closed the opening chapter of bliss. One cold day I was bustled over breakfast, dumped on to the low chair by the kitchen grate, while Harriet pulled on a new pair of boots over my feet and buttoned them with a hook that bit into my flesh during the process. Then we set out as usual, Mother seeing us off at the front gate, and hurrying away to her school next door to the Battersea Polytechnic, a long way from home. She turned right at the gate, going down-street to the poorer end, in the direction of Harriet's rabbit warren, while we turned left, to the quiet Surrey Lane, passing under the spire of the church adjoining the Roman Catholic Convent.

This convent, and all connected with it, was for us a sinister neighbour. Even the children who attended school there were tainted and dangerously foreign. We never met one of them in the flesh. We only heard the faint, despairing cries that came from their playground during intervals between lessons; if what they did there could be called lessons. I often wondered about them, as though they were children in a doomed city about to be destroyed by earthquake.

Every Sunday evening at six o'clock, two mournful bells of a dubious resonance rang from that spire, chilling the air, and lowering the temperature of our snug little home, just at that hour of the week when the human spirit is most susceptible to gloom. I have often inquired of people about this touch of melancholy that colours Sunday evenings, and everybody appears to succumb to it. Is it a purely English malaise, a tincture in our blood inherited from our puritan ancestors? Or is it more general, a symptom of the biological inertia which interposes between all rest and all action, a temporary hesitancy that the lens of the mind magnifies into a mood of fear and dread? I know that, from my earliest years, the ringing of those two bells from the Catholic Church every Sunday evening fettered my soul with iron. This reaction was unreasonable, for not until I was a pupil at Surrey Lane Infants' School did Monday mornings become dreadful, in prospect and in fact.

My first day there was just before Christmas, so that at the start I had the pill gilded by seeing the school-rooms decorated with paper-chains and tinsel stars. The hall, where Harriet left me, loomed up huge and dark in the winter gloom of a Battersea December. My timid wits congealed, and I moved as though I were wholly in a world of nightmare. The floor appeared to be covered by files of children, winding in and out under the guiding hands of several grown-ups, to the thumping tune from a piano, while the decorations overhead swung in

E

the foggy height. I found myself being directed, by a pat here, a pat there, from an adult hand, taking my place for the first time in my life in an organised communal pattern and purpose.

I looked on at this, marvelling at the strangeness; and at the same time I saw my own self-conscious withdrawal, a kind of obstinate refusal to be absorbed, to have my identity cancelled out. This process of conforming and criticising was probably not unusual, for I believe that self-awareness, and the faculty for observing oneself in contact with circumstances, begin in the cradle, and that the infant is already acting a part while at the mother's breast.

All that I recollect now of that first day at school is a scene of vastness: the enormous hall, the class-rooms, the endless files of children constantly on the move; the big Christmas tree and the grey-haired figure standing by it, handing out gifts taken from its sugary twigs as another woman shouted numbers. The meaning of all this arithmetic escaped me; but I was aware of a *firmness*, a cold impersonal pretence of benevolence in the air, which I resented as though it were mocking the sanctity within my hitherto solitary self.

Bewildered by this psychological novelty, and the physical strangeness of large spaces and huge numbers, I found myself being pushed forward to the tree, and taking from the old lady a sugar pig. It had a pink-mauve snout, and a blue ribbon round its neck. Its hide sparkled, hard and crystalline. I accepted it as part of the exaggerated unreality of this world into which I had been betrayed. I was half-afraid, half-exalted, but when, with equal unaccountability, Harriet and Jack suddenly appeared, to retrieve me, and I was withdrawn to become myself again, the sugar pig lay clasped in my arms to be taken home as a token of that strange adventure over the frontier of a new life, just as the scouts sent by Joshua into the Promised Land came back with bunches of grapes and jars of honey.

CHAPTER SIX

Hornbook in Hand

DURING MY NEXT THREE YEARS spent in fairly regular attendance at the infants' school on the ground floor of the red-brick building called Surrey Lane Higher Grade School, I had no support from my brother, for he was on the second floor, in the boys' school.

The régime there increased his aloofness, and this tempered our old intimacy. We walked to school together, Harriet no longer escorting us, but I quickly noticed a monitory attitude in the way he spoke to me. I withdrew into myself, and began to have some reserves toward him too, though I lost none of my worship.

Slowly and laboriously I learned the alphabet and the spelling of two-letter words, sing-songing them in a class of sixty infants, following the red-tipped cardboard pointer in the teacher's hand, as she wrote the symbols on the blackboard. What infinite patience children possess! Would an adult sit from 8.50 a.m. until 12, with few breaks, in a hard wooden desk, with a spit-rubbed slate and a shrieking pencil, tonguing out pot-hooks and hangers, content to make no seeming progress, day after day; and then resume the dusty and evil-smelling task from 1.40 to 4.30? Those were our hours in the infant school, at the ages from five to eight. My brother, in his more spartan circle of men teachers, and boys ranging in age from eight to fourteen, stayed in school until 5; and had home lessons to do in the evening.

The routine was accepted as nothing to grumble at. Jack worked at his lessons, and brought home excellent reports. I was wayward, quickly bored, and subject to the first signs of those internal pains that later grew more concentrated and

59

violent. But slowly I learned to spell, and found an interest in
the mystery of words. I carried the mystery home with me,
and its power began to work upon the books there. Hitherto
I had spent much time in sitting back in an arm-chair in the
long parlour, front and back rooms thrown into one by opening
folding doors.

I never saw those doors closed. The arch above them, and
also the two fireplaces, were hung with plush curtains edged
with tassels. I remember how carefully I had to move about
in that long room, for odd tables, stands, corner shelves, were
dotted about, filling the floor space, and displaying a wealth of
vases, photograph frames, decorated boxes, folded ivory fans,
and convuluted glassware, almost as fragile as the soap-bubbles
that I delighted to blow, on warm days in the garden.

The space before the bay window in the front was impene-
trable, being filled with bamboo stands carrying enormous
flower-pots, out of which rose a jungle of aspidistras. They
were the pride of Mother's heart, and she spent half an hour
every Sunday sponging the leaves with soap and water. The
surface of the soil in the pots was hard, and crusted with a film
of green. From time to time, flowers appeared at the base of
the leaves, like miniature shields, hard, round and roughly
enamelled.

Mother's love of plants was like all her other emotions, fierce
and constant. She drifted towards green things as though
bewitched. She could not be out in the streets of Battersea for
a quarter of an hour, without coming home carrying a root of
some kind, either found in a wall or crevice, or bought for a
few coppers from the barrow boys. Foliage rather than flowers
delighted her, and this speciality drew her to an interest in
ferns. Thus our backyard, in spite of its burden of bare
concrete and the cycle-house, had an Amazonian character by
midsummer, lush and sombre under lavish clusters of leaves
whose thick texture was beaded with seeds on the underside.
Hart's tongue was her joy, and she turned the dreaded cycle
rides to good account by insisting that a basket be carried on the
back of the parental tandem, to be filled with plunder from the
Surrey commons, the lanes of Kent, the copses of Hertfordshire.

It may have been this dominance of deep-green shades in
house and garden that gave the home atmosphere a touch of
sombreness, of brooding beauty. 'It made a harmonious background to Mother's personality, and even to her physical
appearance, the warm brown of her hair and eyes, the firm
mouth, the blood-mantled cheeks, and the undecided conflict
between joy and melancholy that affected each movement of
her over-expressive features. Her forefinger seemed always to
be soiled with mould, for she could not refrain from poking
about in the garden-beds, or among her flower-pots, if only to
touch these green things that meant so much to her and offered
her some gift or consolation not to be shared even with her
husband and sons.

It will have been noticed by now how every other object on
the screen of memory fades back when my mother appears
there. It was so in life, for she was a dominant wherever she
might be. I cannot explain why, for she was never assertive.
Indeed, the first noticeable quality in her was a Daphne-like
shyness, easily alarmed into suspicion and even hostility. But
this was obviously an induced social habit, due to old unhappy
far-off things, and it could not restrain her deeper and truer
self, the lyrical and laughing spirit that shone through the
melancholy, the caution, the expectancy of pain.

It was this capacity for enjoyment that made her so positive
a character, and prompted her to grasp at life with ambitious
hands. It fed her instincts, giving her confidence and insight
both into the present and the future. Thus she *knew* my father,
and she *knew* Jack and me, as we were incapable of knowing
her, and she ruled us accordingly. But the responsibility was
to kill her prematurely.

Long after I started school, my cumbersome efforts to learn
to read went unrewarded; I still ploughed my way through the
volumes of bound magazines, the *Welcome*, the *Boys' Own Paper*,
the *Family Journal*, which, for some reason that I still cannot
understand, my parents had sent to be bound in red, with
fierce red leather backs and corners. This gave a bright homo-
geneity to our two glass-doored bookcases that stood on each
side of the fireplace in the back half of the parlour, dimly lit by

the french window that crouched under the kitchen extension
of the house and veiled itself in jasmine during the summer.

I studied every detail of hundreds of pictures in these annuals,
and were I to meet them now, over half a century later, I should
be startled by a recognising familiarity. I can see myself, thrust
by the weight of the book to the back of the arm-chair, my legs
sticking out straight from under the scarlet covers; my attention
flickered over the riches, like a butterfly over an herbaceous
border, pausing to sip here and there, every day differently, but
always with a quick intensity that fed my imagination abund-
antly, until the small body housing it was also affected, flushing
and pulsing under the intoxicant.

So I drank there, careless and enraptured, the only cloud
being that dark blur of print below or around the pictures; a
blur that tantalised and reproached me now that school had
taught me of something concealed in those shadows on the page,
which hitherto I had disregarded as a mere framework to the
pictures, whose drama was more than enough for any fervent
mind.

That shadow grew during my terms in the infant school.
Conscience lay concealed in it like thunder, for I knew that I
was not trying to learn to read. My idleness of mind was
beginning to show itself, and had been noticed both at school
and at home. Mother and Jack frequently exchanged glances
while trying to help me over this first moral hurdle. I was
quick and instinctive enough to intercept those signals of misgiving, for what I lacked in intellectual fibre I made up in
nervous sensibility. I *thought* through my skin, as a cat does: a
dangerous and capricious way of entering the estate of
civilisation.

Still more abject was my sloth in the matter of figures.
Belated in mastering letters and words, I was still more behind
in grasping the significance and relationship of number, and
this provoked an inhibition that hardened into a mental scar,
so that I have passed through life slightly crippled in the field
of mathematics and the manipulation of money.

That early weakness was aggravated when I entered the
boys' school, following my brother, who soon departed with a

scholarship to the Polytechnic Secondary School. My timid reluctance to use my wits logically in mastering problems in arithmetic and geometry was given a medicine that only inflamed the sore. Caning after caning, the reflex accompaniment for me to every mathematics lesson, paralysed not only my brain but my nerves, and to this day I have remained almost totally without the equipment for grasping those elements of pure reasoning which lead, on the one hand, to the solitary delights of astronomy and music, and, on the other hand, to the social powers of engineering and finance.

This has been a lifelong deterrent, leaving my reasoning power half-starved, to be fed only on the overgrowth of my nourishment from language. I realise too late that my appreciation of such a divine philosopher as Spinoza must remain only tentative because I have never mastered the processes and assumptions of the world of number.

The disturbance in my mind grew, and still I could not master the elements of spelling. Any word of more than one syllable floored me and I fretted over the shame of this defeat. By the time I had been struggling for two years in the infant school with this problem, I had begun to have frightening dreams, and to wake in the night, sweating so freely that my flannel night-shirts tortured me. They might have been woven of horsehair.

Such was my nervous condition when, on that first day of the new century, I went with Jack to pick up the aquarium from Mr. Abbey's house in Tite Street, across the river. I was not, of course, wholly obsessed by my failing, for there was much to be enjoyed, hour by hour, in the procession of small events, and fancies. But not a day passed without this spectre touching me on the shoulder, at school and at home.

It may have been the nervousness resulting from this failure to spell that made me follow my brother with such dog-like devotion. For he was now eleven, and could read fluently. Moreover, he had begun to take an interest in the pianoforte that stood against the wall in the back parlour, with vases and picture frames on it that rattled and danced during our Sunday evening concerts, when Mother's overture, Sidney

Smith's 'Tarantella', opened the feast, to be followed by a violin
or flute solo from Father, or a richly emotional baritone song,
'Ora Pro Nobis', 'The Deathless Army', 'The Vagabond', 'The
Lost Chord'. The repertoire was small, but melodious. So
was the range of the instrumental pieces, which by constant
repetition week after week became lodged irreparably in my
mind, like bullets in the flesh of an old campaigner, too deeply
embedded for the surgeon to remove. I have only to hear
today the melodies of Raff's 'Cavatina', or Godard's 'Berceuse
de Jocelyn', Handel's 'Largo' and 'Harmonious Blacksmith',
and one or two hackneyed melodies from a Haydn sonata or
symphony, to be carried back instantly on the wings of nostalgia
to that parlour with the tasselled hangings, the aspidistras, the
gas chandelier that gurgled when Father had neglected to fill
the cup-like socket at the top with water: and I hear these
tunes not as they are being played by a tea-shop ensemble, or
on a radio programme, but in the hesitant tones of my father's
violin and flute, with the felted accompaniment of our solid
Broadwood-White piano, whose device for producing a
pianissimo (what was called an under-damper action) had
the effect of removing the whole performance from the parlour
to a remote bedroom.

Every evening before bed-time, Mother patiently went over
my picture books, trying to persuade me to give my whole
attention to words picked out here and there, so that I might
memorise them and the letters from which they were built. I
did my best to help her, for I was still so much an extension of
herself that her fears, disappointments, as well as her moods
of pleasure, overflowed into my veins. But try as I would,
eager in my devotion, I could not learn in the normal way of
deliberate memorising, through exercise of will-power. And I
have never been able to do so. I have to make the effort, for
intellectual conscience demands it, and I can feel only contempt for sleight-of-hand tricks in the processes of any kind of
work, mental or manual. But the scholar's method, the patient
accumulation, memorising and ordering of facts, comes down
upon me as a stifling burden. I force myself to it, but the
process remains unrewarding even after a lifetime of applica-

tion. The planning of a book, the constructing of a plot—all seems lifeless and mechanical still. If I had not faith in another motive power, I should be ashamed of my inability to work by scientific method, and of my lifelong habit of surrendering to a state of self-hypnosis before plunging into the actual process of creative writing.

If I had not faith! In that phrase lies the motive of my journey over the bridge of time into the past, and the setting up of a transparent theatre into whose fluid element I can stare at the living creatures evoked there, almost forgetting that I myself am one of them.

CHAPTER SEVEN

A Second Birth

I THINK IT IS THE GNOSTICS who believe that the soul is born when we are seven years old. I am inclined, from my own experience, to believe this dogma, and I base my belief on the events of that wonderful year, the first of the new century.

It began with the setting up of the aquarium in the bay window of the kitchen, overlooking the long and only flower-bed in the yard. The afternoon sun struck the back of the house, and threw a thwart beam across that window, penetrating into the aquarium and lighting up its occupants, so that they shone like lighted ships.

Jack's constructive genius first fully showed itself, in all its dogged persistence and ingenuity, in the furnishing of the aquarium. He was disappointed in the result, for his plan had been too grandiose: a matter of rubber tubes joined permanently to the kitchen taps, to supply the aquarium with running water. He had to content himself with that element called, during the 1939-45 war, 'static water'. But he made the most of it, and every night he scooped out a jugful, and poured in an equal amount from a vessel held above his head, while he stood upon a chair.

Thus the aeration of the 'static water' was assured. I knew, because I pressed my nose to the frontier of the aquarium, and watched the solid bubbles of air rushing around, gathering greenness as they travelled, changing from diamond to emerald in the process, before they dissolved to enrich the element.

Before disappearing, however, they lit up, by their iridescence, the fairy world created by my brother in that glass-bound continent. Tearing like comets through the firmament, they entangled themselves in meshes of water-weed, clung to the trunks and undulating tendrils of the underwater plants, dodged through the apertures of the grotto, and the branch of coral borrowed from a glass case in the parlour, bombarded the flanks of the three goldfish and their odd flunkey, a drab little roach who contrived, in this magic universe of light, to shine with an inky glow like a hooded lantern.

I cannot count what hours I wasted, if they were wasted, gazing into that distant world. When the slant sun of summer evenings struck the aquarium, the effect was so overwhelming that I stood there almost in tears. Sometimes at night, when the gaslight threw a sombre beam into the tank, I was equally moved, but with more tragic and foreboding an emphasis, for in this refraction the weeds had become dark emblems of despair, and the golden creatures subdued to a sluggish resignation, their tarnished sides immobile, except for a petulant movement of cavernous mouths and the supporting rhythm of the transparent fore-fins, no longer luminous.

It may be that the other-world scenery within the glass walls of Jack's aquarium so played upon my imagination that my sluggish wits were at last awakened. I know that about that time, the end-of-winter weeks before my seventh birthday in March, the concentration with which I stared into that small tank (much to the amusement of the family) began to be applied to the rest of the world around me. I saw things with much more particularity, and I was aware also of my curious pleasure in this recognition of detail.

No doubt the improvement was optical as much as mental. A medical examination at school had revealed the fact that I was short-sighted. The doctor took me solemnly between his knees, looked into my face, and said, "If you don't get some glasses, you'll be blind by the time you are fifteen, and I shall tell your parents so."

I was rather proud of this distinction. Fifteen! That was so far ahead that it meant nothing to me, except a sort of twilight at the end of life. My parents thought otherwise, and one Saturday afternoon I was taken, via a steep road called Pig Hill, to a chemist's shop on Lavender Hill, Clapham, opposite the first theatre that I was ever to enter, 'The Shakespeare'.

Behind the shop was a room where my eyes were tested in the rough and ready way customary in those days. The chemist hung an open framework that felt like the Forth Bridge around my ears and on my nose. Lenses were slotted into this, and twisted about, while I was instructed to read the card of letters beginning with a large 'E'.

I remember still the astonishment with which I saw the smaller letters change from a dark blur into separate items of the alphabet. I thought about it all the following week, and found that by screwing up my eyes when I was out of doors I could get to some faint approximation of that clarity, for a few seconds at a time.

This made me surmise that the universe which hitherto I had seen as a vague mass of colour and blurred shapes might in actuality be much more concise and defined. I was therefore half prepared for the surprise which shook me a week later when, on the Saturday evening, we went again to the shop on Lavender Hill, and the chemist produced the bespoken pair of steel-rimmed spectacles through which I was invited to read the card. I read it, from top to bottom! I turned, and looked in triumph at Mother, but what I saw was Mother intensified. I saw the pupils of her eyes, the tiny feathers in her boa necklet; I saw the hairs in Father's moustache, and on the back of his hand. Jack's cap might have been made of metal, so hard and clear did it shine on his close-cropped head, above his bony face and huge nose. I saw *his* eyes too, round, inquiring, fierce with a hunger of observation. He was studying me with a gimlet sharpness such as I had never before been able to perceive.

Then we walked out of the shop, and I stepped on to the pavement, which came up and hit me, so that I had to grasp the nearest support—Father's coat. "Take care, now, take care!" he said indulgently (though he disapproved of all these concessions to physical weakness). "And mind you don't break them!"

I walked still with some uncertainty, carefully placing my feet and feeling their impact on the pavement whose surface I could see sparkling like quartz in the lamplight.

The lamplight! I looked in wonder at the diminishing crystals of gas-flame strung down the hill. Clapham was hung with necklaces of light, and the horses pulling the glittering omnibuses struck the granite road with hooves of iron and ebony. I could see the skeletons inside the flesh and blood of the Saturday-night shoppers. The garments they wore were made of separate threads. In this new world, sound as well as sight was changed. It took on hardness and definition, forcing itself upon my hearing, so that I was besieged simultaneously through the eye and through the ear.

How willingly I surrendered! I went out to meet this blazing and trumpeting invasion. I trembled with the excitement, and had to cling to Mother's arm to prevent myself being carried away in the flood as the pavements rushed at me, and people loomed up with their teeth like tusks, their lips luscious, their eyes bolting out of their heads, bearing down on me as they threw out spears of conversation that whizzed loudly past my ears and bewildered my wits.

"Is it any different?" asked Jack, in his proprietary voice. He was never satisfied until he had collected all possible information on everything which life brought to his notice.

"It makes things clearer," I replied, knowing that I had no hope of telling him what was happening to me. I was only half-aware of it myself, for this urgent demand upon my attention made by the multitudinous world around me was the beginning of a joyous imposition to which I am still responding today, breathless and enraptured, though the twilight of the senses begins to settle.

My excitement must have communicated itself to the rest of the family, for Father proposed that, instead of our going home to supper, we should have the meal at The Creighton, an Italian restaurant near Clapham Junction. This was the first time in my life that I ate in public, and I remember it so clearly because the table-cloth appeared to be made of white ropes in warp and woof, and the cutlery had an additional hardness, beyond that of ordinary steel and plate. When the food came to the table, the steam rising from it was as coarse as linen. I saw the spots of grease on the waiter's apron, and the dirt under his finger-nails.

All this emphasis made me shy, as I would have been, indeed, without this optical exaggeration that had the effect of thrusting me forward, to be seen as conspicuously as I now saw everything and everybody around me. But I ate my fried plaice, dissecting it with a new skill, since every bone was needle-clear. Our parents drank stout, their usual supper glass. Jack and I had ginger-beer, a rare luxury that added to the formality of the feast.

By the time we reached the darker streets near home, my head ached under the burden of too much seeing. Perhaps the grease of the fried fish, and the lateness of the hour, had something to do with the exhaustion that almost destroyed me as we trailed homeward. The new spectacles clung to my face, eating into the bridge of my nose and behind the ear-lobes. I longed to tear them off and throw them away into the darkness. I tried to linger behind, so that at least I might secrete them in the pocket of my blouse.

But before I could further this purpose, something caught my attention. I realised that, after all, the side-streets were not quite dark; that the yellow pools round each gas-lamp, now as clearly defined as golden sovereigns, were augmented, pervaded, suffused by a bluish silver glory. I looked upward, and saw the sky. And in that sky I saw an almost full moon, floating in space, a solid ball of roughened metal, with an irregular jagged edge. I could put up my hand and take it, ponder its weight, feel its cold surface.

I stopped walking, and stared. I turned up my face, throwing back my head to look vertically into the zenith. I saw the stars, and I saw them for the first time, a few only, for most were obscured by the light of the moon; but those I saw were clean pin-points of light, diamond-hard, standing not upon a velvet surface, but floating in space, some near, some far, in an awe-striking perspective that came as a revelation to my newly-educated eyes. I felt myself swept up into that traffic of the night sky. I floated away, and might have disappeared into space had not a cry recalled me.

It was Mother's voice, in alarm, for she had looked round, perhaps impatiently, to urge me along, only to see me lying on

my back on the pavement, in a state of semi-coma. Father
picked me up, and I was still too far gone to resent being
carried like a baby. I knew, however, that Jack would have
something to say when we got to bed, for he would accuse me
of showing off, or creating a scene. He had a horror of any
form of demonstration, and he discouraged extravagance and
self-indulgence, two weaknesses which he was always prepared
to detect in me, and to correct.

CHAPTER EIGHT

The Fourth Dimension

FOR ME, the new century was certainly coming in like a lion, as we have seen from these miraculous events at the very opening of the year. I find it difficult to cope with the speed and emphasis of those that followed. I could now stare into the aquarium with augmented curiosity, observing the tiny details which had hitherto escaped a pair of myopic eyes. The bronze armour of the goldfish, the exquisite sculpture of the water-snails, the green flesh of the weeds, the microscopic solids suspended in the water, settling down to the sandy bottom, and swirling up with its lighter grains under the flick of a transparent tail: all these precise features of this fairyland of nymphs attracted my eyes for the first time, and began to draw my mind into a similar habit of particularity, feeding it and training it.

This was a fruitful discipline, so effective that my parents noticed a difference in my response to the common happenings of our daily life. Father thought so much better of my promising intelligence that he began to talk openly of his long-laid plan, the ordering of two tandems to be built of Chater-Lea parts, so that he and Mother on one machine, and Jack and I on the other, might be equipped to take the roads of England as our province, gypsies for the rest of our lives, free to say, with George Borrow, 'to the right, or to the left' whenever we should come to a parting of the highway.

This plan involved a serious economic reorganisation. The joint income at that time, made by my father as a sorter in the Post Office and my mother as a teacher employed by the School Board for London (a body taken over by the London County Council in 1902), was not more than £240 a year, though Father made a few pounds extra for a week or two before

Christmas, in compulsory overtime. During those weeks of strained excitement he was on duty night and day, and we saw nothing of him until Christmas morning, which he spent in bed, cosseted and petted after his heroic labours.

Out of this income, modest even in those days of low prices, when Britain was on top of the world, Mother was contriving to buy the house, through a building society. The owner, who formerly lived in it, was a rubicund character who worked on the *News of the World* and smoked cigars on weekdays as well as Sundays; a sign of prosperity. I remember the day he came over to see my parents, to clinch the bargain, and how he led a procession, consisting of himself, his wife, and a daughter of my age at whom I looked incredulously, and our family. He took us round our own home, pointing out its virtues from the builder's point of view. He had a reiterative phrase which I have never forgotten, for he drilled it into our minds as though he were hammering red-hot rivets into armour plate. Smacking a door-post or stamping on a concrete surround to a drain-pipe, he shouted, "Take a load o' dynamite to move that, old boy!"

'Old boy' was my father, though the landlord ought rather to have addressed himself to 'old girl', for Mother was the really interested party. Father would willingly have lived in his cycle-house, content to be near his steed and unhampered by static possessions.

Once a quarter, one of my parents took the carefully sequestered sum of money to the office of the building society, at the foot of the steps of St. Paul's Cathedral. Sometimes we boys were taken, and later on the task fell to Jack and me alone. How terrified we were on the journey there, weighed down with the responsibility of the money, and the instructions to "be careful, and not to speak to anybody in the street or on the bus". Dogged by highway robbers and footpads, we sneaked our way from Battersea to Ludgate Hill, timidly deposited the money, and emerged from that formidable office free of care, light of heart, triumphant.

People in a wider economic field do not realise the intensity of the mood of thrift which possessed my mother, and other folk in like circumstances. There was something of the Norman peasant's mania about this preoccupation with pennies. Mother had every coin earmarked, and what makes me admire her is that in spite of this elaborate planning, so nicely determined week by week and year by year, she seldom rebelled against my father's Olympian disregard when from time to time a new wave of enthusiasm moved him to buy a later brand of bicycle.

Like the ant, she moved round the obstacle, and started all over again on her schemes of thrift. I am not sure what her final aim could be, for she never discussed it. Perhaps unconsciously she was trying to draw her little household up to a standard of living such as she had been used to in Benjamin Orton's castle. Maybe she was propelled from behind, in horror, by the spectacle of the other grandparents in their squalid rooms in Hampstead; the drunken old soldier, the servile old woman whose handsome features not even time and stupidity could wholly ravage.

If her ambition was cultural, I never discovered it, for she appeared to be content that her sons should go to an elementary school, as near home as possible; and her economy made no allowance for buying books or music. During the whole of my childhood, my parents never bought a book, and I remember their puzzled silence when, out of my first week's wages of fifteen shillings at the age of sixteen, I bought for myself a Palgrave's *Golden Treasury* in the 'World's Classics', bound in red leather, for eighteenpence. I still use that copy, and it is little the worse for wear, though it has been carried in my pocket on hundreds of bicycle rides and tours, and in my luggage to many countries in Europe.

The only journals in our home were the weekly *Titbits* and *Cycling*, and the *Boys' Own Paper* and *Chatterbox*. Yet my parents went to considerable expense in having the monthly parts of the *Boys' Own Paper* bound in firm boards, with red-leather backs and corners.

It was as though Mother's intelligence and taste were deliberately held latent. She painted in oils, and most of the pictures in our home were her work, including the sumptuous cluster of German iris that enhanced the huge drain-pipe set as an umbrella stand in the front passage. She played the piano with skill, and could read music at sight so well that she was always commanded as accompanist at the sing-song parties customary in those decades. She was a good teacher, and Jack and I were instructed in the elements of music, both in fingering and reading. But she never took us beyond those elements, and appeared to be content to repeat, every Sunday evening, her performance of Sidney Smith's 'Tarantella', and the Victorian ballads which Father sang with such pathos. She urged him on with his flute-playing and his brave efforts on the violin, but here too the repertoire was limited to half a dozen pieces, repeated week after week, year after year.

Both parents were similarly confined in their literary range. They seldom read books. Mother, no doubt, was too exhausted by having to live two lives in one. As soon as I was able to trot to school alone, Harriet left us, and the price of her wages and keep went toward the quarterly allotments for the building society. Mother ran the house, doing the shopping on her way home from school. She made the beds at lunch-time (it was then called the dinner hour) and frequently scrubbed the kitchen floor after the midday meal, before going off to the afternoon session at school. In the evening she had the rest of the cleaning to do, the household sewing for four, the supper to get, and the rest of the tasks that usually keep the mother of a family busy from morning to night.

Yet she was an efficient teacher, and the fact that she was appreciated and loved was shown by the way pupil-teachers (young girls about to enter a training college) at her school were constant visitors to our house. Even the headmistress, a formidable dragon named Mrs. Parker, terror of the slum mothers, came to us from time to time, rustling in stiff black, with jet ornaments sticking out of her like broadsides of naval guns.

With all these people from the school, Mother was easy, informative, and listened to with affectionate deference.

This was her intellectual side, and I suspect that it had to be confined to her life with these colleagues. Father could not follow her there. He became uneasy, puzzled, even hurt, when on rare occasions, after some outside stimulus, or under the warming influence of a glass of whisky, Mother released her latent powers, and talked of matters other than the Post Office, the cycling world, and the sentimental to-and-fro of our family life. Father's grey eyes would grow cold, and if Mother did not accept this warning, he would make some sly and falsely humble remark that immediately brought out a likeness to his incalculable old mother. His wife's response to this was to drop her intellectual bravura, and to win him back by a gesture of affection. Sometimes, however, if she were over-animated by circumstances or good company, she would rebel; and then Father was instantly annihilated by a rapier of wit or sarcasm, against which he had no defence. A cloud would come down over the home, lasting for a day or two, while Father's fear-born sulk, and Mother's impatient mood of revolt, gradually dissolved, leaving our honey-sweet domestic happiness unimpaired.

But it was Mother who lost these battles, for she was fettered by her own passionate instincts. She loved us all with a fierceness that was desperate. It consumed her, as it subdued us. I responded to it, because I inherited some of it: a dangerous inheritance, that commits one into relationships that can become an incubus. Mother clung to Father like a tigress, and she was equally primitive and feline toward her sons. Her life was a losing battle, waged by her intelligence against this fever in her blood.

In everyday matters, and the more tangible problems of material ambition and the control of our budget, however, she was cool enough. Thus, when Father again mooted the idea of having the two tandems built, she staved him off, using my increasingly painful attacks of back-ache as an excuse. He, on the other hand, advanced the theory that the weekly exercise on a tandem behind my reliable brother would rapidly put me right.

The matter remained in suspense during the early months of that year, while our seemingly humdrum life moved on. It was during this period of calm that I stepped into the Fourth Dimension.

I attribute the miracle to the new spectacles, for it happened only a week or two after that Damascene Saturday night when I walked out of the chemist's shop and saw Lavender Hill, and the sky above it, filled with a Presence of which during my first seven years I had been unaware.

During the succeeding days I never lost for one moment the consciousness of my heightened faculty. I felt it in my finger-tips, and in that queer, observing self who had been my companion since I first began to look about me from the cot in my parents' bedroom.

It was a faculty, and it was also distinctly a power. It persuaded me that I *knew* objects, and had some kind of monitor-ship over them by reason of the vision with which I now could pierce into the heart of their being. And it was a universal power. I looked up at the plane tree, and I felt my authority touching its topmost twig. Near or far, nothing eluded my scrutiny: the sugar in the bowl on the tea-table, with tiny, flashing crystals; the dusty texture of the salt.

The excitement of this optical stimulation may have put me into a mild fever, for my sleep at night was peopled with great globes of flashing light; and in the daytime I felt my cheeks burning. The second self, the observing self, stepped forward to an even sharper alertness, and I moved under its guidance as though entranced.

Such was my condition one evening after school, when I was sitting at the kitchen table, drawing on a sheet of paper an underground labyrinth, and peopling its corridors and recesses with tiny matchstick figures, a line for the body, four lines for the limbs, and an open dot for the head. This was a pastime to which I had been long addicted but I could now pursue it more minutely.

Tonight, however, I was restless, and I wearied of the game. Bedtime loomed ahead, and I had no inclination to start a new game. Mother or Jack would soon be driving me upstairs. At the moment, they were absent from the kitchen. I looked about me, and saw nothing. I was tired, and not unwilling to go to bed. I looked up at the Swiss clock, in its wooden case on the high shelf over the stove. And I read the time!

At first I could not believe my eyes. The family had wasted hours trying to instruct me in the mystery of the clock face. I was just as dull over this as in the spelling of simple words. The impact on my mind in that instant was so sharp that I have remembered the position of the clock-hands ever since. The time was twenty minutes past six, and the gaslight above the table, over which I leaned and stared, hissed with an occasional impure splutter.

Then, still incredulous, I turned my attention to other objects in the kitchen. On the sewing machine lay Jack's library book, a dirty brown object disguised in a uniform binding with gilt numbers on the back. I picked it up, opened it at the first page, and began to read *The Swiss Family Robinson*.

It is an understatement to say that I began to read. I stepped into another life. I was one of that family on the wrecked ship, passing through the barrier of words, enlarging my small suburban existence by this new dimension. I could not know what was happening, or the scope of this vast inheritance. I heard the sea breaking on the shore of that fortunate island and I shared with Fritz, Ernest, Jack and Franz in establishing ourselves under the palm trees, and in offering up thanksgiving for our safety. I have never lost that island. I have since found Prospero on it, and bewildered princes, learning from them to question destiny and the appearances of the material world. But it remains, and has grown into a larger universe than either intelligence or imagination can comprehend. There have been times when I have confused it with actuality, much to my material detriment, for it is a mistake to come back to this solid earth, still wearing your crown, and making the gestures of a prouder office with which you have invested yourself elsewhere.

At that stage, the enlargement was not literary. The words themselves were not endeared to me. I had merely caught the knack of using them: and how I did it I shall never know, for to say that the subconscious self must have been learning under the dunce's cap does not explain the irrational process.

Mother found me sitting at the table, with the book in front of me, and my breathing body in front of the book. Then Jack followed her, and both of them stood watching for some moments before I jerked my head, saw them, and broke the spell.

"I can read," I said.

Jack frowned; and his frown was always an intimidation. He stepped forward and looked over my shoulder. "Twenty-five pages!" he said, turning to Mother. "Now read a bit more. Read it aloud," he commanded.

I read a few sentences, without stumbling.

"Ugh!" he exclaimed. "Now you'll have your stomach-ache!"

And I did; but not immediately. Mother made our supper cocoa, and I ate a slice of cold roast pork with bread and butter. Nobody mentioned this visitation which had blown the roof off our little house in Battersea. The pain came on in the night, and I tossed, writhed, sweated, until my groans woke Jack who lay beside me, and he went and woke Mother, who so gravely needed unbroken sleep, after her habitual double burden of day's work. It was the recollection of Jack's remark, however, with its grim realism, that brought the tonic to my startled nerves.

CHAPTER NINE

Irresistible Forces and Immovable Objects

THE CHANGE IN MENTAL and sensuous capacity brought about by a first pair of spectacles altered my whole way of life. I became, overnight, a bookworm. The novelty of my new power had much to do with this. I read the whole of *Swiss Family Robinson*, and was not deterred by a bloodstain which had oblitered half the print on a page in the middle of the book, at the point where Ernest fitted retractable blinkers to the ostrich, so that he could guide it to right or left while seated on its back, riding the whirlwind.

I read the book four times before venturing further. This lingering at the threshold of the Fourth Dimension shows how strongly I was affected; though I was not conscious of any timidity. Living for weeks with the Robinson family, and sharing the abundance which the island offered them, I quickly carried that wealth into our home circle. Every Sunday afternoon the kitchen furniture was rearranged, becoming the doomed ship, and Jack (indulgent of my novice enthusiasm) took part with me in the wrecking scene, and the setting up of our camp under the palm trees.

The new faculty had to be fed, however, and my eye fastened on all printed matter. I read passages in the *Daily Chronicle*, which had just replaced the *Daily Mail* in our home, as a result of my father's increasing rancour toward the governing class with which he had an unhappy, sinister connection. From that time, the period when the conduct of the Boer War was shaking many people's confidence in the impeccability of the set-up of the English social structure, my father began to air equalitarian views. They were neither coherent nor clear, and they had little political stamina. They emerged rather in moods of muttered resentment, as distant thunder, following lightning flashes that came not from him, but from Mother. I heard the word 'Socialism', and it sounded like a dying echo of 'Serve 'em right', ricocheting from the walls of the great country houses of England, as Father turned his back on them.

I remember reading the war news in this *Daily Chronicle*, and feeling my mind rising up inside me like a cat waking from sleep. What interested me was the sensation, rather than the material that fed it; for many years of social and mental bewilderment and unacceptable helplessness were to pass before I learned the secret of joyous living with an eye on the object and not on self, and a full confidence in that 'negative capability' which the young Keats discovered to be the true talisman of all poets. I would apply it still more widely, to every human being who desires freedom from the prison of self, and a confidence to grapple with the most outrageous of circumstances.

My parents made little comment on this new development, and it was Jack, not they, who opened the way further by taking me to the public library, in a back street unknown to me, where I enrolled in the Juvenile Department, and carried home my first borrowed book, *Masterman Ready*, another tale of shipwreck and desert islands. My visits to the library became regular, and within a short time I was going there twice a week to change my book. I read nothing but tales, and most of them were sea-tales, so that I soon had a working knowledge of the Pacific Ocean, and of life at the Poles.

For my seventh birthday in March, my mother gave me a Bible, and here for a while I was puzzled by the language. It puzzled and it worried me, and at first I put it aside. But the very bulk of print in the double columns, the delicious thin paper, the leather binding with flaps, drew me back to the book whose appearance was so different from all others.

During that summer I began to read the Book of Job. I had no comprehension of it, but it acted on my seven-year brain as a lashing of ship's rum would have acted on my stomach. I mouthed the wonderful phrases to myself, rolling them round and round, growing daily more word-drunk. My reading in other books, and upon the newspapers, was affected by this intoxicant. A consciousness of the way things were said dawned within my mind, kindling a light never to be extinguished.

I spoke about this to Mother one day, and she was critical, telling me that I ought to be thinking what the Bible was about, and not of the way it was written; that, after all, being rather old-fashioned. I looked at her in dismay, finding myself for the first time doubtful of her guidance. This made me so remorseful that I gratefully accompanied her, Father and Jack to the Congregational Chapel, almost opposite my school, the Sunday after that conversation.

So my wrong approach to the Bible started a new family habit. Perhaps Mother thought that the beauty and Jacobean grace of the Church of England service would only encourage me in my 'art for art's sake' tendency. Perhaps Father's growing interest in Socialism influenced also his religious mood, if he had such a mood, and disposed him to revert to the idol-breaking Protestantism of his mother's family.

This Congregational Chapel was filled every Sunday, because it had at that time an eloquent pastor, whose sermons boomed and thundered for nearly an hour, so that when he stood at the door to shake hands with every individual of his departing congregation, his face shone with sweat. I noticed, too, that his teeth were riddled with decay. This may have been the cause of a slight whistle and hiss in his delivery during moments of fervour, as though the grand organ were ciphering.

I listened to these outpourings of words, so that they became tributary to the river of language down which I was now being carried in that frail little boat, a childhood personality.

It was as though all incidents, all the purposes my parents unwittingly contrived, flowed together, augmenting the flood which I could not then control, and have never since been able to. By the time, less than eighteen months later, that I was transferred from the infants' to the boys' school, I could read freely, and took a lively interest in the way words were made. Lessons in spelling at school were thus an agony of frustration, until I was given permission to take a book with me and lose myself in it while my classmates struggles with constructions such as 'the cat sat on the mat'. They were quite indifferent to my withdrawn studiousness. I was to find this tolerance did not accompany my promotion to the boys' school.

That dreadful translation was not to come until the following year, when I was eight. The year 1900 had yet more miracles to offer, before our home life entered a period of more or less serene uneventfulness: but to call a child's life uneventful is to be clumsy in recollection, to forget that the smallest event in his crowded day is probably a pristine experience, startling his imagination, and putting a permanent impression on his mind.

Spring moved into summer, and the aquarium was now taken for granted in its place under the bay window of the kitchen; something that the home could not be without and could never have been without. Jack tended it regularly, and one afternoon Mrs. Brown, the cab-owner's wife, brought him a tiny jet-black fish, who was added to the company of gold, causing a violent acceleration of traffic in that confined world, which went on for a day or two, until the blackamoor was accepted, though he remained a Ganymede among these golden gods, ever restless, nervous, darting in blue-black diagonals across the tank, a perpetual foreigner.

Mrs. Brown herself was a black figure, a small old lady always neat in sequined cape and a high bonnet with flowers that bobbed as she walked. She had rosy, wrinkled cheeks and blue eyes that flickered in a constant summer lightning of benevolence. They fastened especially on me, because I was nearly always at home when she called. "Take care of that child" was a kind of theme-song in her chattering conversation with Mother, to whom she was devoted.

Mrs. Brown never came empty-handed. I was always presented with a stick of Cadbury's chocolate, which I preferred to eat by nibbling at it, mouse-fashion. Its flavour was deeper, more solemn than that of the flat squares of Fry's chocolate, which was our domestic brand. Mother was given a lace-edged handkerchief, or a pin-cushion; sometimes a pair of gloves. Evidently Mr. and Mrs. Brown did well on the profits from the four-wheeled cab. The old lady lacked nothing. She walked in jet and amber, rattling as she went. Her loose adornments flowed over the kitchen, or the parlour, like water from a duck just come to land: bags, string-bags, an umbrella, a veil, a smelling-salts, handkerchiefs and gloves, and various odd things such as thimbles, spectacle cases, reserves of earrings and brooches carried loose, and even, on one occasion, a bone shoe-horn.

She sat, bobbing and chattering like a cheerful little blue-tit, through the tea-hour until about six o'clock, when she would make an habitual exclamation of surprise, consult a jewelled watch after searching for it among the intricacies of lace over her bosom, and cry, "La! My dears, I must be off. Mr. Brown will never forgive me!" Mr. Brown being as rosy-apple-cheeked and as loosely accoutred with symbols of benevolence as his wife, but in a masculine way, such as ruffled silk hat, pocket-knives, nosegays, a long whip, and a voluminous blanket of double texture, one side being red wool, the other black waterproof: Mr. Brown being thus a male complement to his wife, it was impossible to believe that he was likely to harbour even the shadow of a suspicion that a person, least of all his wife, might need to be forgiven, under any possible circumstances.

On one of her visits Mrs. Brown produced what looked like an enormous sausage, some nine inches long, as hard as one of the solid rubber tyres on her husband's cab-wheels. She handed it to Mother, flickering her lance-blue glances over me and nodding the bonnet-blooms in my direction. "Make him a cup every night," she said, speaking of me as though I were absent. "He's a tender mite behind those spectacles." Certainly Mother would have taken this ominous counsel from no other person in the world but Mrs. Brown. It may have been because Mrs. Brown was not of this world, but created through a compromise between Charles Dickens and Hans Andersen. Therefore, while the sausage lasted, I was given a cup of Brand's Extract of Beef every bedtime, the essential solid needing to be slivered off the block with a shoe-maker's knife.

In spite of portents of physical weakness, I went regularly to school, becoming so self-dependent that I ran home alone twice a day, at dinner-time and in the afternoon, groping for the back-door key hidden behind the pan of the water-closet in the yard, and letting myself into the empty house.

Mother prepared the midday meal every morning before leaving for school; I needed only to add salt to the saucepan of peeled potatoes, and put it on the gas-stove. If the meat was a steak, or chops, I would light the grill, and get the pan hot in readiness before Mother came hurrying home, often short of breath and flushed, her eyes brighter than they need be. Jack, who followed me home, took a share of the jobs, either laying the table, or filling the scuttle, though he was usually distrait, in pursuit of one of his creative dreams, a slave to his own clever hands, which led him into many a fruitless pursuit, where after patient trial and failure he emerged pale with fatigue, as obstinate as the earthly materials which he had been trying to command to his invention, only to fail.

One such failure had a glorious moment of triumph. Out of his savings he had sent to the *Boys' Own Paper* for a set of brass castings, parts of a model locomotive. Following the instructions in the columns of the paper, he worked for weeks, polishing and filing, soldering and screwing, until one day the strange-looking locomotive was completed. It had a brassy appearance, its cylinder as prominent as a camel's hump.

It looked too heavy and massive for its size, like 'Puffing Billy' or 'The Rocket'. But its wheels, with their shining flanges, and its rotund boiler gave it a defiant character.

The wide circle of rails was set up in the yard, under the kitchen window, the lamp was filled with methylated spirit and pushed into place beneath that very cold boiler, the match was applied, and the blue flame flickered half-invisible in the summer afternoon air. Then we waited and watched. The monumental engine was quite indifferent to the persuasive fire under its belly. It stood still.

Jack refilled the lamp after the first charge of spirit had burned out. He relighted it, and set up two bits of board each side of the locomotive to keep the draught away. A faint, simmering sound was heard. It was only the locomotive sleeping.

Again the fuel was exhausted, and again Jack replenished the lamp. His face was now white with anxiety, and his eyes smouldered back in their caverns like panthers at bay. If I ventured on a remark, I was snapped at, and found it advisable to retreat a little, looking on from the middle distance, concerned rather with my monitor's humiliation than with the cause of it. My interest in mechanics was perfunctory, like Mother's interest in bicycles.

After the lamp had been filled for the fourth time, Jack made one or two drastic alterations, and even condescended to take Mother's help, by emptying out the now luke-warm water from the boiler, and replacing it from the boiling kettle. The combined operations worked. Internal noises were heard, and when Jack gave a flick to the cylinder, a single oscillation sent a jet of steam up his arm, making him jump back. But I could see the gleam of hope in his eye. Again he flicked, again the locomotive spat at him. He waited, while the internal irruptions and spittings grew more touched with temper. Then suddenly, without coaxing, the engine shuddered, belched, and began to move.

Slowly that stubby cylinder nudged the driving-wheel, a half, a whole revolution, then a second revolution. The engineer rose to his feet, looked at Mother, then at me, and nodded. He was too overwrought to speak.

I ventured nearer, knowing that the thunder no longer threatened. There we stood, Mother as spellbound as her two boys, while the brazen locomotive gathered momentum, moving round the circle, rocking the rails, faster and faster, settling into a steady pace, rattling round now, circle after circle, until it seemed to blur into a continuous ring of angry brass, rushing after its own tail with the intention of consuming itself, like the worm Ouroboros.

As indeed it succeeded in doing, for after a sudden acceleration, and amid a cloud of steam, there was a loud report, and fragments of the engine flew past our heads like shrapnel. The trial run was over.

Mother, terrified for her brood, forbade further experiments in locomotive engineering, and our next model railway, set up some years later, was to consist of ready-made rolling-stock and engines.

After this glorious defeat, Jack turned to one of his other intense enthusiasms. He had been working up to it for some time, putting in a spell every day at the Broadwood-White piano. His small but shapely hands appeared to be a part of the keyboard, so easily and so quickly did they fit themselves to it. His patience was unlimited, and he rattled up and down with the studies in a collection of Czerny's Exercises, and a book of scales which he had unearthed from the pile of sheet music that filled a bamboo frame beside the instrument, in a dark corner, as though it were stuff of a dubious quality.

Jack must have regarded it in that way, for after rummaging through it several times, with exclamations of disgust, he picked out only these books of scales and exercises, and one piece of music that to my infant eye looked more impressive than the rest of Mother's repertoire because the notes were so much more crowded and black, and the cover was decorated with a giant medallion containing the portrait of a grumpy old man with long, untidy hair. Round this medallion, and drawn out over most of the page, were outpourings of laurel, scantily-clothed ladies, and harps, trumpets and stringed instruments. The title-page contained a lot of printed matter too, but this was in a strange language and I could not read it.

Jack, now near his twelfth birthday, looked into this heavily-engraved piece of music, and at once his attention concentrated. I was sitting at the table in the back sitting-room, at the time he found this treasure, and I watched the familiar frown settle on his old-young forehead, below the cropped hair. He bent over the sheets of music, opened on the table, staring at the staves as though at a bull-fight.

"Look out!" he said, pushing me out of the way; for I was sitting with my back to the piano. I retreated to the other side, and went on with my drawing, though my interest in it was now divided, for when Jack was fastened upon a project, his intensity of will drew me after him, a feather caught in the draught of a comet.

He set the music up on the stand, and began his attack. To

my ear, the result was a confusion of sound most unpleasing. It was so to him, for he stopped, frowned more savagely than before, and made a fresh start. He got very little further before breaking down. But he would not be defeated. Again and again he started, and at last a smile of pleasure lit his face. He turned to me and said, "I know! This isn't the same as all that!" And he nodded contemptuously at the contents of the bamboo stand, which contained, no doubt, Sidney Smith's 'Tarantella' somewhere in the three or four-inch pile stored on-end in the dark corner.

I cannot explain what attracted my twelve-year-old brother to this sonata of Beethoven, the only piece of worth-while music in our home. His only instruction at that time had been given by Mother, to the limited extent already described. She had neither time, opportunity nor energy to further her own interest in music, and I am not certain that she possessed more of that interest than she exhibited on Sunday evenings, with her husband or a few friends who showed even less musical sophistication.

Then one day a gaunt young man with long hair and a nervous cough came to tune the piano. I noticed his thin, dirty hands, with finger-nails like claws, that rattled on the keys and scratched the face-board behind them. He smoked cigarettes the whole time he was at work: and that was an unusual habit in 1900.

Jack and I were vastly interested. We stood side by side watching him that Saturday morning. He took out the front of the piano, exposing the strings and the rusty pegs. That was wonderful enough. But he talked to us while he worked, break-ing off the conversation at intervals while he struck a note and called forth a clank from the three strings whose neighbours had been muted by a metal tool stuck through them. He talked to Jack, over my head, and my attention wandered.

Jack, however, was doubly interested, for two sides of his nature were engaged by this long-haired professional. He saw the mechanism of the piano at work, and learned, by demon-stration, how the pressure on the soft pedal brought up a long damper of felt and applied it to the strings, to cause that far-away effect which made the listener urgent to run upstairs, or into the kitchen, seeking the music so ventriloquially removed.

I could feel, by the tone of the conversation between Jack and the tuner, that this method of inducing a pianissimo was not approved. Jack's face wore the bleak inscrutability habitual when he was bored or disgusted. His nose became bigger and bonier, and his eyes retreated into their sockets.

In spite of his disapproval of the structure of our Broadwood-White, Jack was able to give particular attention to the other part of the tuner's flood of soliloquy. It was about music, and it poured advice over the bullet-head of my brother, who stood gravely beneath it, like a religious enthusiast receiving baptism by total immersion.

During a pause, after the tuning was done, he produced the Beethoven sonata, and asked the tuner to give him an inkling how it should be attacked.

The result was like that of opening a weir. The thin, bow-backed figure of the piano-tuner shook with latent energy. He tossed his hair back, cracked his bony knuckles, and began to play the sonata in G major, Opus 32, No. 1 (published in 1803), which, as music-lovers will recollect, opens with a startling statement, a running gesture, and then the assertion of a theme whose dogma is beyond all doubt.

The tuner emphasised that dogma with the vehemence of a Savonarola castigating the pleasure-loving Florentines. Jack and I swayed like water-weeds in the flood, making the same mesmeric movements under the invisible punches of the music. Then, after the violent assertion and running to and fro, the second part of the sonata, heard by us both for the first time in our lives, came out with a long, rapid melody that tore us up by the roots and flung us downstream; the main stream of the art of music.

The musician was equally touched by his own magic, for as he played this melody, he leaned over it, watering it with his flowing hair, which almost touched the ivories. I was deeply impressed, as much by the spectacle as by the music. All was new to me: the performer, his odd manners and appearance, the nature of the music and the fluidity of the performance.

G

That is why I have never forgotten that half-hour, as long as one of the half-hours spent by Adam and Eve in the Garden, before their Disobedience set the clocks ticking.

When the performance ended, the pianist sat, nervously working the muscles of his cadaverous face, and wiping his dirty hands on a dirtier handkerchief. He was sweating freely and emitting an odour as of mice, or bats. Then he turned to Jack, and looked at him. But Jack was lost. He stood before the keyboard, staring at the notes, settled into a shy obstinacy. I could read that index. He was struggling with something; an emotion against which his cautious and sardonic mind was warning him. He ignored the unhealthy figure at the piano, and he ignored me.

Thus, for several moments, we made a statuary group, the musician and I waiting for my brother to show some sign. But we were to be disappointed, for suddenly he looked up, quietly thanked the tuner, and left the room. He must, however, have gone to Mother and spoken to her, for when she appeared, without Jack, to pay the tuner, she asked him if he would give the boy some lessons, a request to which he agreed.

From that time, Jack put in some practice daily, and went regularly for a weekly lesson. He did not let this interfere with his other interests. He always had some constructive project in hand, one in particular giving me great pleasure. It was an aerial railway, whereby little buckets suspended under a double-flanged wheel were run along lines of thread set up intricately round the back yard, with graded slopes to ensure a steady flight of the buckets. One terminus was inside the kitchen, beside the aquarium, the line entering through the open window. We sent pencilled messages to each other, I being stationed by the goldfish, and Jack far abroad in the cycle-house. Our communications often took the form of spelling lessons, for Jack was determined to teach me to be accurate. He carried this purpose almost to excess a year or two later, when I had sufficiently mastered the piano to be able to leap, in a stepping-stone progress, over the bass parts of several books of duets, mostly by minor German composers, such as Kirchner and Volkmann.

Our games of spelling by aerial railway, and our playing of
duets on the Broadwood-White, were always accompanied by
a sort of screwed-up, highly-tuned patience on his part, marked
by a nervous sensitiveness in the muscles round his mouth and
eyes. The least stumble by my duller mind or clumsy fingers
would cause those muscles to twitch, as though Jack had bitten
on a gumboil. His whole body would shrink, and wait in this
protective contraction until the shock was absorbed. Then he
would quietly instruct me to start again, and once more the
opening theme of the overture of 'Masaniello', or 'The Barber
of Seville', or 'The Arlesienne', boxed and muffled by that
esoteric combination Broadwood-White, was launched on its
doomed journey.

Though Jack was undemonstrative, indeed almost secretive,
in his pursuit of music, he did not drop the more practical
business of his life, the inventions, the engineering feats, the
drawing and painting. But within a few weeks of that
thunderous introduction to Beethoven, Jack had brought into
the home Bach's 'Forty-Eight' and the 'Well-Tempered Clavi-
chord', and sonatas by Haydn and Mozart, the volumes all being
borrowed from the Music Department of the Public Library.
The Broadwood-White stood up to it doggedly, though without enthusiasm. This unresponsiveness was bound to cause
trouble. I saw it coming. One wet Saturday at the beginning
of the summer holidays, during that gloom of apprehension
while we counted the hours of the three or four days prior to
setting off, Jack was struggling with a sparkling passage in a
Mozart sonata. But the damp, hot weather of the Battersea
marsh had clogged the action of the piano and swollen the
damper felt; so that the music was Mozart with a cold in his
head and a sluggish liver.

Suddenly Jack stopped playing, struck the obdurate keyboard with his fist, and began to sob. This conduct was so
utterly out of character that I stared at him aghast. I could not
bear the misery and embarrassment.

"Jack! Don't! Don't!" I cried: and I began to weep too,
for I happened to be in a highly emotional state that day, a
condition due partly to the excitement of anticipation and

partly to the influence of the book I was reading, Mark Twain's
Life of Joan of Arc, an incredibly pathetic piece of work.

I found that book by chance in the Surrey Lane Library, and
it has haunted me ever since, in association with a sad *étude* by
Stephen Heller, which Jack was playing repeatedly at that
time.

The distress in the drawing-room must have communicated
itself about the house, for Mother appeared (flustered and tired,
being engaged in packing the huge tin trunk ready for Father
to cord-up and label). Jack's head was soon in her bosom, and
I was clinging shipwrecked to her skirts.

Then Jack found voice. He was seldom articulate in words,
preferring to exercise his authority by nods, grunts, salted
monosyllables. But his occasional outbursts of rhetoric had an
Old Testament ferocity of denunciation about them. And
here was one such occasion. He damned Broadwood-White and
all their stubborn works, their boards, their frames, their
dampers, which never in all the history of the art could unite
to make a musical instrument. He called our piano a mangle,
a wheelbarrow, a plough. He demanded that Mother should
sell it, or burn it, since he was determined never to play on it
again.

Mother was angry: and also she was hopeless. She, too, wept
a little, and pushed Jack from her. But she knew what he
meant, and I could feel the sympathy in her anger.

After the emotions died down, she said that she would speak
to Mr. Brown about the matter when he brought his cab to
take us to King's Cross station, a day or two later. The idea
of selling one piano and buying another was revolutionary, in
those late Victorian days, even in a household which had been
shaken up by the evidence of an unusual talent in my brother.
There was small reserve of money, for the payments to the
building society had to be found, quarter by quarter, ill or well.

We could see that Mother was worried by this wholly unreasonable demand from Jack, normally the most cool and
rational member of the family. But she promised to see what
could be done and to talk things over with Father.

At that last suggestion I felt a twinge of misgiving, for only a few days before I had overheard a bedroom conversation between my parents, in which Father had argued most persuasively that if only we bought the two tandems, money need not be wasted on these annual railway fares up to Rawcliffe on the Humber, where Mother's sister lived with her dentist husband in a long, Georgian house on the village green.

My misgiving was soon justified. Jack's personality was already so pronounced that, although he was only twelve years old, he took part in the family conference on this crisis of his making. It was held one Sunday evening after tea, during that hour of foreboding when the two bells of the Catholic Church were ringing their ominous vespers. I was present, lying on the rug behind the sofa, unseen but alert.

Mother had evidently opened the attack earlier, for Father now broke abruptly on the matter by addressing himself to Jack, who sat at the table reading the new monthly number of the *Boys' Own Paper*.

"What's this about a new piano? We've got a piano," said Father, ready to be jocular. Jack retreated into his cave, and glowered. This both annoyed and frightened Father. He hated trouble and would always contrive to walk round it, or to persuade it away. He was adroit at both methods.

"Mother and I have been saving up ever since you were little chaps," said Father, now with a note of grievance, as though Jack had done him a grave injury. "We've always hoped and planned to get you boys on the road with us, so that we can be free, the whole family, to go where we like, do what we like, and be beholden to nobody. We've got the world in front of us, Jack, my boy. Think of that! I'll take you to the mountains of Wales. We'll go to the Highlands and the Lake District. And Dick and Mother with us! Think of that! But we can't do everything, my boy. You know how hard Mother and I work for you boys. You're our lads, and we're proud of you. We want you to have the best of everything. And there's no better and stronger machine built than one made from Chater-Lea parts. I won't tell you what the two tandems are going to cost us: but Mother and I have gone into that; and we've decided to do it now. I've been round to the agent and ordered them. It's going to do young Dick a world of good; fresh air, plenty of exercise; that's what he needs. And you too, my boy. Not always this crouching over books. Get up with the sun and breathe the good air. That's the order of the day—out, and on the road!"

By this time Jack, the habitual pessimist, had realised that he was faced with an accomplished fact. He emerged from his fastness, his face pale, his eyes hooded by those heavy lids. He studied Father in such a way that Father appeared to be much the younger of the two antagonists, as no doubt reincarnationists would believe him to be.

Before Mother could intervene, Jack accepted the situation: but by the strength of his personality he contrived to do so without uttering a word, or committing himself in any way. The Catholic bells suddenly clanged together three times; harsh, dissonant notes, as from a very raven of religion. A black silence fell, and Jack sat in the midst of it, more inscrutable than ever.

CHAPTER TEN

Excursions and a Miracle

JACK'S CLOUD OF MELANCHOLY did not lift. Not even the prospect of a brand-new tandem bicycle could cheer him, for his obsession with music was already a tyrant over his whole nature, absorbing his sense of justice. Father was devoted to him, as to Mother and me, and this desire to have us all with him on the white roads of England was a true and elementary passion, like that of a child who picks up a bird or a kitten in its hands and crushes it convulsively.

The holiday in Yorkshire was darkened by my brother's mood. Fortunately for me, the rambling country house and the long garden with its orchards, fruit-coverts, stables and yard, and the two servants with their Yorkshire dialect, intrigued me so completely that my attention was distracted from Jack's grievance.

My aunt and uncle were amused that a child of seven should be so interested in the way Yorkshire folk talked. My widowed Grandmother Orton gave me particular attention, reading to me and hearing me read, and making me whistles from balsam stalks. She was a calm, gentle person, at peace after the removal of her savage-tempered husband. I loved her, and was delighted that she came back to Battersea to stay for a few weeks, before going on to her youngest daughter in North London.

During that early autumn she filled our home with a serenity like evening sunshine, a quality that my parents, happy as they were, could not dispense because they were still too urgent in the affairs and responsibilities of the noonday of life.

I recall one instance of the comfort which Grandmother gave me.

Mother had spoken gravely to Jack about this business of the piano, and she promised him that she would now begin to save, in a special fund, in order to buy a more sympathetic instrument. He must practise meanwhile on the Broadwood-White, and avoid using the soft pedal. It would be a good habit to get his pianissimo by delicacy of touch, rather than by mechanical means.

I was privy to this compact and took it much to heart. Jack's disgust for the Broadwood-White communicated itself to me, and I criticised its dull, clapper-like tone and its bilious walnut case. But I did my daily bit of practice on it, making little progress, being reluctant to overcome an increasing physical laziness that made all movement a weariness of the flesh. I preferred to sit and draw even more and more intricate underground chambers and tunnels, peopling them with ant-like figures of a useful formality, whose hordes I could command to my liking.

But my quick understanding of Mother and Jack, and of their half-secret compact, made me eager to help it forward. Our immediate disappointment was softened by the gift from Grandmother of a musical box, a lovely thing with inlaid work on the lid, and a second lid of glass fitting down on velvet edges.

The works gleamed golden, and the barrel through its close wire bristles shone with a sun-like splendour as it rolled slowly round, its bristles plucking at the metal teeth of the comb against which it rotated. It played only three tunes, for we had no reserve of barrels: but this repertoire could be endured over and over again. It was fairy-music. It came from a land of miniature sorrows, and pleasures so tiny and exquisite that they were more heart-breaking than the sorrows. Inside the lid was a picture of German peasants, a dark forest, a mountain village.

One wet day I ran home from school at noon, concerned because I was wearing a new pair of boots. Thinking that it would be a good plan to dry them in readiness for the afternoon, I took them off and put them in the oven of the kitchen range, while I busied myself with setting the potatoes on the gas-stove, as usual. Grandmother, who had been unwell, was upstairs in her room.

Jack appeared, and Mother followed. She was tired and worried about Grandmother's failing health. There had been some bother, too, about money, for the cost of the tandems threatened to be much more than at first estimated. Father had done a little dodging over this, passing it off as a mere nothing. It needed great patience to appreciate him when he was in one of these equivocal moods evading responsibility.

Mother entered the kitchen that day, set down her large black handbag (she was like Ellen Terry in this, for she went nowhere without it, and never had another one); she set down her bag and sniffed.

"What's smelling?" she asked.

I knew at once. A sickening sensation gripped my stomach, as though I had been winded by a blow in the solar plexus. "I put my boots to dry," I whispered as I opened the oven door. A cloud of steam arose and I drew the hot boots through it.

Mother collapsed into a chair, and stared at the boots, then at me. She wept and grew angry. I stood numb with misery, holding the crinkled boots in my hand.

"Put them on!" she commanded, suddenly. "Put them on! And go to the off-licence for some stout. I must have something to revive me. I can't slave like this, day after day, trying to keep the home together, and not a soul to help me; not a soul!" The emphasis she put on this last repetition was tragic and desperate, neither Jack nor I could withstand it. I struggled into the boots, sobbing blindly, and groped for an empty beer bottle. Then, degraded and shamed, I hobbled up the street on those corrugated soles.

The man and his wife who kept the off-licence also kept a huge bulldog, brindled and slavering. This monster, emblem of the British brewing industry, had always shown a friendly interest in me and came slouching round the counter whenever I entered the shop, dribbling over my stockings and muttering canine endearments.

On this occasion he stopped short, sniffed, and sniffed again. Then he approached gingerly, and nosed around the baked boots, looking up at me with so marked an inquiry that both his master and mistress were made aware of the calamity.

This so put me to shame, and I was in such discomfort from the boots, that I wept afresh, and confessed what I had done and how Mother had made me come out in the boots as a punishment.

The off-licencee and his wife petted me, and gave me a stick of sealing-wax, which I put forlornly into my trousers' pocket, while the bottle was filled with stout, the cork stamped in, and sealed from the pot of boiling wax on the counter.

, By the time I got home, Mother had recovered from the shock. I was forgiven, the boots were removed from my cramped feet, and Grandmother, who now appeared from her room, undertook to buy me a new pair. Poor Mother hurried on with the belated meal, and peace reigned.

That gift was the last Grandmother gave me, for she took to her bed shortly after, and died in our house.

For several days the home became a foreign world, filled with relatives.

I have no recollection of the death or of its immediate consequences. I saw no demonstration of grief. Jack and I were sent away for a few days to the other grandmother, in the unsavoury rooms in Hampstead by the horse-tram terminus, overlooking a fever hospital. We spent much of that time with the pseudo-grandfather, wandering about the frontiers of the heath, and waiting for him outside the public-houses. But he was not unpleasant company, and told us tales of his life at Malta. He told them with zeal, especially after calling at several pubs.

Much of his reminiscence was unintelligible to us, though the facts must have entered our minds, for I have them lodged in mine still. They were connected with a Maltese girl whom he had by this time deified. He described her charms, and lingered particularly on certain ecstasies, and how, when they were over, this Mediterranean goddess would fling her arms round him with unabated ardour. The tears ran down into his beard as he recalled this touch of tenderness. I was moved too, though I could not understand why. It was impossible not to sympathise with him, knowing that he now had to go home to the tumbled puritanism of his old wife, who was incapable even of cooking him a decent meal, or cleaning the three rooms which were his last home in this world.

Jack and I returned to Battersea to find one aunt still with us: the youngest, a riotous woman who had lost an eye and wore a black patch. She had remained to help Mother clear up. I had little to do with her, for Mother and she did not get on together, and we were kept away because she swore frequently and blasphemously. We decided, Jack and I, that she must have inherited the temperament of her father, old Benjamin, whom we dimly remembered as a pincher of cheeks and ears.

One day before this aunt left, she struggled out to the yard, carrying a double-bed mattress from the room where Grandmother had died. She called us from our play and made us help her shake and beat the mattress, describing with un-Victorian candour the uses to which it had recently been put, and to which it would in future probably be put, by way of compensation. Thus, during the upheaval caused by Grandmother's death, Jack and I were given some insight into the beginnings and ends of life in the flesh. But we made no comment to each other about this widening of our knowledge.

At last Mother got the house cleared of her relatives, and her relief compensated for the exhaustion. Her black clothes made her look thinner, and a slight habitual difficulty in breathing became more pronounced. She turned to Father, and to Jack and me, with even more than her usual ardour of love. What is more, she broke through her discipline of thrift, urged by an impulse of restlessness following the emotional disturbance of her mother's death. She must have come into a little money at the time, though we were not told of this, the subject of money being taboo. I do not know the cause of this; but it has had a lasting influence on my attitude to money. I find it still a most embarrassing matter to discuss, especially when it concerns a fee for a professional job. Even when I buy something in a shop I ask the price with a slightly self-conscious hesitancy, half-expecting the man or woman behind the counter to share my discomfort. As for bargaining, I find that wholly impossible and undignified. The neurosis, persisting lifelong, must have been expensive.

Mother's revolt against thrift consisted, first, of having the kitchen redecorated in a wallpaper of gay, open pattern, that appeared to double the size of the room. For the first time, 'art' entered our Victorian home, bringing light and gaiety.

Her next step was to buy Father a new bicycle, with a modern invention called a 'free-wheel' and Bowden brakes. He had hungered for this, tempted by the advertisements in *Cycling*; but had restrained himself because of the larger project, the bespoke building of the Chater-Lea tandems, with handle-bars to his own design.

Mother's act in buying this bicycle was no doubt diplomatic, for her next plunge was to ask Mrs. Brown about the deferred problem of the pianoforte.

One evening, while Jack and I were playing in the yard with our aerial railway, the four-wheeler clip-clopped up the street and stopped outside the house. We rushed under cover of the jasmine-roofed side-way, and peered through the lattice of the garden gate. We saw Mr. Brown set his whip in its socket, stand up on the box, unwind his rug, drop it over the horse's back, and climb wheezily down. Then he disappeared behind the back of the cab, and emerged with a nosebag, which he fixed securely for his beast to feed. Finally, looking the whole outfit over with a methodical eye, he turned in at our gate and pulled the T-shaped handle that rang the bell behind it, inside the front door. Mother let him in.

I was prepared to return to our game; but Jack stopped me, telling me to wait, and remain hidden at the garden end of the jasmine tunnel. We thus were concealed beside the house-wall, near the open french doors of the back sitting-room, into which Mother had invited Mr. Brown.

Father was at work, on late duty. He seemed always to be at the office, or away on one of his cycle rides, whenever Mother had some major project afoot.

We heard Mr. Brown cough, and accept a glass of port (from a bottle surviving the funeral feast). Then Mother invited him to inspect the Broadwood-White, and to say what contribution it would make toward buying another instrument. Mr. Brown was doubtful and reluctant.

This opening conversation, so clearly overheard, threw Jack into a deadly stillness. He seized me by the arm and motioned me to stay behind him, while he waited for further developments. The aerial railway was forgotten.

Mr. Brown explained that he was not properly in the musical instrument business, or indeed in any business; but that 'things came his way, my dear'. He met all kinds of people, in all walks of life, and had many regular passengers who were ready to give him a tip, or put him on to a good thing. If he *did* hear, for example, of a piano, Mother might be sure that it would be a bargain, at a knock-down price. She must understand that these odd bits of trading with which Mr. Brown was put in touch were usually the result of some unfortunate loss, or personal crisis, connected with the vendor. Ready money was always the immediate consideration.

The conversation retreated as Mother saw Mr. Brown to the front door, and Jack and I were left to wonder what conclusion had been reached. We watched Mr. Brown go through the several operations, but in reverse, which had assisted his arrival. Seated on his box, he flourished his whip at Mother, who stood at the gate watching him. The horse clip-clopped up the flinty road, Mother shut the front door, and Jack and I returned to our game. But it languished. We played no more that day.

Days, weeks, passed, and nothing was said to us, nothing further happened. Jack would not ask. At first we lived uneasily, hoping and expecting. Jack's irritability increased, and one day he was so sarcastic to me that I threw a toy at him and cut his forehead. The screams that followed were mine, not his. He led me into the house by the arm, and told Mother that there had been an accident.

"Yes," she said, "I saw it."

This outbreak cleared the air, and the temperature of our daily life dropped to normal. The year began to close in, the jasmine blossoms disappeared, and the tall sunflowers in the tile-bordered bed became skeletons. The first cold weather drove me indoors to more and more reading; my first winter

as a literate mortal, so that I welcomed the dark evenings and
the fireside stool.

Then, one day toward Christmas, Mrs. Brown paid us a visit,
shutting herself up with both my parents in the sitting-room.
The following day was a Saturday, and Mother cut and packed
sandwiches and gave us the pennies for our bus fares to South
Kensington, from the 'Rising Sun' at the corner of Surrey Lane.
We spent hours at the museum, staring at the mastodon and
the stuffed animals. I was wholly lost in wonder, but Jack
obviously was merely filling in time. He answered my inquiries
patiently, but with an incoherence most uncharacteristic. I
suspected nothing. I had, perhaps, forgotten the promises, the
conflict, the scheming about the pianoforte.

But when we got home, there, in the front parlour, stood a
new instrument, another upright, but in a plain black case,
severe, formidable. No piano-slip, no photograph frames, no
vases, softened its professional outline. It stood apart, like a
priest, expressionless, different from the fussy life around it.

"You'd better wash your hands," Mother said. I cannot
recall a better example of understatement. It came after she
had followed Jack into the sitting-room, where he had gone to
look for a book. But he had not come back to the kitchen,
where I was already seated at the table, hungry and tired after
our day at the museum. So Mother left me alone there: but
the silence of the house was eloquent. I felt it communicating
something to me, through the hair on the back of my head.
Everybody knows that prickling sensation over the skull when
some supra-rational intelligence is being unloaded at the door
of consciousness, while the door is still closed.

I slipped down from my chair and crept along the passage.
Mother stood just inside the doorway of the back room, looking
at Jack framed in the arch between the rooms. The light
(which she must have kindled in readiness for this moment of
drama) struck downward over his bony head and the ridge of
his nose. He looked severe, his adult mouth set grimly. His
eyes were dark. He was in one of his moods of retreat.

Mother waited. I felt cold and clung to her, pressing my
face against her apron. She put her arm round me, but still

stared at her elder son, waiting for a sign. Then he spoke, but hardly to us. The whisper was the surface of a deep soliloquy going on inside that monk-like figure.

"It's overstrung," he said.

"How do you know?" asked Mother, as gently as though she were waking a sleepwalker.

"I've looked," he went on. "And it's a shift-key action!"

I could hear that he was awe-stricken. The terror of perfection was upon him; an emotion familiar to his cautious nature.

"Well?" asked Mother, puzzled, and perhaps a little crestfallen.

Jack did not reply. Slowly he advanced towards the piano, his face expressionless, though a false diagnosis might have described it as sulky. I leaned forward to peer round the archway. I saw him pause, then open the lid. The keyboard, dead-white instead of the colour of old teeth, was as austere as the ebony case. He drew up a chair, sat down, and raised his hands above the keys. Another pause followed. He may have been afraid, or incredulous.

Then he struck a chord and ran up and down a scale. Even my childish ear recognised at once the quality of tone. It had a velvet softness, but there lay upon this velvet a clear-cut diamond of sound.

Jack leaned forward as though he were losing his senses. Then he began to play, and I recall the piece; it was a Spanish dance from an album called 'From Foreign Parts', by Maurice Moszkowski. He had memorised it before returning the book to the library.

I do not know who was the more entranced and surprised, Mother or I. We stood, clinging to each other, listening to those crystal notes, and I had the illusion of *seeing* them as well as hearing them, so hard, so clear, dropping into the incongruous cosiness of our Victorian sitting-room. I had the impression, too, that the old Broadwood-White, in the dark recess of the back parlour, was brooding jealously, clumsy with reproachfulness. I could almost have been sympathetic toward it, had I any emotion to spare.

But I had not. Here was an experience that demanded more than I was capable of at seven years of age. I stared at the black beauty, and at my brother seated at it, back bent, a frown on his face. I identified the two. They were creatures of a kind. They belonged to the same incarnation, remote from the world of suburban Battersea, the pawky good humour, the complete unconsciousness of other values than those of domestic warmth, simple family virtues, elementary pleasures.

It might be hyperbolical to suggest that Jack and the new piano recognised each other: but so it seemed. And my brother instantly became more than ever a changeling, a creature utterly unaccountable in this environment and of this heredity.

Mother and I were so completely hypnotised by the music itself, and by the quality of Jack's technique revealed through the connivance of the new instrument, that Father came home unperceived, without either of us noticing that he was later than usual after his nine-to-five duty at the Post Office.

He came in, clapped an arm round each of us, interrupting the music with a loud:

"Why? What's this? The new piano come?"

Jack stopped abruptly.

Father bundled us forward, and the three of us stood over Jack, who still sat at the keyboard.

"It's made by Klingmann, of Berlin," he said, reading the inscription on the face-board. Then he demonstrated the soft-pedal action, showing how it brought the hammers a fraction of an inch to the left, making them strike only two strings of the tri-chord.

By this time, however, Father's patience was exhausted. He picked me up gleefully, rubbed his handsome black moustache over my face, and cried, "I've got news for you! I looked in on the way home. The tandems are ready! They'll be delivered this week!"

And he herded us out to the kitchen, to a high and noisy tea, his excitement so open and healthy that we felt quite sunburnt by it, and dusty from the macadam roads of England.

CHAPTER ELEVEN

Father Opens a Campaign

THE ARRIVAL OF THE TANDEMS WAS DELAYED, however, until Christmas Eve. In the meantime, Jack concentrated all his energy into one mania—piano practice. Nobody objected, because the dulcet voice of the Klingmann pleaded for him.

A few days after it had taken its prime place in our home, the tuner came to attend to it. And Jack attended to him. A new phrase entered my vocabulary, 'Continental Pitch'. I rolled it round my tongue, and my imagination fastened on it with the aid of the engravings on the albums of music that now flowed into the house from the public library. I pictured a foreign country, with snow-covered alps, and villages with onion-topped church towers, and castles on crags above a turbulent river. 'Continental Pitch'. The phrase was to lodge in my mind like an acorn in fertile soil. At that time I had never heard of such a thing as an orchestra. The only musical instruments known to me were the piano, Father's fiddle and flute, and our musical box. Occasional whiffs of music from outside the home—the Salvation Army brasses and drums, a barrel organ or a hurdy-gurdy, were too infrequent and too distant to impress me. The only choral music I heard was that of the carol singers at Christmas time; but this was not of our earth. I heard it in a waking sleep, out of the winter darkness.

Jack's musical experience had been equally limited, and the wonder is where he found his fastidious taste and his technique. And I am also puzzled by my Mother's timidity and my Father's complete unconsciousness over his talent. There he was, a child of twelve, struggling unaided with the difficulties of Bach, Mozart and Haydn, reading books on counterpoint and harmony, and burning himself up in the process, so that he grew more and more monk-like in appearance, his nose protruding startlingly during these years of puberty when physical development tends to be uneven, so that one day a boy or girl is all feet and hands, and a week or two later the head becomes top-heavy.

During that week or two of uninterrupted piano-practice before Christmas, Jack's skill in performance improved so much that Mother and I often found ourselves relinquishing any job that we were at, to creep into the sitting-room, and stand or sit, listening to the surly little musician frowning at the reading desk, his neat fingers flickering with a stylistic disdain over the keyboard. "Fine! Fine!" Father would say, when he happened to be indoors. But his new bicycle and the prospect of the tandems kept him preoccupied, and I had the feeling that he was biding his time, to introduce us to what he conceived to be a larger and more worth-while life.

That time came on Boxing Day, two days after the arrival of the tandems.

The machines were the latest thing in the cycle trade, especially the smaller one specially built for two boys aged twelve and eight. The handlebars were so designed that they could be adjusted through an infinity of positions, and the saddle-pins were elongated for a like purpose.

It was impossible not to share Father's triumph and excitement. His pleasure might even be called delirium, except that the idea of fever within so perfect and healthy a body was inconceivable.

Although he was still sleepy on Christmas Day, after so many eighteen-hour stretches of work during the postal rush over several weeks, he got up early that morning, as soon as Jack and I had unpacked our stockings, and was out of doors before breakfast. While Mother cooked the Christmas dinner, he was busy with spanners and rags, tightening nuts and polishing spokes, summoning one or other of us in turn to see if our respective saddles were at the right height and pitch.

Mother had to summon him in several times, with some sharpness, so that he should be ready for the ceremony of Christmas dinner; but there he was, in his wooden arm-chair at the head of the kitchen table, skilfully sharpening the old carving-knife on the steel, the stag-horn handles of both clasped in his square fists. Before him lay the aitch-bone, a mountain of meat shaped like the rock of Gibraltar, still sizzling and spitting beads of fat and oozing blood-gravy into the little well at one end of the willow-pattern dish.

"Ah!" cried Father: and his teeth gleamed under his black moustache as he smiled at us, his small family seated with him at the table on that first Christmas Day of a new century, with all the roads of the world open before it. His grey eyes reflected those limitless vistas, and I could see his mind busy with the prospect of pleasures ahead to which he would introduce us now that we were equipped to accompany him.

Mother, flushed and tired after the hard morning's work in the hot kitchen, sat opposite him, and the steam from the joint and the mounds of potatoes, sprouts, and mashed swedes clouded her spectacles; or maybe they were dimmed by the heat from her face. She took them off and wiped them on the edge of the tablecloth, while Father carved the beef, filling our plates with thin slices, wielding his weapons with a flourish, while maintaining a gay discourse on his wife's genius as a cook, and how lucky we boys were to have such parents who could feed us like this and show us the glories of nature and the far cities of the earth.

Mother's brown eyes, without the disguise of her spectacles, looked at Father where he sat enthroned in his enthusiasm, like a god in a nimbus of light. I saw her worshipping him and I wondered which of his family round that table admired him most, Mother, Jack or I.

What a meal it was; the plates covered with a layer of roast beef, batter pudding and vegetables piled on that British base: the Christmas pudding that followed, black in its ripeness, and flaming with brandy: then the crackers, the almonds and raisins, and a glass of port for each of us.

When the feast was finished, and Jack and I had rolled like young Roman patricians from the table, Father overrode Mother's protestations and ordered her upstairs for a rest, while he and the boys would wash-up.

Two large black kettles of boiling water from the kitchen stove (a stove now lazily slumbering in its ashes after a hard morning) were consumed in this task as well as the contents of auxiliary saucepans on the gas-stove in the scullery. Father, with Mother's apron round his best suit, stood at the sink with the dirty plates and cutlery piled beside him. He talked and sang as he washed, jockeying Jack and me along when we fell behind with our wiping-up. The cat, also replete, sat on the mangle behind us, staring with an Egyptian inscrutability at this display of energy amid a cloud of steam, shot with half-lights from the surfaces of tumblers, plates, forks and spoons, polished by our towels.

Then the last saucepan was scrubbed with Monkey Brand soap, the bowl and sink flushed down with hot water and soda, and the job was done.

"Now, boys," cried Father. "We'll have a lesson in mounting!"

By this time my distended stomach was beginning to rebel, but I dared not say so. We went out to the yard and the cold air struck through my super-heated skin, waking me from my lethargy, so that I realised, with a shock, the ordeal confronting me.

Father brought forward the smaller tandem, as proud of it as a cavalry officer of his horse. I stood shivering on the concrete, my swollen belly fluttering as though I had swallowed a live bird instead of a plate of beef. I was frightened as well as cold. This lesson was my initiation as a cyclist. I looked helplessly at Jack, who took the occasion calmly because he was already experienced, having possessed a small machine of his own for the past year or two.

"Come along," he said quietly, "you'd better try now. It'll make things easier when we have to go out on the road."

So I took my position beside the rear saddle of the tandem, while Jack held the front handlebars. Father seized my right foot and my posterior, hoisted me into the saddle, explaining at the same time how I must push off on the right pedal, in time with Jack. After several repetitions of this exercise, we tried the process together, and to my terror I found myself in the saddle and the tandem rushing up the yard. Jack, not used to the length and weight behind him, wobbled and applied the brake. Whereupon I fell off and barked my shin on the rat-trap pedal. But again I dared not give in, and for the rest of the afternoon we went through the movements of mounting and dismounting, until by tea-time the ritual was mastered and I felt some confidence, though by now Jack was bored and grumpy. Father, however, was jubilant. He patted us on our strained and aching backs, and promised us a real ride next day, and a lesson in correct pedalling, with the ankle dropped and heel at the correct angle to get the most power in every push.

Darkness saved us from further drill. Silent, exhausted, we crept into the house, leaving Father to bed the tandem down in its stable and to follow us indoors, as cheerful as ever, where he greeted Mother with a kiss and drank half a dozen cups of tea, while describing the route which we were to follow next day on our first family ride.

The pleasures of Christmas evening were shadowed by that vigorous prospect. I call them pleasures; but every child must know the anti-climax that follows the impossible excitements of the earlier stages of Christmas Day: the day that began in the small hours of darkness, with toes groping under the blankets, trying to feel the laden stockings at the bed-end. Then, with wakefulness increasing at each rustle of wrapping-paper, there followed the decision that we could start, where-upon Jack scrambled out of bed, slowly struck a match and lingeringly lighted the gas, commanding me not to be so impatient. So came the moment to unpack the stockings, to show each other, item by item, the carefully-chosen gifts until we came to the formal apple and orange at the bottom.

After that, the removal of ourselves with our swollen and con-fused riches to our parents' bed, where we sat up, demonstrating our treasures, while the elders dozed half-sincere in their occasional displays of interest.

Throughout the morning these gifts and the larger ones given us at breakfast would keep us in a state of delirious ecstasy, an exultation that could only result in a corresponding fall.

It came always after tea, and it usually lasted right through Boxing Day, by which time the more fragile of the treasures would be broken, and those left whole would have lost their savour.

That Christmas evening our gloom was deepened by fore-boding, as Father sat tuning his fiddle and giving us our march-ing orders, or rather pedalling orders, for the morrow. He proposed to take us for our first family excursion to Virginia Water and back. That was his idea of a gentle ride, without strain for Mother, and bearing in mind that this would be my introduction, as a cyclist, to the 'rolling English road'. Only Father knew the mileage and the weight of the tandems.

"Are you sure it's all right?" asked Mother.

He pooh-poohed the misgiving and reminded her that he and Jack would be at the head of the tandems, bearing the brunt. Then he gave himself to the present task, the performance of Godard's 'Berceuse de Jocelyn', with Mother playing the accompaniment on the old Broadwood-White, because Father said an English piano, tuned half a tone lower at English pitch, was good enough for him and did not strain the strings of his fiddle. His attitude toward the Klingmann was a criticism, only half-concealed, of all that new instrument stood for: a too serious interest in music, Jack's precocity, and Mother's encouragement of it. Our family musical *soirées* were therefore always held in the back room round the Broadwood-White, which remained unsold, to be carried with us five years later when we left Battersea.

Boxing Day dawned bleakly with thick fog and frost. Mother refused to set off, as had been proposed, after breakfast. Father was annoyed and took himself into the back room, where he played his flute in solitude until dinner-time.

We all sat in silence round the table, consuming cold beef, bubble-and-squeak, and cold Christmas pudding. "Tom!" said Mother, suddenly, at the end of the meal. Both Jack and I detected the note of warning in her voice, and we looked at each other apprehensively. It made us shy and miserable to see Father rolled over and bounced in the flood, as though he were no older than ourselves, though we knew that in the end, as the clouds rolled away, Mother would contrive to restore his dignity and set him up again as the head of the house who could do no wrong and whose word was law.

But this time the heavens were on Father's side, for the fog broke and a gleam of sunlight, like a dusty yellow handkerchief, flicked across the bay window of the kitchen and almost brought the aquarium and its inmates to life.

It also flicked the sulkiness and disappointment out of Father's grey eyes. He looked up, squinted at the sky, and said:

"You were quite right, my girl. We've done better to wait. But it'll have to be a short ride round the houses today. After all, there's a lifetime before us."

Mother could not deny him a second time, and we got ourselves ready for a local expedition. Father wore a short covert coat of fawn, a cap, knickerbockers, stockings and spats. Mother veiled her straw hat as though she were a bee-keeper, fastened the edges of her skirt with clips and yards of elastic to the insteps of her shoes, and carried a little fox-fur tippet round her neck. Jack and I both wore buckled knickerbockers, black stockings, marine jerseys, and cloth caps. I was also wound into a long scarf made of squares of red and black knitting (like the quilt on our bed), and I wore a pair of woollen gloves.

The front door was locked, the cat put out, and we all emerged into the backyard.

"Now then," said Father, "we're off, my dears! I'll lead the way, Jack; and we'll make for the park, ride round once or twice, then come out by the Queen's Road and beat the boundaries of the parish. There will be no traffic about on Boxing afternoon."

He was right, as he always was, in outdoor affairs. The streets of Battersea, after the revels of Christmas Day and the morning of fog, were deserted. We had no need for self-consciousness as we wheeled the long tandems round to the street, accompanied by the cat, who sat on the coping mewing with dismay at being turned out of her arm-chair on a cold and frosty afternoon.

Mother and Father mounted and left the mooring of the kerbstone. "Come on," said Jack, "or we shall lose sight of them."

I shivered, gulped, and obeyed. Jack was already in his saddle, grasping the handlebars and balancing the machine beside the kerb, with the offside pedal raised and his foot on it ready for the push-off.

I put my foot over the low centre bar and took my seat.

"Now push!" cried Jack.

We were afloat. We glided on, and the pedals carried my feet round with them. Gradually feeling the regularity of this movement, I began to take my share in keeping it going, leaning forward convulsively and pushing on the downstroke. But I forgot the other pedal rising on an unaccented syllable, and the foot on it was lost, was waggling in mid-air, and the ankle was angrily bitten by the rat-trap pedal.

The pain was sharp and unexpected. Tears streamed down my face, and the cold air chilled them to pellets of steel. But Jack was desperate, and wholly concerned to keep the machine on an even keel. He was fighting against the weight and length of the monster and the useless lump of mortality seated behind him.

I could do nothing but hang on, my hands convulsive on the brown felt grips. Jack urged me to push, for he could not propel the tandem alone. I did my best, and slowly the numbed foot came to life again, though by now my fingers were frozen to the bars.

We rounded the corner safely at the top of the street, and this gave us confidence. After all, the tandem was a handsome specimen, and unique. Our parents were sailing on ahead and I heard Father call aloud:

"Come along, boys, keep close."

His voice floated merrily over the ghostly parish, and I saw a window curtain drawn aside and a face peering out at us.

On we pedalled, and by the time we reached the park gates near the Prince of Wales's Mansions, I had caught the knack of free-wheeling at the same time as Jack, though this meant a slight lag in my rhythm, the difference between pushing with him and being on the alert for pushing with him. This gave him the burden, though neither of us knew that I was not taking my share.

I could see little ahead; only the faded blue of Jack's jersey and the nape of his neck. But to right and left I had a prospect of Battersea that commanded my attention by its stillness. I have never forgotten that quiet scene, so negatively emphasised. Even the fashionable bicycle track round the park was empty. We circled it twice, Father and Mother slowing down and riding abreast of us, so that Father could give us a taste of his vitality as an open-air guide. Nothing quelled his high spirits. I watched his shapely calves working as steadily as the pistons of a locomotive, his ankles and heels dropping on the turn, regular, exact. The pressure needed no exertion and he still had all his breath to feed that flood of conversation, buoyed upon outbursts of song, usually a stave or two from his favourite ballad:

"Oh merry goes the day
When the heart is young "

His heart was congenitally young, and appeared to be totally unaffected by the hardship and humiliations of his early life. Like Hardy's 'Darkling Thrush', he poured abroad his triple repeated ecstasies:

"When Frost was spectre-gray,
And Winter's dregs made desolate
The weakening eye of day."

These words from Hardy's poem, written that week, on the 31st of December, aptly describe the afternoon of Boxing Day and the boskage of Battersea Park, where the morning's fog still lingered under the bare trees, though their higher branches 'scored the sky' with some faint suggestion of colour and form, brown against pink, but all of it dusted with the gathering consolidation of frost.

That frost deadened my feet, which moved round, each in its cold circle, like corpses in a whirlpool. Even Father's animal warmth could not thaw them, though he rode beside us and from time to time put an encouraging hand on my back, a giant's gesture that caused our tandem to leap forward as though the road were suddenly declined beneath it.

Battersea is never a sun-drenched district. It lies in what used to be marsh and mudflats, a stretch of land succumbed to the lazy embrace of a wide curve of the Thames. In primeval times the mists must have lingered there winter and summer. In the Victorian Age of smoke and iron they lingered there still, but deepened with an overhead obscuration never wholly dispelled. That may be why, in those days, few birds inhabited there; only a desolate colony of sparrows, their feathers mono-toned and as drab as their feeble twitterings.

The inhabitants of Battersea tried, instinctively, to brighten their lives by a copious use of lime and whitewash. Human resistance to environment is always marked in some way, and we find that the cleanest and most arduous housewives inhabit the dark industrial towns. I think of the white lace curtains, the flashing window-panes, the vividly reddled or whitened doorsteps of the dwellings in Leeds, or Manchester. So too in Battersea, where now the natural canopy of river mists was augmented and riveted with the heavy underside of factory smoke, the dreary streets were diversified with a thousand eccentricities of domestic pride: a front path paved with bottle-ends or even the metal caps from bottles; a figurehead rescued from the ship-breaker's yard; an old mast erected on a deck of concrete before the house; and, hung before his gate by one neighbour, a lifebelt kept bright with white paint.

This was the little world round which we rode that day, during its suspension from the welter and moil of normal life.

Leaving the park, by an eastern gate, we followed the parental tandem over Chelsea Bridge. Father had evidently changed his mind. I was to discover that once on the road he threw all consecutive plans to the winds. Often, on a tour, he would start off in the morning by wetting his finger, holding it up to feel which way the wind blew, and choosing our course by deciding to run before the wind 'to help the boys along', but also, I suspected, to enjoy a greater sense of freedom and to spread the wings of his panic heart in a justified irresponsibility.

Over the bridge, we turned westward along the Chelsea

Embankment. Here we passed one or two broughams carrying
rich children to the parties of other rich children; fabulous
creatures wholly outside our ken. The sooty gardens in front
of Cheyne Row lay dead. How sombre, how ominous was
Victorian London in winter, especially to a child susceptible to
colour and clean line, and to whom cold and damp were
specially abhorrent because they increased the periodical bouts
of pain in his stomach.

Father pointed out the place where he had thrown the pickled
onions at Thomas Carlyle, but the story meant little to me, for
the name was unknown, and I was beginning to flag. Our
tandem was built not of light alloys, but of the steel that was
the chief foundation of the British Empire, permitting it to pile
superstructure upon superstructure of wealth. I felt as though
I were propelling the whole of the steel industry at each rise of
the pedals. But Jack did not think so. He grumbled at me for
being a mere passenger, and he was probably right, for he had
to lean over his handlebars and groan as he pushed.

"Drop your ankle! Drop your ankle!" cried Father, dis-
approving of this uncontrolled exertion. Jack only muttered to
himself, and I could see from the pose of the back of his head
that he too was at the point of exhaustion. I began to feel
miserable, and I looked at Mother, but she was still veiled and
she sat behind Father like Patience upon the monument, though
I was certain she was not smiling.

We passed the end of Tite Street, and though by this time I
was too enfeebled to give attention to any matter, I recalled
how Jack and I had crept timidly on to the Embankment,
bearing the precious aquarium.

Father now proposed that we should plunge past the house
where the painter J. M. W. Turner once lived in squalor, into
the district so aptly named the World's End, and that we should
continue westward along King's Road, Chelsea, to Walham
Green, ultimately to cross the river by Wandsworth Bridge and
so home by the York Road past the malodorous candle factory.

But the veiled figure of Patience riding behind Father
suddenly came to life, and an angry life. She insisted on dismounting. Accordingly we drew into the side by the river-

pavement. Jack's strength, however, was not enough to support the tandem while I jumped off. Nor was I capable of jumping, my inadequate body being by now rigid with cold. We both collapsed and lay on the pavement with the tandem on top of us. The situation was not graceful, and it offended Jack's over-mature dignity. After we had struggled up, unhurt, he stood white with anger, and not daring to vent it on Father he picked upon me as the scapegoat. I was past caring. I stood in a coma of general discomfort, every part of my anatomy aching, except those parts too numbed by cold even to ache.

There followed, upon the pavement of Chelsea Embankment, still happily deserted, one of those scenes when Mother broke through her usual policy of government by seeming acquies-cence, and staged an open revolt.

Without a word, she brushed us both down, leaving Father to pick up the shining tandem and rest it against the trunk of a plane tree. Then, snatching off my gloves, and feeling my hands, then Jack's, in search of evidence, she opened her attack. She cursed the tandems, their weight, their length, their manœuvrability. She referred to the disabilities of the female body and particularly of mothers of children, she pointed out the singular delicacy of her own children and enumerated several reasons for it, all connected with Father's heredity, personal stupidity and callousness. She called upon God to witness the universal unfairness between the sexes, with woman as the eternal victim and slave.

Jack, during this oration, retreated to the balustrade, and looked at the ebbing tide and the seagulls lamenting over the mudbanks of Chelsea Reach.

Still Mother had not finished. She was flushed, as I could see because she had unfastened her veil. The smoky sunset clouded the lenses of her spectacles, otherwise the fire of her eyes would have annihilated poor Father, who stood quietly waiting as though being photographed beside the new machine.

Mother's vehemence terrified me by its extravagant range. I wanted to implore her to stop, to leave the rest unsaid, so that the whole universe of nature and man should not be made to depend upon my father's innocent impulses, his premature opening of the summer campaign for the conquest of the English roads.

At last Mother's breath gave out. She stopped, and drew me to her as though we were now to face the spears of a hostile tribe, or the rifles of a firing party.

"That's all right, old girl," said Father. "We'll take a short cut home over Battersea Bridge."

CHAPTER TWELVE

Sunshine and Shadow

LIFE HAD BEEN ALL ROSES during the three years in the infants' school at Surrey Lane. Promotion at the age of eight to the boys' school introduced me to the thorns. No doubt my experience was like that of most boys of the same age who leave home to start at preparatory schools for Eton or Winchester. But boys in that walk of life would probably be more hardened for the shock by having been brought up in nurseries, removed from an over-warm emotional contact with their parents.

The change from women teachers to men made a difference that affected every aspect of life. Everything, and every relationship, became less personal and more formal and official. Contacts, favours, privileges, and justice itself, lost that element of caprice which enables the genius and the rogue to flourish. The human male is like the Jehovah whom he created in his own image: administrative, legalistic, inexorable, reluctant. He prefers to proceed by seniority. That is how he has built up civilised society and its institutions.

To a child emotionally over-stimulated by the close intimacy of a lower-middle-class home, during the years before the Welfare State put in its foot to prevent the front door being slammed against the outside world, this introduction to a standardised environment was bewildering. At eight years of age I had been permanently conditioned, so that I have never wholly been able to surrender myself to it. The machinery of officialdom, which works in school life, in business, in politics, on committees, and particularly in the Government services and the law, has made me feel like a gypsy in court, or a butterfly on the wheel. Though later in life I spent a quarter of a century in the Civil Service, the wonderful organisation

founded on the Stoic philosophy, I have never been able to
prevent myself from shrinking with dismay and a twinge of
humiliation whenever I go into a bank, or a post office, or a
big departmental store; any place run on impersonal, institutional lines. These perturbations are, of course, concealed. I
fancy that the man who becomes a master of men, a statesman,
a tycoon, is one who never feels these perturbations, and is thus
able to grasp, without a moment of misgiving, the controls of
that machinery of government, of finance, of all large-scale
activity.

Yet I fear that I may be generalising dangerously from my
own particular case. Many of the exemplary officials of
modern life, the men whose blood has been transfused with
ink, have come from homes like mine: cosy, passionate, instinctive, and almost completely isolated. It is not even safe to
say that this early environment is the cause of the nonconformity of certain characters who develop into masterly
manipulators of that large-scale machinery of modern life. If
certain self-made men are unorthodox, men such as Lord
Beaverbrook or Ernest Bevin, is not also Sir Winston Churchill,
whose childhood knew neither the inner nor the outer suburbs?

How dreary, and how bog-like, all this generalisation
becomes. I feel it choking me, giving me the same sensation
of dismay as grips me when I go into a post office to buy a
stamp, or sit down to fill up one of the forms with which our
State-controlled lives are littered.

So I found myself in the boys' school, and there I endured
its processing until I was twelve, when we left Battersea. My
brother's career was the model on which I was expected to
shape my own. Unhappily for me, the school had a system by
which a master went up with his class of boys, standard by
standard, from the first to the seventh, the ex-seventh being
run by the deputy-Head, a gentle, bearded scholar who walked
alone. It was he who finally took my brother under his wing,
and made him win a scholarship to the secondary school
attached to Battersea Polytechnic. Fifty years ago such scholar-
ships were rare. All through these school years Jack's health
was faultless. He never had to stay away from school, or avoid

doing his home-work, on which he spent a couple of hours every evening, after a day at school that lasted from 8.40 a.m. until 5 p.m., with a midday break from 12 until 1.40.

The lower standards up to the 5th finished at 4.30. Otherwise, the boys had to work just as hard. I found it heavy going, especially as the emphasis was on arithmetic. The arts were not encouraged at Surrey Lane, perhaps because it was a higher-grade school, though to what that aspiration pointed I did not discover.

The system of the master remaining with his class for several years, from standards one to seven, which meant practically the whole six years of a boy's life in the school, was unfortunate for me because I had the master who had formerly led my brother through the same groves. His name was Mr. Meek, and he was trusted by my parents because he had always been so helpful and favourable to Jack, a brilliant pupil. There was some professional fellow-feeling, too, between him and Mother. Thus he received me with marked interest and was prepared to further my education, as he had furthered my brother's, with some particularity and enthusiasm.

Perhaps the fact that I was a precocious reader gave him false hopes. He may have expected that I should bring the same precocity into my dealings with vulgar fractions and the decimal system, and, later, with mensuration, the elements of Euclid and the measurement of water flowing in and out of tanks, sumultaneously, through pipes of differing diameters.

He was quickly discomfited. He soon found that I had no aptitude for figures because I was not rational in my way of life. He also found that I was an apprehensive boy, groping my way through the world as a snail does, by the aid of instinctive horns that retracted with lightning speed before the least opposition. Mr. Meek evidently disliked snails, and before long he began to treat me like one. This tended to make me keep my horns permanently withdrawn, while I was in school and subject to his increasingly chilly criticism.

Before long, this unhappy relationship began to tell upon my health, and more and more notes from Mother had to be sent to school excusing my non-attendance.

My nervous condition was aggravated by what went on in the playground before and after school, and during the so-called 'play-time' break each morning and afternoon. It was anything but play for me, at least during the first year. Jack's position as a member of the Seventh forbade him to have anything to do with me at school, and I had to try to stand on my own feet.

I was not always successful. This was due to a game popular with the bigger and heavier boys, who formed themselves by joined hands into a living lasso, which hurled itself across the concrete playground and wrapped itself round the small, shrinking *fauna* of the lower standards, throwing them to the ground and dragging them to a corner, where they were released with velocity against the wall, to whimper there, and ruefully staunch the blood flowing from grazed knees, elbows, or noses, and to wonder what would be said at home about their torn garments.

But the innumerable forms of minor torture, bullying, and mischief which boys can serve to boys, as a portent of the ways of the adult world, have been written about too much because of the deep impression they make on the infant mind. There were compensations: the tiny joys, equally pristine and impressive, which the grown man and woman have to relinquish as their sensibility hardens. It was a pleasure to chew pieces of orange-peel in school, or those withered tubers called 'tiger-nuts', or a dried bean called 'locusts', bought in the one-room sweet-shop in a slum dwelling opposite the school gate, kept by a crone who subsisted upon the farthings thus gathered from the scholars.

I recall, too, the seasonal games, such as the mid-summer sport of 'cherry-oggs', when ingenious boys made castle façades of cardboard, with doors through which their mates were invited to pitch dried cherry stones, so many being paid out if the stone passed through. I have no doubt that some of the more persistent of those promoters are now successfully running football pools.

After the 'cherry-ogg' season, which ended with the expert manipulators carrying large cotton bags full of this stony

I

currency, there followed the autumnal jousting with horse chestnuts, or 'conkers'. A certain amount of research went into this game, in the matter of toughening the nuts by soaking them in oil and drying them. One social factor worth recording is that a boy's word as to the promotion of his 'conker' was always accepted. It might be a 'fiver' or a 'tenner'; or it might have smashed a hundred adversaries. No doubt was ever thrown on the claim by its wielder. That should make us confident that ultimately the United Nations Organisation will be an accepted and trusted authority.

With the coming of cold weather, iron hoops were heard trundling to school, driven by boys with an iron hook in a wooden handle. Both hook and hoop wore smooth and polished under this mutual friction, while the skill of the trundler in guiding the hoop, turning, stopping and bouncing it, served as an apprenticeship to later dexterity with a bicycle; a skill transmitted perhaps hereditarily to sons and grandsons, to emerge in the driving of sports cars and the piloting of jet planes.

These are only three of the group games which enriched street and school-yard life, kindling mass enthusiasm overnight, and as suddenly being dropped to give place to another. Toward the coming of spring, which brought radio-activity even to the dust of those Battersea streets, a racial craving for colour seized the children and they would be seen walking abstractedly along the pavements, or crossing roads recklessly in front of the hooves of wagon- and omnibus-horses, while giving all their attention to a cotton-reel into one end of which they had hammered four tin-tacks. Round these tacks they wound a thread of coloured wool from a ball carried in the pocket. With a pin, or a sharpened match-stick, they raised a second turn of the wool over the tacks. This operation of alternate treatment of each round produced a tubular rope that made its way slowly through the central hole of the cotton-reel. Inch by inch, foot by foot, it grew, coloured according to the choice of the young weaver in his selection of skeins. When this rainbow rope was long enough it was made into reins, sometimes with the addition of knitted harness. For weeks, during the lengthening evenings of March and April, these gay caparisons would be worn by one boy, as the horse, and held by another, as the driver.

Such tribal activities are not seen in the modern, mid-twentieth-century suburbs. Anthropologists may be able to explain why they have disappeared: but to me it is a paradox that the democratic standardisation of life, especially urban life, should result in the disappearance of these folk games, leaving children that much the poorer and a prey to passive, inert pleasures usually enjoyed in darkened rooms, behind drawn blinds and closed doors.

Jack and I took a share in these seasonal delights, though we were perfunctory because of our closer, small-family interests. The tandem, that Moloch, demanded all the physical energy that we could summon up, leaving none for a vigorous sharing of our school-fellows' games in park and street. Further, I had now become a bookworm, living by proxy on Pacific islands, or up the Amazon, or on the central prairie of North America. Marines, cowboys, Red Indians were my companions, more real to me than the urchins with whom I shared desks in school and made quarrelsome friendships in the streets.

Only in reading did I find serenity and self-confidence. As soon as I put down my book and took off the armour of words, I felt the winds of life blow cold upon my nakedness and I shivered with apprehension. Even at home in that calm, protected enclosure, I was not wholly secure. Demands were made of me which I feared I could not meet: small domestic duties such as dusting, cleaning boots, running errands, all needing alertness and immediacy of mind, a faculty still dormant.

In the boys' school, this apprehensiveness grew month by month under the eye of Mr. Meek. It was a grey, contemplative eye, and I knew by instinct that it did not approve of this younger brother. Some allowance at first was made for my puny appearance: the thin limbs, the swollen stomach, the flushed face. But I soon found myself burdened with home-lessons to be done on the days when a bout of sickness and backache kept me from school.

I was given cards of sums to work out, or the names of rivers and capes to learn by heart, and these dull tasks prevented me from crossing the Atlantic in a windjammer, or rounding up buffalo with the Sioux Indians, or serving with Midshipman Easy against the French.

Mr. Meek's suspicions of my integrity communicated themselves to the Headmaster and the pupil-teachers who from time to time assisted in the class-rooms. One of these young men, trying to waken me to a sense of duty, took me by the ear and pulled so hard that the lobe broke away. Blood streamed, consternation followed, and for a whole morning I was a school hero.

Mother interviewed the Headmaster next day; but she did not improve matters, for he was an august figure enthroned above all minor strife. His name was John Burgess, and he was ten feet high. He carried his head flung back, with a grim mouth and chin set against the world. He wore large brown shoes, highly polished and hooded by spats, summer and winter. He flung out these feet at an aggressive angle as he advanced (rather than walked). He was terrifying.

His throne was set at the end of the big hall, surrounded by windows, so that he sat in a blaze of light that hovered round his severely brushed hair. His pince-nez flashed fire. In front of his desk, as a kind of altar, stood a long chest, open during school hours to reveal a set of canes of varying thickness and colour, from light switches to heavy cudgels; some strawblonde, others dour as mahogany as though impregnated with congealed blood. Lying on the array of canes was the Punishment Book, the register of shame. A record of every chastisement was entered therein, after the event, with a broad pen, and in deliberate calligraphy that possessed an Hebraic quality, as though the angry god of the Old Testament himself had made the entry.

Boys sent by their class-masters for punishment by Mr. Burgess had to stand in the hall, toeing a white line in front of The Desk. To wait there, facing the grim figure, or even the empty throne, the open chest of canes within sight, was ample torture, especially if the ordeal were prolonged from a quarter to half an hour.

It broke the nerve of a classmate of mine, when both of us

were sent up for persistent talking in school. We had been standing side by side for some time, through a whole session and a playtime, when school was resumed for the last session of the morning and the Head decided to give his attention to us. I saw him rise from his chair, remove his pince-nez, thrust them on their black cord into the breast pocket of his dove-grey waistcoat and replace them by a second pair from the opposite pocket. My legs began to tremble and I felt faintly sick, for the mere act of standing for long always set up the pain and dragging sensation in my back.

The Head moved slowly to the chest and began to inspect the canes, a ritual that he performed with theatrical technique. Finally choosing one, and flinging open the Punishment Book, he turned to the row of urchins.

At that moment the small, inoffensive little boy beside me revolted. He uttered a loud, hysterical cry, dashed to the desk, seized the inkpot and flung it at the awful figure of Majesty. It burst on that dove-grey waistcoat.

For a moment the laws that govern the sun and the stars were suspended. The universe froze into stillness. Then the frantic child flung himself, after the inkpot, against that universe. With another shriek he snatched at the cane in the hand of authority. The Headmaster, towering above him, looked down at this commotion round his feet, while he took out a handkerchief and, with as grave a deliberation as he had changed his pince-nez, dabbed at the ink-stain on the ruined waistcoat. Throwing the handkerchief into the waste-paper basket, he picked up the struggling and impassioned child by the middle of his back and carried him face downwards along the hall, the small limbs making violent motions of swimming in air.

The disturbance had brought two masters from class-rooms adjoining the hall. The Headmaster gravely passed his burden to them and disappeared through the double doors, followed by the masters with the boy.

I looked along the line. One urchin, whose muscles had succumbed to shock, stood in a pool, crying. None of us dared to speak, and we were still there, foot to the white line, incapable of digesting so vast a drama, when the Headmaster returned. He had changed the waistcoat for one of dark red, and this made him look like the Avenging Angel. Even the spot of ink on his trousers, and another on one of the fawn spats, did not compromise his dignity. His eyes behind the pince-nez gleamed, and his large mouth was set firmly.

Picking up the cane from the desk where he had dropped it, he replaced it in the chest *and closed the lid*! Turning, still in slow motion, he faced us, looking at each boy individually. Then the oracle spoke. "Let that be a lesson to all of you," he said. "Dismiss!"

The rebel did not appear again in Surrey Lane Higher Grade School. Rumour and legend gathered about his name for a while. Schoolmates who lived in the same street said that inspectors had been to see his parents. There were stories of dreadful punishments; nakedness, flogging. Some said that he had gone to prison and that his father had been sacked from his job at the insistence of the police. Then the hero was forgotten, and the white line resumed its whole and fatal significance.

Seasons passed, and standard by standard I groped my way, half-hypnotised by the critical grey eye of Mr. Meek. My brother, winning his scholarship, left the school and went to the Polytechnic, which stood at the other end of Battersea approaching Nine Elms, next door to the Board School where Mother taught, and near to the famous Dogs' Home. That district was a foreign land to me, hostile and sinister.

Jack now wore a school cap, and had exercise books whose covers bore the same device as the badge on his cap. He became a little more removed from me; more serious, more sardonic. At fourteen, his features were increasingly inharmonious; the huge nose protruded, the small severe chin and mouth receded, the brown eyes took on the startled, guilty expression with which Adam must have confronted his Maker after biting the apple. Whether or not Jack, at that time, had contemplated the forbidden fruit I did not know. I never knew, for reticence on all such matters was a law which we accepted without question. Yet this atmosphere was maintained without prudery. Mother especially was no puritan. She would, for example, sit on the water-closet, leaving the door open in order to maintain a conversation with one of us. I was sometimes vaguely shocked by natural gestures of that kind.

The austerity of life in the boys' school did not improve my health or my character. The bouts of pain increased, and sometimes left me so languid for a day or two that I drifted about the world in a state of semi-coma, a prey to day-dreams and illusions, some pleasant, others monstrous and frightening. But these periods were of small significance in comparison with the fullness of my normal days. Everything was grist to my mill, even illness.

Gradually, and with no desire on my part, I began to feel removed from other people, especially those of my own age. I spent more and more hours alone. My frequent absences from school provided long stretches of solitude at home in the empty house. It became quite a routine for me to be left in the morning after eight o'clock, when Mother and Jack went off together. They gave up coming home at midday and I would have the house to myself until tea-time unless Father returned about 3 p.m. after an early 'duty' at the Post Office.

The house became a fastness, half-fabulous, half a theatre-property. I touched everything about it and in it, its walls, crannies, curtains, furniture, with my wand of imagination, piling up intangible riches. My mind indeed to me a kingdom was; and a constant stream of immigration poured into it from the books that I consumed during those days of crowded solitude over a period of two years during which the mechanical round of family life moved uneventfully.

I read the Bible, because the words enslaved me. I also read *Titbits* and the *Boys' Own Paper*. The juvenile section of the local library was soon exhausted, and I borrowed novels from the adult side, rosy fiction, and sentimental tales sodden with emotionalism. This indulgence was unconscious and unobserved. Mother was too over-worked and harassed; Father too intellectually limited and concerned with his own healthy

interests for either of my parents to be aware that I was stupe-
fying myself in precocious reading.

Jack spotted it. He found the home-lessons imposed by Mr.
Meek and took me to task for neglecting them. His contempt
put me to shame, and I writhed under the lash of his tongue
when he read out some love-passages from one of the novels
which I was consuming; my age at that time being nine years.

After this discovery of my mental and moral torpidity, Jack
gave some close attention to my reading and resumed his earlier
habit of confiding in me his own purposes and interests.

I responded instantly, for my increasing physical discomforts
and the consequent long periods of loneliness were beginning
to sap my vitality. I found myself drifting into shadowy places,
a prey to fear and inclined to secretive suspicions of life. The
clouds passing over the murky skies of Battersea threatened
me. The two bells of the Catholic Church brought the menace
nearer. The music of a barrel organ in the street so disturbed
me that I would have to stand still and clasp my arms round
my own body to control the beating nerves and prevent myself
from bursting into tears. The music at home; all music, the
banal ballads sung by my parents, the Haydn and Bach and
Mozart which were now my brother's daily fare, threw me into
a torment of strong feeling that turned my bowels to water and
brought on bouts of sickness.

For relief against this effect of all music, I turned to drawing.
I drew the sleeping cat, the leaves of the aspidistras, the
nasturtiums in the garden. On my tenth birthday Mother gave
me a box of water-colour paints, and I began to use the brush.
But this was too exciting, like the music, and I was thrown into
such ecstasies of happiness and *discovery* (in the mystic's use of
that word) that the well-known symptoms of burning cheeks,
suffused eyes and the slow, grinding pain in my back too
frequently followed my efforts to paint flower studies.

Jack's renewed friendship—it was something more than
friendship—offered a tonic to my courage. He came frequently
with me to the library and supervised my choice of books. Thus
I was introduced to Stevenson, S. R. Crockett, Kingsley, and
Lamb's *Tales from Shakespeare*. The quality of the prose of these

writers sent me back with more word-awareness to the Bible.
That tenth birthday, my aunt in Yorkshire sent me a Prayer
Book, and I found the Collects in it, those prose poems so
exactly worded, so concise, so crystalline, that they focused my
weakened eyes on purity and precision. I never returned to the
rosy fiction.

This more attentive reading of the Bible and the Book of
Common Prayer set my imagination to work in another
direction than the grammatical. The character, the very
physical person, of Jesus began to loom up as a constant
acquaintance. He became a companion of my long days at
home, and we talked together as freely as though he were a
member of the small family: more freely, indeed, for here was
somebody who, like Mother, held some mysterious power, some
pull of the blood; without, however, letting it slacken through
sickness, preoccupation, or other mortal deterrent. For
Mother's two-lives-in-one was beginning to tell on her strength.
Some of her gaiety, her lyrical response to people, things and
events, were subsiding, just as the crest of a sun-drenched
fountain falls back into itself as the distant source diminishes.

Sometimes, when I ran to meet her at the wrong end of our
street, she came towards me with a stoop in her shoulders, a
drag in her pace. Even the great black handbag sagged. And
she began to worry. She worried about paying for the house,
about the cost of food and clothes, about the future, about 'her
boys'. When she voiced her fears, Father flung his arm round
her and laughed, jockeying her out of these moods of anxiety
by giving her a hearty kiss behind the ear, or lifting her from
the ground and setting her down with a bracing jolt that made
her glasses slip down her nose and tumbled her hat. She took
these affectionate embraces gratefully, even with a response of
passion. But I could see that they did not answer her unspoken
questions, or solve the problems that lurked in the darkening
shadows of a nature that had been too sanguine, too spontaneous.

Nor did Father's boisterous good nature lighten my moments
of misgiving. His handsome, healthy figure was a welcome
feature in my life, as in Jack's. He smelled of fresh air and

cleanliness. Mother had good cause for being so jealously in love with him, for he was as upright and well-groomed as a cavalry officer. His simplicity and frank loyalty were endearing, too, and demanded a response that was content to ignore his limited range of consciousness, his bewilderment when confronted with an abstract idea, or an æsthetic value. He was so sure of himself, so apparently fearless.

His character was therefore in itself a certitude. If there should be anything to fear, or some matter beyond his comprehension, he breezily denied its existence. This would restore us all, Mother, Jack, myself, creatures of misgiving, to the full light of day—but only for the time being.

So frequent was my absence from school that I lost the possibility of winning a scholarship. The vacancies were so few. I began to feel that I was merely a visitor at the school, making no friends, and achieving no place there. Mr. Meek finally gave up trying to model me on the example of my brother. This made my school life more comfortable, but it also gave the impression that I might be unregenerate. I began to accept the fact that, though not the black sheep of the family, I was, at best, the grey.

This led to a period of stalemate. I might have become a mere beachcomber, but for my increasing obsession with words and my box of paints. I loved pencils, too. I collected them as a connoisseur, according to their grades of hardness and softness. I kept them in a black ebony box, savagely carved on the lid, one of the odds and ends picked up by Mother on the stalls, or in a pawnshop. In those years a pawnshop with its sign of three golden balls stood at a street corner in every small shopping centre.

Jack introduced me to Nuttall's Dictionary, and a set of Chambers's Encyclopædia of an ancient vintage, but brightly bound in scarlet leather backs and corners, to match the volumes of the *Boys' Own Paper* and a periodical called the *Welcome*, a journal that suffered from literary leucorrhœa.

Thus, with hard and soft at my disposal, both in pencils and reading matter, I fed mind and spirit, while my body was left to look after itself. Though the new century was now some three years old, the Victorian view of the body and its place in life, survived in our home, as in millions of others throughout the country.

Brother Body, that patient ass, was about to revolt. In 1902 our summer holidays were spent at Leighton Buzzard, a centre from which we explored the countryside in a horse and trap belonging to my father's relatives, children of the cousins who had befriended his mother at the time of his birth. I can recall little of the holiday because by that time I was beginning to sink under the burden of pain and general physical distress. I would sooner sit than stand, sooner absorb books than exert myself to talk, observe, or think. I remember that we visited John Bunyan's cottage at Elstow, outside Bedford. This austere pilgrimage was counterbalanced by a visit to the races at Tring.

One day Father received a letter in a crested envelope. It caused some head-shaking and argument by innuendo, between him and Mother. Finally, Jack and I were told that we must amuse ourselves for the day with our cousins, and Mother and Father drove away, smartly dressed, in the trap. I felt a vague disquiet, as always when my parents took some unexpected action after an emphatic debate. I must have inherited Mother's dislike of being left out of any conspiracy, however minor. Jack welcomed the opportunity for exploring at leisure, without the responsibility of the tandem, though by now he was expert at handling it, with me as the appendage.

We spent that day with our cousins, idling on the banks of the Grand Junction Canal, which runs through Leighton Buzzard, a neat ribbon of water rippled from time to time by the narrow barges towed by ponies that plodded along the path, their hooves dusty and freckled with buttercup pollen. I enjoyed this well enough, stirred by Jack's enthusiasm for the brightly-painted cabins on the barges, the pots and pans, the gypsy-like bargees and their families; gypsy-like, but reminiscent also of the Battersea costers who went off with their carrier pigeons every Sunday in little carts painted in the same tradition as these barges at which I stared with eyes bleared by too much reading, and abstracted by the nagging query as to what lay behind my parents' sudden excursion that day.

My curiosity was satisfied when we got back to the town, for the old great-uncle, head of the house and a bluff old patriarch, was just heading the horse into the stable yard, through the archway from the street, when we returned. I heard him shout, above the clatter of the horse's hooves on the cobbles, "Hey, Tom! Too late in the season for strawberries and cream! Though the strawberries at Woburn are extra large!"

That remark, puzzling to my young ears, told me at least where my parents had been. They were both subdued that evening, though Father broke out into one of his moods of sly vindictiveness when his old cousin began to speak of the Coronation arrangements for August 9th, the day Edward the Seventh was to be crowned. Father said something, so savagely out of character that I have never forgotten it, about having had enough of crowns and coronets, and that it was time an end was put to all that sort of thing. I remember too that this unexpected outbreak of Socialist sentiment, in a provincial town and during a moment of Royalist excitement, caused an embarrassing silence broken deliberately by my mother, who laughingly declared that she was prepared to wear a crown of roses at the ceremony in the Market Place, below the Eleanor Cross which had been erected there by another King Edward many hundreds of years earlier.

In my nine years I had seen a Queen's Jubilee and a Queen's funeral. Now I was to see a King's crowning, or at least a provincial celebration of it. For days the townsfolk had been decorating the market square, the Eleanor Cross being dwarfed by a high stage topped by a canopy. Flowers and bunting changed the puritan Midland town, and for a few hours the ghost of Oliver Cromwell was banished to the flat fields and ditches of the surrounding countryside. Cardboard crowns, the colour of milk chocolate, pinned every knot of festoons on buildings and painted poles.

I had never before seen such public rejoicing and the coloured spectacle, with the anticipation of fireworks and a municipal bonfire, so excited my hopes that I could not sleep at night and had to spend the morning of Coronation Day in bed. It was a cold day, so that when I got up I had to wear a borrowed greatcoat. But the evening cleared, and the fireworks and bonfire fulfilled my hopes. I saw people with flaring torches, and unexplained figures on the stage in the Market Place, sitting on gilded chairs, while several of them came to the front and made speeches which nobody heard, but everybody cheered. Faces flickered in the torchlight. Feet shuffled in the shadows. The excitement grew wilder and louder, and grown-ups began to tumble and stagger, confusing the solidity of the crowds, and relapsing in side-streets and doorways.

I felt the cold night-air creep up my legs and seize my back, and I had to lean against Father to keep myself from falling, like so many other citizens, into a clumsy heap on the cobbles of the Market Square. So, having assisted at the birth of the Edwardian Age, I was carried to bed in my father's arms, wholly unconscious of the part I had played in the procession of the history of England.

CHAPTER THIRTEEN

The Outside World

IT WAS, of course, impossible that so cloistral a régime could go on without interruption from the outside world. Sooner or later Mother's defences had to weaken. In spite of her unexplained fears, she would have to open to the invader. Her own nature betrayed her. She was ambitious for her boys. Having discovered that it was impossible to push her husband on to accept larger and wider responsibilities, either in his work or more generally in life, she turned to Jack and me. We were still too young for her to be specific in her plans for our future; but she talked frequently of careers, the advantage of a good education, and the stark need of ensuring that we should equip ourselves for 'the battle of life', a phrase that still echoed from the receding walls of the nineteenth century.

Jack's steady development obviously bolstered her hopes, though I still cannot understand why she did not fasten on his outstanding talents and guide him toward a career where they could be used. It may have been that his talents were so many. It may have been that Father prevented her by his stubborn resistance to any course outside his ken. About that time, I first heard him state the axiom that what was good enough for him should be good enough for his boys, bless them. This statement was made then, as always subsequently, with a warmth of parental love that demonstrated itself by a tremulo in his voice, and an outstretched arm to gather us to him.

No doubt the poverty and hardship which he had known in boyhood had fixed in his character an obstinacy born of dread of hunger and degradation. He was too innocent and too lacking in intellectual confidence, perhaps even too fundamentally cowed, to contemplate going out to fight for himself in the open

market. He had a curious belief that money-making was a
dirty game, something not even talked about, and all he asked
was that he should be assured of a regular income, no matter
how small.

He saw the Civil Service as the only way for himself and
therefore his sons must follow him. This acceptance of his own
course as the best was evidence of the contradictions and self-
thwartings in his nature. Humble in his claim on society, he
was enclosed in an arrogance that made him incapable of
accepting another point of view, even if he were taught to see
it. Mother had given up trying to teach him. She got her way
only by her periodical outbreaks of angry masterfulness, before
which he instantly succumbed.

His loyalty to the Civil Service, and to his colleagues in it,
was that of a soldier to the regiment. But he remained content
without promotion, and whenever a junior was posted above
him he professed to prefer it that way, though his explanation
of this unworldliness dwindled away into incoherent phrases
and vague gestures in dismissal of the subject. It had the effect
of a smokescreen through which Mother's reproaches could not
penetrate.

"That's enough, old girl; that's enough," he would say,
deeply hurt, at every attempt to prod him into competitive
action. His mind havered at any form of mental or moral
conflict, and he was incapable even of argument or debate.
This gave him great advantage, maintaining him in a perpetual
age of innocence. But it gave Mother the task and burden of
two. Her double daily chores as housewife and school-teacher
were paralleled by her double responsibility in bringing up her
sons.

Perhaps she too was afraid of Jack's talent, and perplexed by
the way in which it showed itself so variously; in music, in
drawing, in mechanical inventiveness. How to harness it to
the pursuit of a career would have puzzled parents with much
more knowledge of the professions, much wider cultural range
and experience, than our mother and father possessed. Like
most people at that time, and in that walk of life, they were
grateful for small assurances: a safe job, a respectable anony-

mity, a local esteem. Outside that limit lay a dangerous unknown which included crime, genius, fame, notoriety, and exalted rank. All the people who came to our house (few and infrequent) were of this persuasion, unanimous in their social and moral quietism. Behind my own parents' acquiescence in this lay an element of mystery, revealed only occasionally by oblique remarks and references, and by my father's perverse attitude toward the aristocracy and to all manifestations of ambition, or of pursuits larger than he could comprehend.

Jack's ability as a pianist was among these last. I remember one autumn day in that Coronation year, when we were home again, with our monotone of life humming along before the approach of winter, with its blanketing of fog. Jack brought from the library a volume of Schubert's songs. He was then under fourteen, but he could read music with enough ease to be able to indicate the voice-line while playing the superb accompaniments.

He was thus engaged, when Father came into the sitting-room to 'do a bit of practice' on one or other of the half-dozen pieces in his repertoire. He listened for a few minutes, while Jack's fingers nimbly dabbled in the lovely undercurrent of the 'Boating Song'. I saw his grey eyes grow colder and his mouth set obstinately.

"What are all these *lyder*?" he demanded, deliberately mispronouncing the German '*lieder*'. "*I* like something with a tune in it."

Jack's fingers froze over the keyboard, and the river ceased to flow, with its freight of flower petals and romantic lovers.

"There *is* a tune in it," he said in that quietly emphatic tone which touched its victim like a flick of Mr. Brown's whip. "It goes like this." And he thumped out the voice part with his thumb, giving it a banality that made him wince at the caricature.

"Well," said Father, "now let's have one of our old favourites. There's nothing like the old friends."

I watched Jack's head; the way it bowed from the neck; and his hair, cropped yet silky, like a priest's skull-cap worn to protect the tonsure. He made a venerable figure, infinitely patient, infinitely resigned. Father stood beside him, tuning up, plucking and screwing, humming to himself in sheer good-will and vitality, like a beehive in winter.

"Oh!" he cried. "I can't tune as high as this foreign piano. Let's go to the old Broadwood-White. We know where we are with that!" And they retreated to the back room, leaving me to watch them through the archway from my seat under the shade at the verge of the aspidistra forest.

Just as a soldier's loyalty is to the army, but more particularly to his regiment, so my father's to the Civil Service was concentrated upon the Post Office. I never heard him criticise one of his colleagues adversely. The worst he would say was that an overseer or a superintendent was 'a funny chap'; a generous euphemism to disguise a toady or a bully.

Certainly the fellows of my father whom I met (mostly cyclists) were various in character and hobbies; for all of them had hobbies. One was a pioneer in photography who ranged the dusty and motorless English roads on a tall, bony bicycle loaded with a massive equipment of tripod, bellows camera, black cloth, boxes of half-plates and spare sets of lenses as big as telescopes. His pictures were as good as those taken by Lewis Carroll. He was also a microscopist, and many a flea's leg and drop of contaminated water did I see through his instrument. Further, he ran a branch of the Boys' Brigade at Clapham, and my parents were persuaded by him that my attacks of abdominal pain would be alleviated by my learning to form fours and to handle a musket. So for a month or two in the summer of 1903 I went on two evenings a week to a chapel hall on Lavender Hill, a couple of miles from home, where I put on a belt and buckle over my jacket, and a tiny pill-box hat over one side of my head. But the eurhythmic drill and the long walks, the carrying of a heavy dummy rifle two miles there and two miles back, had no remedial effect on my stomach, and I was bored and depressed by the monotonous exercise of forming fours.

Another colleague of my father, to whom our Battersea house was subsequently sold, had a different theory about my complaint and its cure. He had been in the Volunteers during the

K

Boer War, and while in South Africa had won the Diamond
Sculls as an oarsman. He was still an enthusiastic river man,
and went every Sunday to Putney, where he rushed up and
down the Thames like one of those water-walking beetles whose
dainty feet tickle the placid surface of pond water to faint
grimaces of laughter.

He was a man of great muscular power, but gentle and inarticulate. He never spoke. He left that task to the dark and
luscious widow whom he had married after his return from the
war. She had an equally ripe daughter, who made a living as
a female bass singer on the music-halls. She often sang in our
sitting-room, accompanied either by the Broadwood-White or
the Klingmann, and the corner-stone notes of 'Out on the
Deep' or 'Abide with Me' would make the floor vibrate beneath
my feet.

This champion oarsman, whose figure seemed to be set amid
a constellation of silver cups, tankards and shields, all as silent
as himself, suggested (through the widow) that a little rowing
would do me good. So that same summer Father took me, for
Sunday after Sunday, on the tandem to Putney, where I was
put into an outrigged skiff and taught the finer motions of
sculling, with feathering, and turn, and steady length. This I
enjoyed, because I liked the silent kindness and strength of my
trainer and also because I was enchanted by the river and its
activities, the boats, the steamers, the tides, the swans, all
unified under the delicious undulation of the lapping water that
made a double world of substance and reflection.

What awe I felt, toward that fearless athlete, one moonlit
summer night when the two families were returning to the
Putney boat-house after a Sunday on the river, the river of
Jerome's *Three Men in a Boat*, with two heavy boats laden
with adults and children, creaking wicker baskets full of
provender, plates, bottles and cutlery, and a loose assembly of
fishing-rods, oars and boat-hooks. The males wore striped
blazers and tiny caps, the females were stiff at the top in straw
boaters, but relaxed below the neck in endless miscellanies of
lace and linen.

Slowly the tired revellers oared down the river, half-borne

by the ebbing tide. The merriment had died away. Night on
the waters is always slightly ominous. The moonlit surface
took on a deep unction, gleaming here and there with a slightly
satirical lip of light where the moon struck a ripple. The trees
on each bank doubled their height, to loom over the scarves of
mist beneath them. Sounds from the shore rang hollow and
distant, and from time to time a human cry, or a forlorn bell,
sounded a note of appeal, or warning.

Parents and children alike were subued. The oars creaked
in the rowlocks, and their blades carved the thick water,
sucking and clucking. A murmur of sound came from the
prows of the two boats, and a tiny disturbance of wavelets
trickled and danced away behind us.

After the excitement and adventure of the day I was half-
asleep, but still alert enough to be affected by the glory of the
moonlit waters, now touched with a hint of danger and something supernatural. I lay in the bottom of the boat, staring up
at the velvet night and the stars scattered over it, few because
of the glare of the moon.

Then suddenly the boat jerked, a rasping, sandy sound ran
along the keel, and the two oarsmen, my father and another
Post Office man who looked exactly like Edward Elgar, caught
crabs and were almost deposited in the laps of the ladies. We
had run aground in mid-stream, and the tide was falling!

The womenfolk raised their voices in protest and alarm, while
the two men recovered their balance and began to experiment
with the boat-hook. But we were held fast, and every effort, as
well as every passing moment, forced us more securely on the
hidden shallow.

The other boat, captained by the Diamond Sculler, lay off
the sandbank, shouting instructions which my father and
Elgar's double practised, but without success. There we stuck,
weltering gently in the sensual caress of the tide.

What happened next was one of those incidents which affect
an onlooker for the rest of his life, as I am now proving. My
mentor, the silent champion who was to cure me of my childish
ailments, left the second boat there in the middle of the river
that was sliding down so relentlessly; he stepped over the side

of the boat and *walked upon the waters*. That, at least, is how I saw this miracle.

He waded to us, seized the gunwale, and shook. But still we were held fast.

"Come on, Tommy," he said, which for him was quite an oration, conjured by the drama of the moment. My father snatched off his canvas shoes, removed his socks, rolling up his trousers, and stepped out into the unknown. By doing so, the lightened boat, and the further efforts of the two men, together with the prowess of Sir Edward Elgar with the boat-hook (his huge moustache vibrating with the effort), succeeded. The boatload of women and children glided free, and my father had to jump aboard hurriedly or he would have been left standing in the middle of the river.

The heroes were duly praised as we resumed our homeward drift, and the grateful mothers rummaged among the débris of the stores to produce a bottle of ale to celebrate our survival.

Neither the scientist nor the athlete, who gave so much time during my tenth year to improving my physical stamina, had any noticeable effect upon it. My bouts of sickness and pains in the back increased in violence.

They were particularly virulent when we went out on Sunday evenings for a musical and social gathering, excursions comparable to those of a football team playing an 'away' game. Such occasions always involved a hearty supper of cold meat, pickles, pies and blancmange, with beer and whisky for the grown-ups and cocoa for the children. This heavy repast would be staged at about nine o'clock, two-thirds of the way through the festival. I found, invariably, that a cold pork chop, or a plateful of roast beef, with gherkins and onions in vinegar, followed by a jam tart or a mince-pie, washed down with a large cup of creamy cocoa, had a bludgeoning effect upon my digestive sensibility, frequently bringing on the dreaded attack before we had left the domestic auditorium.

This always happened at the flat, in Harringay and miles from home, of the colleague with the remarkable likeness to Elgar. Perhaps his wife's hand was unusually heavy at the pastry board. Maybe the climate of North London disagreed with me, or reminded me too nervously of visits to my paternal grandmother. Whatever the cause, there was no escape for me on those Sunday evenings at Harringay, so it was anticipated that I should threaten to upset the evening's pleasure, and a blanket was folded ready on a sofa pushed discreetly out of sight behind the piano, where I could be retired with a pile of the *Strand* and the *Windsor* magazines, through which I would glance with an eye made atrabilious by the pains within my distorted body, and by the critical reluctance with which my ear accepted the ballads and instrumental solos in process of execution on the other and more festive side of the piano.

What always puzzled me was my brother's attitude toward my indispositions. Like Samuel Butler, he assumed that sickness was a crime, and he condemned me accordingly. Father, on the other hand, was inclined to overlook the weakness, believing the antidote to be a little healthy bustling, and that to make light of it would show it up for what it was, a mere fancy.

Mother was the only one who indulged me, and I exploited her sympathy with all the frantic egoism of a drowning kitten. Thus I spent day after day away from school, losing valuable lessons and wallowing in my morbid solitude with over-stimulating literature. I had discovered Thackeray, and I read *Vanity Fair*, *Pendennis* and *The Newcomes* at feverish pace, so eager was I to share that world which (like the large rooms in the house in Tite Street) awoke in me a sense of recognition, a pre-natal familiarity. I also found a novel called *The Silence of Dean Maitland*, about a man who allowed another to suffer unjust imprisonment, which so shattered my nerves that I was prostrate for days.

One Saturday, toward the end of the summer, I was sitting reading *Villette*, again with an intensity of emotion that made the sweat stand in beads on my forehead and run down over my spectacles, so that I had to take them off and wipe them, while dipping my head closer into the book to continue reading with the naked eye. This wonderful book, soaked in an atmosphere of mild despair, was almost more than I could bear. It was my introduction to the Brontës, and those three sisters have haunted me ever since.

While I was thus absorbed, old Mrs. Brown called, bringing Mother the gift of a cucumber and the usual stick of Cadbury's dark chocolate for me. I heard Mother greet her at the front door, and stand engaged with her in the passage beyond the open door of the sitting-room where I was reading. I read on, for, like the lonely narrator of that tale, 'I liked peace so well, and sought stimulus so little' that I often resented the interruption of visitors, rarely though our home was thus disturbed.

Suddenly, with that sixth sense we all exhibit and employ when ourselves are under discussion, I heard Mrs. Brown say, "You know, my love, that child ought to see a doctor."

That may sound an ordinary and casual statement today. Fifty years ago it implied a serious break in normal life; a consulting of the oracle, a descent into the unknown, and an expense likely to disrupt the whole economy of life. I heard Mother draw a deep breath. The chill of fear had struck her. "Why? Why?" she whispered; vaguely, wildly. Then the two women passed into the kitchen. I sat pondering for a moment, and then returned to Belgium and more academic company.

A week or two later, however, after I had been laid low again by a bout with my adversary (now almost a second self), the passing remark by wise old Mrs. Brown was acted upon. Father took me to see the official Post Office doctor, who had the Flemish name of Brabant (which made me prick up my ears, having just read *Villette*).

This meant a long walk over Chelsea Bridge, round by the pumping station, into the sinister labyrinth of Pimlico, where row after row, through street after street, of mid-Victorian houses with pillared porticos still stand flaking away gradually into a squalor that is not even brutal. A kind of lethal greyness, like the scurf of leprosy on doomed human skin, covers the whole district.

To this forbidding neighbourhood my father and I came one Saturday afternoon, when he was conveniently off duty. The doctor was tall, quiet and courteous, an old and rather a sad man, whom I could not see distinctly because his consulting-room was subfusc, with deep-brown walls, heavy curtains, and windows covered with netting that had once been white; but perhaps not so long before, decomposition surely being quick and active in that acid-laden atmosphere.

I was desperately frightened, not because of the assumption that I was ill, but as a result of my passage through the sinister approaches to this rendezvous. I trembled when the old doctor put his hand on my shoulder and looked gravely into my face, without speaking, for several moments. Then he drew down my lower eyelids, and looked at my teeth. After that I was asked to bare my stomach and to lie on a dusty couch under the dustier window.

This was terrifying because so unexpected. "Gently, Richard," said the tall figure, as his thumbs and fingers prodded and tapped around my abdomen. It was novel to be called Richard. I felt at once that he had opened the door into my private world, where of late not even my brother had entered. And these exploring hands touched my tender bones and flesh with knowledge both gentle and sure.

"I think I had better see you and your wife," said Dr. Brabant. "There are several things to be discussed."

With that, we were courteously dismissed, and Father and I walked home again, my arm in his, while he pointed out to me the geographical singularities of the route along the Embankment: for Father never would return by the way he had come. He regarded that as a waste of opportunity. So though Mothers doubtless was biting her fingers with anxiety to hear the doctor's verdict, Father and I lingered over our return journey, and he would even have made a detour to the King's Road to show me the house where Ellen Terry lived had I not reminded him that Mother and Jack were waiting for us to come home to tea. He was content to show me Whistler's house. This interest in the stage and art was purely postal. He appeared to know the names of every householder in the South-West District of London. They often knew him also, for while walking in the streets or the parks he would be greeted with a nod and a smile by strangers, whose names he would reel off to us when they were out of earshot; and it was exactly as though he were reading an address on an envelope. Thus, through this impersonal postal medium, I met Campbell-

Bannerman, later to be Prime Minister; Baron Reuter, founder of the News Agency; Seymour Hicks, and many other public figures in all walks of life. My father reduced them all to one walk, however, the small continent of a postal district within whose frontiers he was omniscient.

Tea-time that day was almost noisy with a crossfire of questions and Father's unsatisfactory answers; unsatisfactory because Father would not or could not face unpleasant facts, or matters beyond his concise mental grasp. "Everything's all right," he said airily, "you can trust old Brabant; a thorough gentleman; treats everybody alike!"

This did not satisfy Mother, and a storm threatened: but Father happened to let slip, amongst his euphemisms, that Dr. Brabant was coming to consult her as well, when he would also give me a further and more detailed examination.

This plan matured about a week later, and after I had submitted to a severe pummelling back and front and had my chest listened to through a primitive wooden stethoscope like a toy trumpet, Dr. Brabant (who shook hands with me in a manner that assumed I was his own age) retired with Mother to the sitting-room, where they consulted alone. Father had forgotten the occasion, or he may have decided that too much fuss was being made; and that, if anything serious might be involved, it were best left to what he always called 'the women-folk'. Or sometimes, on like solemn occasions, he referred to them as 'man's helpmate'. That day being fine, he was awheel and away, so that plans for my immediate future were decided between Mother and Dr. Brabant.

They began by my being kept away from school. For a month, during the melancholy days of autumn, I spent the time reading an author whom I had newly discovered—Charles Dickens. *Pickwick Papers* filled my solitude with good living, enabling me to survive the spectacle of dying sunflowers and falling sycamore leaves in the backyard. I was instructed to spend most of the time with my legs up, a command which I willingly obeyed, since it enabled me to live in the proxy of books, without the interruptions of daily life such as dodging kerbstones, road traffic and school-fellows, and all the myriad petty annoyances that accompany material reality. At that time my purpose was to move my body as little as possible to avoid disturbing the intense drama going on within my rudimentary mind.

During those blissful weeks, Jack did his home lessons in our back bedroom, to which I had to retire at six o'clock. He sat there working at his exercise books with the heraldic covers, silent and dour. But from time to time he would give me a severe glance of inquiry, that was curiously comforting.

"What's this?" he asked, one evening when he had finished his work and was about to go down to supper. He picked up a notebook, the pages ruled in columns for pounds, shillings and pence (an adaptation of which I have never made use), and found that I had filled it with my uncertain handwriting.

"It's a story," I replied. "It's about a lady and a motor-car."

His severity increased, and he grunted.

"I'd better read it," he said. "There are sure to be spelling mistakes."

That was the beginning of an activity which was not followed up at the time; but later it became my master and has commanded most of my interest and vitality.

Jack took the notebook down to the kitchen, and when he came up to bed he leniently said nothing about my story except that he would keep the book for a while. I had not the energy to object; and further, my vanity was roused; that projection of self-consciousness which is the unavoidable shadow cast by the light that creative purpose kindles in the mind.

A few days after this seemingly abortive incident, a letter came which Mother read to me. It was a notification that a place was now vacant in the Yarrow Convalescent Home at Broadstairs. My parents were instructed to deliver me, on such and such a day and hour, at Holborn Viaduct station, to the charge of a nurse who would be conducting a party of children by train.

This was a revolutionary step. Never, in my life, had the family been parted, one member from another. We all fell silent, and I had the sensation amidships of having swallowed a live bird, whose wings were fluttering beneath my ribs. The idea of leaving Mother was so unreal that it did not even disturb me.

"Fine!" said Father at last, to break a tension which he could not endure. "Do you a world of good. We'll ride down to see you. It's a good road once you get past Eltham. Of course, there are two routes, Old Watling Street and the mid-Kent through Maidstone. We'll go one way and come back the other. Make a nice *winter* ride!"

At the word winter I took a greater interest in Father's day-dream. The season now was late September.

"Shall I have to stay there for long?" I piped. "For more than a week?"

"A week?" cried Father, with even greater heartiness. "You've got to get rid of that swollen tummy, my lad. You'll never be a good man on the road until you do. And we've planned to go to Hampshire for next summer holidays, taking our luggage on the tandems. A holiday on the downs, in a cottage I've heard about! That'll do us all good, you and Mother. And look at *me*! I've got a graveyard cough!" And he imitated a hacking cough so comically that we all had to laugh—even Jack. He also, perhaps, thought the situation was becoming over-charged.

The days that followed oppressed me because of a weight of secretiveness in the air. Nobody behaved quite naturally. Mother slaved away, repairing my underclothes and buying replacements for those garments beyond repair. Only four more days remained, and still the subject of my departure had not been mentioned.

Then, on the Saturday morning, Mother being home from school, she took me to buy a pair of boots. This task fulfilled, we prepared to return home; but suddenly I noticed that she was very red in the face and on the verge of tears. I took her arm and tried to coax her into a lighter mood.

"I'm going to have your photograph taken," was her response: and she clutched me convulsively. That, like a visit to the doctor, was a ceremonious matter fifty years ago. We found a photographer's shop in the Battersea Park Road (the

Dantesque thoroughfare which spat sticks of carbon), whose window was adorned with pictures of bridal groups, clubs, and individuals fixed in a *rigor mortis* at all ages from infancy to late life.

It may have been a touch of irrational anguish in Mother's mind that next moved her.

"You may as well wear your new boots," she said, while we waited in the studio for the executioner to appear. So there, against a background of marble balustrade, in cardboard, a bower of roses and a cottage, I sat down and put on my new American boots which we had bought as an odd line at William Whiteley's, having heard of this opportunity from Mrs. Ritchie, wife of the Scottish liftmaker, a great woman for bargains.

The photograph did not reach home until I had gone to Broadstairs; but on my return many weeks later I was to see a pinched face, with startled, apprehensive eyes staring through a pair of spectacles, a veined hand resting on the balustrade, an unnecessarily emphasised Eton collar—and the American boots, long and suave.

Jack was responsible for the last ceremonial gesture with which my departure was to be marked. Everything was now ready, and in two days' time the dreadful separation would be complete. We were seated at the kitchen table, Father, Mother, Jack and myself. I was toying with a quaker-like beverage called Benger's Food, Dr. Brabant having proscribed a supper diet of pork chops and cocoa.

"Dick ought to see an opera before he goes," said Jack suddenly.

Mother looked at him reproachfully. Had I not been present she would have accused him of being cruel in harping on the possibility that my days were numbered. Father, however, seized on the suggestion as a means of lightening the sombre atmosphere, as of a Greek tragedy, which had been closing down over our home for the past month.

My last evening at home was a break in the strict *regimen*; for I did not go to bed at six o'clock, I set off with Father and Jack (Mother being too busy and too distressed to go) for the Shakespeare Theatre on Lavender Hill, Clapham, to assist at a performance of Gounod's *Faust*.

Jack had proved himself again unerring in psychological insight. My private fears and my physical discomfort were swallowed up in a vaster cataclysm of emotion. The music (I had never before heard an orchestra) rolled over me like a Pacific surge, lifting me up and sucking me down, a raw-nerved piece of flotsam; while the scenery, the characters, the plot, and the pervading sense of moral conflict, with Faust's horrible sin, poisoning the air in the over-heated gallery of the theatre, all combined to drive me into a frenzy of feeling that froze solid, turning me to stone. I remember still the cold fury of compassion with which I witnessed the end of Marguerite in prison; and the guilty terror that made me apply to myself Faust's last moments, when he descended through the trap-door into Hell, supported by Mephistopheles and a nimbus of coloured fire.

Nor had Jack remained unaffected. His Spanish complexion was touched with an unusual flush, and his great brown eyes shone with that upward-looking fire which El Greco carried into the features of his saints and martyrs.

We walked home from the theatre, down Pig Hill into the Battersea marshes, Father discoursing to us and neither of us listening, each being still under the spell. I shivered in the night air, after the fever and the ecstasy, and my teeth chattered in rivalry to Father's happy monologue.

Sleep vanished that night. Jack and I lay whispering in the darkness, a darkness still lurid with hellfire, and sonorous with the first orchestral music we had ever heard. What had given Jack the premonition of this wonderful thing, that he had suggested the visit to the opera? How had he heard of the touring company, and on what sources did he draw for his prescience of what we should hear?

At that time in his life he appeared, at a casual glance, to be a secondary schoolboy of fourteen, rather solemn perhaps, rather slow in movement. But there he was, in his school cap and reach-me-down suit, his dark hair rather more close-cut than is usual among English schoolboys. He sought no company and depended on nobody. But other boys clung to him, as I did, just as later in life, when he was a grim, sardonic schoolmaster, a later generation of scholars was to gather in twos and threes at the front gate of his house, seeking the privilege of walking to school with him: a practice for which he gave them only a reproving scowl.

Yet beneath the saturnine exterior there worked this sleepless personality, exploring in fields of thought and cultural sensibility, utterly unknown to his parents, outside their tradition, foreign to their taste. By this time he had discovered for himself (the help of the piano-tuner with the taloned fingers having long been discarded) the pianoforte music of Field, Chopin, Schumann and Brahms, which he attacked with a fastidious dexterity that gave his playing character and beauty, though his fingering was amateur and no doubt unconventional.

I shared in all this, willingly entering his world and feasting there gluttonously. I even tried to work at the piano so that I could be worthy to accompany him in duet-playing, a pastime which we were to share (with frequent mortification for me) until his death. His music flowed with its balm into my own private world, gracing the scenery of Dickens, Thackeray, and the lesser Victorian novelists who were my continent with an atmosphere that was aromatic and pulsating with light.

Next morning was bleak October, with the first intimations of Battersea's river-fogs smearing the window-panes. After the restless night Jack was grumpy. He shut himself up within himself, remarking that the wind was in the north. He had already shown this singular faculty, a sense of the north which I have found referred to only once in all my life of reading: by George du Maurier in *The Martian*.

Jack first demonstrated this gift when we were lost in the labyrinth of South Kensington during one of our Saturday visits to the museums. We were on our way home, and had wandered too far west. Suddenly Jack stopped, raised his great beak, and sniffed upward. Then he turned a quarter-circle, saying, "We're going the wrong way. *That's* the north!" And he pointed like a setter dog, emphasising the direction with a nod. Accordingly, we took the next left-hand turning and soon made our way to the King's Road and finally to the river.

"How d'you know that?" I asked, after we had been trekking south for some minutes. "I *don't* know," he said. "It just *is!*" And it was. The gift was as good as a binnacle, for Jack never lost his way, as I was to discover some years later when we rode out on our bicycles every fine Saturday into the network of lanes in north-west Kent, frequently returning after dark, guided by this useful instinct secreted somewhere in my brother's nervous system.

I, too, might have known that the wind was in the north that morning, for I felt wretched: my limbs numb, my belly full of lead, my vision askew; regular symptoms which have appeared all my life whenever the wind veers to the northern half of the compass. I have often inquired of doctors what might be the cause of this malaise, so unfailing in its prognostications; and the doctors have invariably replied, "Bunkum!" I have also asked several professional psychologists. They have merely looked wise, or grave, and said nothing, so that I have been left with a sense of guilt, as of some dreadful ancestral inheritance.

That morning, however, there were several causes to which I could ascribe my misery. Looming ahead lay the ordeal of leaving home. The wonder and glory of the opera, the introduction to orchestral music, had stretched me to straining point: and here I was after that cruel release; flaccid, collapsed. We had been late to bed, and we had been sleepless.

I crawled to the bathroom, but felt little better even after that refreshment. I returned to dress myself, and was confronted with a picture that wrung my heart. Mother had just preceded me into the bedroom, which was empty. I saw her walk round the bed, pull back the clothes where I had been lying and fling herself in a paroxysm of grief on the pillow still bearing the impress of my head.

I felt my throat close, and the tears scalded my eyes. What could I do for her whom I loved so desperately? I stepped back, lingering behind the door, trying to control my own grief and the shameful exultation with which I realised how much I meant to this dear being who was the very pivot of my world.

I waited there until her passion was spent. Then, hearing Jack's footstep on the stairs, I forced myself to go in, lest he should find her and disapprove of such self-abandonment.

CHAPTER FOURTEEN

The Cord is Severed

MOTHER AND FATHER took me to Holborn Viaduct station, a strange place, at a dead hour of mid-afternoon. Jack had said good-bye at home, for he had to go off to some school affair. It had been a curt, gruff farewell, but full of understandings, admonitions and unspoken promises. It was like an amputation, with the lost limb still aching after it had been severed.

I walked stiffly, encased in new underclothes and a new suit. The American boots swung my legs, like the weight on a pendulum. Father carried my bag, and from time to time he whistled a merry tune, which I heard from across the Styx where I was being conveyed; heard and absently recognised as:

> "Oh happy goes the day
> When the heart is young."

My heart must therefore have been old, burdened with centuries of human experience and disillusionment. There was no happiness for me in that autumnal day, as we approached Holborn Viaduct, the chill north wind cutting across and flapping my overcoat between my legs.

Mother held me convulsively by the hand, and I tried not to cling to her, fearing that any such overture from me might produce another outburst of grief such as I had watched that morning. But it was not easy to be restrained, for an emotional battle was mounting to a climax inside me, and I knew that defeat was probable at the moment of parting, which now drew near.

We entered the hollow dome of the station, and it appeared to be deserted except for a little group of people gathered at one of the platform gates. Perhaps I saw no others, my nerves being focused upon this fatal assembly.

"There we are!" said Father. "Perfect timing. Might be Service folk!" And he strode towards the human knot, jockeying me under the elbow, and encouraging my poor mother with "Come along, old girl. We'll see him on the train!"

But they didn't see me on the train, for the nurse, a strong-minded professional, informed the half-dozen parents that it was better to part at the barrier, so that she would not be distracted at the last by possible demonstrations.

This was my first acquaintance with train departures, and I still think that nurse, so cool with her timid flock, was wise in making the break at the barrier. For what is more wrenching, more rending to the human spirit, than to watch a train glide out of a station carrying a diminishing face, hand, handkerchief, seen through a broken medium of strong feeling, as though a local darkness were closing upon one's life, blotting out personality and all private values?

A shyness, like hoar-frost, settled over me when the moment came to part from my parents. Father stepped back, as though preparing to turn and run. He looked straight and handsome, the cleanest object under that gloomy, soot-encrusted dome. Mother and I were near to each other, but both were blinded and our parting words floated away with our bodies.

I sat in the train beside the nurse, facing the engine, with half a dozen other children who had also parted from their parents. I studied their faces, over the barrier of my own distress, but I could see only a kind of sulky curiosity, half-resentful, half-alert for what might happen next. I saw the buildings slipping past the carriage windows, one adding to another, increasing the gulf between me and the forlorn figure in a shiny blue serge coat, with a shabby black handbag, whom I had watched receding on the platform.

The unreality was so great that I began to trespass over the border of common sense. The train stopped outside Herne Hill station and waited there. Even for passengers in a normal state of mind the ordeal of sitting in a dead train is a minor torture.

L

That afternoon it drove me mad. I got up, stumbled over the nurse's feet, and struggled to open the window.

"I must go back," I cried, "I want to go back. I can walk from here."

But then I saw that the train was not in the station. That baffled me. I was helpless, faced with one of those small hitches in the mechanics of life which have always made my existence like a game of snakes and ladders, with the dice too frequently leading me to abrupt tumbles.

Distraught with misery and my first attack of home-sickness, I stopped struggling and stared down at the permanent way far below. I could not contemplate opening the door and jumping down, my small physical vitality being incapable of such an endeavour, or even of suggesting it to my mind. I have always been handicapped in this way, especially in early life when my body should have been vigorous and eager for muscular adventure. Instead, my mind, straining after the bravest experience, would have to succumb because I had no armoury for coping with the small practical tasks which crop up in their hundreds every day: tying up a parcel or opening one, getting out of a chair to reach a book, stooping to pick up a spoon fallen from the table; all such matters have loomed before me as burdens to be taken up only after an effort of will, and against the inclination of the flesh.

My hesitation gave the nurse time to notice me and to see that I was in a desperate mood. She seized me by the loose back of my coat and hauled me to my place beside her.

"Now don't fidget," she said, in a tone suitable to the old lady who lived in a shoe. "The train will start in a while."

My despair was too great for me to try to explain that I did not want the train to start, and that my spurt of energy was due solely to the frustrated hope roused by this long-drawn halt.

So I said nothing and subsided into my inner darkness, that night of the soul which during childhood can be as absolute as it is shortlived. The train rumbled on again, and after plunging us into the Sydenham Tunnel, emerged into a province that was no longer London. I watched the passing woods, hills, fields, still hostile to this relentless accumulation piling up more and more impassable barriers between me and my own world, the world of Mother, Jack, Father and my familiar, old-maidish habits.

By the time we reached Broadstairs I was sunk into an apathy, that callous condition which follows any kind of excess. My body was shifted from the train to a station bus, and from that to the entrance of an institution, a long building full of light, with varnished woodwork gleaming and greenish-yellow incandescent gas-lamps aiding the still adequate glow of the falling day.

Nothing made a concise impression. I wanted to hide, to bury myself, to be able to stir my numbed faculties to life again, so that Mother should not think I was failing her. I could not put away that picture of her abandonment to grief. My conscience still nagged at me because I had felt a spasm of pleasure, a dreadful possessiveness, as I recognised that her grief was for me, because I was being taken from her.

There was to be no solitude, however, while I was a patient at the Yarrow Home. I discovered this novel fact within five minutes of my arrival. The little group of newcomers was taken over by several nurses and added to the main flock, which must have been some fifty or sixty strong—all boys, most of them about my age and size. I could see nothing wrong with any of them, except that one boy walked with a writhing hip, while another (who interested me because he spoke with a full, clear voice) was marked by a medallion of warts on his Adam's apple.

The crowd was friendly, and had I not been so self-consumed I might have responded. But instead, I stared with a blankness misconstrued as hostile, so that very soon I had what I wanted —a clear space round me and a false solitude. That first impression was never quite erased, and throughout the winter spent in that warm, comfortable and friendly place, I was left to my own devices, and frequently excluded from expeditions to the town and beach, being left to lie on a couch by an open window, covered by a blanket, and surrounded by as many dog-eared books from the pitiable library (contained in one small glass-doored cupboard) as I was allowed.

Happily, this book-poverty was mitigated by parcels of reading matter, sent regularly by Jack, with letters in his laconic manner, giving me news of the goldfish, the latest engineering experiment, the well-being and activities of our parents, and the writer's latest enthusiasm amongst the composers. Of the books he sent me, standing in my recollection because of their beauty and the impression they made on me, were *Cranford* and *The Vicar of Wakefield*.

I might have been happy there but for the absurd clamour of my craving to see Mother. It is the most common emotion in the whole gamut of human feeling; and it is the strongest. Not even the lover, drunken on the wine of sex, puts all his universe into the keeping and authority of one person. A child does this, knowing no self-confidence, hardly knowing that it has a self.

Yet I was not so wholly destitute. In spite of this attachment to my mother, umbilical in its directness, I was already mentally and imaginatively loose from that blood-cord, seeing *around* my mother's personality, with humour and sympathy, in the same way that I observed the other two members of my world. But the bond was physical, mysterious, and it was to remain in my nature, a coil of sensual irrationality, long after Mother was dead and I had transferred my fatality to other women, with an overwhelming intimacy, tenderness, and physical understanding; yet always with mind detached and slightly impatient of the captivity.

I wrote to her every day, in serial letters that I posted twice a week. She must have been puzzled by these precocious outpourings of passion; perhaps a little frightened, for her attitude toward me after I returned home, and until she died, was always touched with a half-concealed anxiety, as though I might have one skin less than other folk, and were doomed to take life hard.

One Saturday before Christmas she came down alone to see me. I knew she was coming, and I saved my chocolate money (we were able to buy a stick of Cadbury's every day in the Home) until I had enough to buy one of those little Goss china ornaments decorated with the coat of arms of the town. Mother was making a collection of these fiddlesome pieces, and kept them in a glass-fronted cabinet opposite the Klingmann, the display being shadowed by reflections of that shining black beauty and the green-sword blades of aspidistra leaves, so that the heraldry of English towns and counties appeared to be lost perpetually in an Amazonian jungle, under an ebony sky.

She came, but I was not allowed to go alone to the station to meet her. This put me into a mood of sullen resentment, for I was convinced that no other such relationship existed in the world, and that matron and nurses should have appreciated this, seeing it in my behaviour, my very looks.

Mother had to come to the Home, and greet me in public, where I was indulging in a little Achillean sulk amongst the noisy children who were playing the favourite game of marble railways. This consisted of setting up long and short slats of wood, each with a running-groove in it, in gentle sloping structures on the support of stands. When the stands gave out, stools and piles of books were used. Intricate permanent ways were planned, some dodging to and fro, some long, others abrupt to act as boosters, all gradually leading the descent. Following this continuity, the marble took on a life of its own, seeming to *think* its way along, like a trout in a brook.

Usually I was eager to join in this game, for I was already a slave to rhythm, hypnotised by all moving objects. But that day I sat huddled in a chair, watching the door with shamefast eyes, humiliated and embarrassed. When Mother appeared, in charge of a nurse, I had worked myself up into such a storm that I could hardly greet her. She looked at me with those poignant brown eyes, a mute examination that read every detail of my anatomy and her personal creature inside it. But I could not respond, though I could see how bewildered she was by my reluctance.

The whole day was crossed by that bad beginning. Nor did we have long together, for matron refused to allow me to go out twice into the town. We had to sit in that play-room until lunch-time, then eat a meal in public. After that I was obliged to take the statutory 'rest' with all the other children. Mother and I thus had about an hour alone together, walking on the sands in the bay, before Mother had to leave for the train. I clung to her during that walk, without regard for her weariness, her stoop, her nervous anxiety and flood of inquiries about my internal pains, my diet, my clothes, and all the rest of the dreary mechanism of my daily life. I wanted to ask her a thousand questions about things at home, especially about the sailing-boat which Jack was building ready for my return (and describing, with drawings, in his letters). But the moment of parting came before I could free my mind of this cloud of temper, blown up by too much anticipation, and suddenly we encountered the crocodile of children in charge of a nurse; the sign that Mother must leave me. Before I could realise my loss, she was gone, and I was added to the flock, a miserable little unit.

Suddenly I felt the lump in my pocket. I had forgotten to give Mother the Goss china. Rage seized me. I flung the gift into the sand and crushed it under my boot, the American boot, and burst into tears. Incidents of that kind may explain why visiting parents are unpopular with the authorities of children's hospitals, institutions and schools.

My life at Broadstairs was not usually so disturbed. Indeed, I made several discoveries that enlarged my range of speculation and consciousness, and two things in particular added to my confidence, bringing me nearer to a sense of equality with circumstance.

One heavy morning, when the outside world was iron-bound with frost, I stood at a long french window in the play-room waiting to go down to breakfast. The sun was just risen beyond the ground, and stood above the lawns, his great red disk etched with naked twigs of the bushes. Under these bushes a gardener was chopping down a dead tree. I watched him. The axe flashed red, and fell. It rose again. The movement, steady and sure, fascinated me. Suddenly I realised that the sound of the blows did not synchronise with what I saw. The thud came when the axe was on an upstroke, ready for the next blow.

I disbelieved the evidence of my eyes. Then I thought my spectacles (those miracle workers) must have betrayed me; or that my illness had begun to affect my vision. I stared intently, screwing up the eye-muscles against any possible intrusion of light or irrelevant image. But the picture I saw and the sound I heard remained disparate.

Then, while I stared, knowledge came to me; the knowledge that follows a recognition of fact, of concrete experience, bringing with it a widening both of the universe and of the individual's understanding of it. These moments are rare, and they are wholly vital. For a flash, the recogniser is a god, who can say 'I am', as Jehovah said in the Old Testament.

On that frosty winter morning, between getting up and going down to breakfast, in an antiseptic, varnished institution where the inmates and staff were so dehumanised that they were little more than parts of the mechanism of the place, leaving me in a murmurous solitude, day after day bemused and lonely, elated by the very dreariness of things, there I stood transfigured, with that astounding companion, the Jesus whom I had fashioned from my reading in the Bible; there I stood and turned to him with an eagerness to impart my finding, to share the signifi-cance, the richness of it.

I had found that time and space are not absolute. Their power was *not* law. They were not even unanimous; they quarrelled with each other; and through their schism the human imagination, the hope, the faith, could slip, to further exploration where intuition had formerly hinted, but where logic and fatal common sense had denied.

I felt both power and exultation flooding my veins. The blood glowed warm within me, rising to my brain and pulsing there, like a crowd roaring some racial acclamation. I had found out the cheat of time and space; and if that were so, then other seemingly stable laws of nature might be questioned, to the advantage of this fettered and hoodwinked spirit, this hidden and oppressed self, locked in the dungeon of my body.

I looked again, and still the evidence wrote itself upon the frosty air, against the disk of the sun who had now risen an inch or two higher, like the minute-hand of a giant clock, jerk-ing itself up toward the hour, invisibly visible in its motion. The beauty of this syncopation between sight and sound released me from so much, from the mass of daily life, the burden of the flesh and its strict locality, from the drag of earth.

That last was my most hated foe. The drag of earth, the weight that would pull me day and night, making every movement, even the smooth gestures which we throw in sleep, a labour too heavy to be borne; the putting on of clothes, the passage from chair to chair, the endless travel from one room to another, and that final torture, the treadmill of the tandem, during those Sunday rides behind my brother, as I tried to do my share of the pedalling, under the goad of his tongue, lashing me to it.

But now I was free. Since time and space were deceivers, openly contradicting each other, and at best offering a compromise in place of a law, I was at liberty to doubt further, to carry on my exploration of the horizons of freedom. Still conscious of the warm blood whispering in my veins, I looked down at my wrist and saw the transparent flesh, the bird-bones, the channels of blue beneath the skin. All this was substance as fragile as a plant. It could not possibly outweigh the solid earth under my feet, where I and the rest of duped mankind walked with such docility.

The sun had brightened to a liquid fire that dazzled my sight, reducing the woodman and his brief moment of revelation to a penumbral figure under the shadow of the bushes in the dead grey frost. I stared at the light, and the stuff of life within my body began to increase its speed of flow. I sensed, with a benignancy deeper and more assured than reason, that my limbs and trunk were lighter than they seemed, and that I had only to reduce them by an act of will, perhaps by a mere change of physical mechanics, to command them off the ground, out of the tyranny of gravitation.

I exerted that will, visualising my hands and feet pressing downwards upon the centre of the earth. It was no surprise to me that I left the ground, and glided about the room (which was empty) some twelve or eighteen inches above the parquet floor. At first I was afraid of collapsing, of tumbling and hurting myself. But I had only to draw in a deep breath, and to command the air through the heavy portions of my anatomy, *watching* it flow and dilute the solid bone and flesh through the helpful chemistry of the blood, this new, released and know-ledgeable blood, and I soared higher, half-way to the ceiling. This thoroughly frightened me, and I allowed myself to subside, coming to ground with a gentleness that was itself a sensuous delight.

I could not leave the matter there. I must put my discovery to the test again, and accordingly I drew in a deep breath and was just about to visualise that downward pressure of will upon body, when the door opened, and a nurse came in.

"Why, little boy?" she said. "Haven't you heard the break-fast bell?"

Then she took a second glance at me, stooped and peered into my face. "Is anything wrong? Are you feeling poorly this morning?"

I was almost indignant, and disclaimed the suggestion that I might have a temperature, for that would mean going to bed in the large ward where a pail stood conspicuously in the middle, on a sheet of mackintosh; an improvisation which dis-gusted me.

I hurried away without replying, leaving the nurse looking after me with some inquiry in her manner. The corridor and staircase were empty, for everybody was at breakfast in the vast dining-room below. Here was another opportunity! I drew my breath again, I scorned the liars of time and space, I took the presence of Christ into my hollow, featherweight bones, and I floated down the staircase without touching either tread or baluster. Alighting outside the dining-room door, I entered and took my seat, content now to live incognito amongst these wing-less mortals.

Then I had to give myself to the problem which faced me every breakfast and dinner-time: the consuming of as much mustard as possible. This had been prescribed for me, and the nurses had to see that I practised the cure, which I imagine was intended as a kind of internal poultice. Once having got used to the heat and flavour in my mouth, I rather liked the secondary sensation of burning in my stomach. It was a com-fortable antidote to the drag and rumble which were my usual condition.

CHAPTER FIFTEEN

"Nature I Loved"

I RETURNED HOME in the early spring of 1904, to find the house and garden shrunken, and seemingly smeared with a dinginess, the overtone of London soot. After the sea-air and crystal skies of the Isle of Thanet, that land of poppies and purple seaweed and suns rioting out of the eastern waters, Battersea struck chill to my eyes, as though cataract were beginning to cloud them.

My experience at the convalescent home, especially that of being severed from Mother, had altered me. I was shy when I found myself again in the familiar kitchen, sitting at supper after the day's journey. I looked almost furtively from one to the other of the three faces, and I could say nothing.

Jack was taller, and his nose more pronounced than ever. His face had a hollow fall, so that his cheek-bones were emphasised in such a way that the reposeful cast of the face took on a static dignity. This made him more like Mother, whereas formerly he might have been a changeling, left in our home from the wreckage of a Spanish galleon that by a freak of time and circumstance had been sequestered from the fleet of the Armada in the sixteenth century, to wander about the northern oceans, finally to come to an uneasy rest on the mud-flat of Battersea Reach.

He looked at me shyly too, over the book which he had propped up on the table as a safeguard against I know not what; perhaps a flood of questions from me, or against my father's bonhomie. I could feel his deep-set eyes, that smouldered with secret purposes, searching me with a relentless inquisition.

Mother was even thinner than when I went away. She had been fretting, consuming herself with worry, the reverse action of her passionate nature that in more healthy mood was gay, sensuous, redolent of luxury and creative desire. Her cheek-bones were more pronounced too, because the flesh below had sunken in, drawing her lips slightly so that her teeth gleamed, adding a touch of desperation to every breath she took. And I noticed the effort of that breathing. The winter, another Battersea winter of damp and sulphurous fogs, had not been kind to her.

Only Father was unchanged, except that he looked a little younger and even more handsome. His black hair and moustache glowed with sheer animal magnetism. His cool grey eyes, full of the open country, looked at me with affection. I could see that he approved of my more robust condition.

"No tummy-ache now, my son, eh?" he said, putting his arm round the tea-cosy and patting me on the shoulder. "Look at him, Mother! There's a man for you!" And at once he launched into an imaginary journey, by road, somewhere into the west, where he and his 'old faithful' (as he often called Mother) and his two 'babbies' would ride with him, free at last of the trammels of the rest of the human race, back in the Garden of Eden. I looked at Jack's sardonic face, lowered over the book of Euclid, and I wondered whether he might not be the Cain in that re-statement of Man's prime family, and I the unfortunate Abel.

However, I was not prepared to be critical of Father's warm sentiments. After so many weeks of institutional discipline, I welcomed a little effusion; I lost my shyness, and began to chatter feverishly, adding to Father's fantasy some literary embellishments gathered from the works of Henty, and Gordon Stables, those adventure-story writers in the *Boys' Own Paper*, in whom I delighted as well as in the more exalted authors to whom Jack preferred to introduce me.

Father did not notice my flourishes, for he was intoxicated with his own vision: but Mother and Jack looked on with some astonishment, and I was vain and self-conscious enough (a weakness that I was later to find to be an occupational disease in the literary profession) to see them exchanging glances, as though sharing a conspiracy of forecasting over my future.

I was quickly re-acclimatised to the subfusc climate of my

native parish, and of course the mutual shyness disappeared
almost as quickly as the mist of a self-gazer's breath from a
mirror. Another week was spent at home, during which I
revelled in the absolute solitude of the daytime hours, renewing
my acquaintance with the odd characteristics and pronuncia-
tions of the beloved domestic interor, and losing myself, with
a sighful content, in two of R. D. Blackmore's rich tales, *Lorna
Doone* and *Cradock Nowell*, in which abnormalities of weather
played critical parts in the development of the plots.

I suffered the violent events in these stories, as I endured the
return to Surrey Lane School and the disbelieving eye of Mr.
Meek, with an equanimity due to my new power, in which I
believed so absolutely that I did not even question its validity,
or indeed its actuality. Again and again, during moments of
isolation, when thought or some imaginative fervour so elevated
my spirits that I had to express my worship and devotion to
Jesus, my Companion, in some instant deed, I practised the
now habitual contraction of muscles, the dilution of my blood
with a slow indraught of air, and experienced the divine
sensation of rising from the ground to command a new
dimension. I did not question this faculty, for it was never
called upon except in solitude, and thus there was nobody to
question it, or accuse me of suffering from hallucination.

Suffering! That is hardly a word to use in connection with
an adjunct that, whether real or not, was to give me comfort
and confidence for many years through the remainder of childhood, through the dangers and misgivings of adolescence,
through the losses and agonies of early love, and over the dead
levels of mid-life, with its *longueurs*, its humiliations, and hopes
deferred.

With this invisible armour, I returned to school prepared to
face not only Mr. Meek, but all that matter-of-fact everyday
drudgery of which he was the symbol. Time began to press
about me, but my anxiety in this matter, already weakened by
the experience on that frosty morning at Broadstairs, was
further allayed by the gift from Mother of a silver watch, a
lady's watch heavily chased, the face flecked with motes of
gold, and the hands also of gold. It was a Victorian piece, given

to her in girlhood, and she would normally have worn it pinned to her bosom by a butterfly brooch, or a bow imitated in enamels. But Mother did few things normally. The only ornament she ever wore was a Jubilee half-crown picked out in colours and made into a brooch: that, and her wedding-ring.

Mr. Meek resumed his policy of leaving me to my own devices, and as I was not actively disobedient in school, life there passed more smoothly than formerly. I was also more successful during lessons, and found that I could now spell and commit to heart the elements of grammar, as well as long extracts from the Bible. I won a copy of this Book of Books as a prize.

That was not my only success following my apparent restoration to health. One evening Jack came home from school, and drew from his satchel a copy of the *Polytechnic Magazine*. He passed it across the tea-table to Mother, not saying a word. I saw her open it with mild interest. Suddenly her gaze concentrated, and the colour rose up her neck and over her cheeks.

"What's this?" she said to Jack, in a tone of alarm that instantly changed to confidence, as though she were witnessing the fulfilment of a long-promised guarantee.

"Show him," said Jack.

Mother ignored his instruction, and continued to stare at the magazine, open as Jack had handed it across the table. From it, she looked at me, and I felt that she was determined to see in my elusive features some determinant hitherto unsuspected.

My patience collapsed; I left my chair and, flinging my arm round her neck, peered over her shoulder. I saw my name in print. The story about the lady and the motor (I had actually *seen* a motor-car in the streets of Battersea, for a local doctor had dared to substitute one in place of his brougham, thereby losing several patients), which Jack had borrowed before I went to Broadstairs, had found a home.

I was not greatly impressed because I could not fully comprehend what had happened, or what the achievement signified.

"Is that mine?" I faltered.

"Looks like it," said Jack, in a tone that contained a warning. The warning was not necessary, because I had changed so

much during my absence from home that the self who had
written the tale was no more than a discarded skin. Nevertheless, I looked at my name and saw it as something concrete to
which I could anchor myself as ship to buoy, off the leeshore
of life.

Jack then explained how he had taken my story to the
English master at the Polytechnic Secondary School, a venture
that ended in publication. What Mother thought about this I
never learned. She might have said something at the time, had
not Father appeared, with his usual hearty kiss for all three of
us. Mother responded warmly, and poured out his tea into a
moustache-cup, breaking a fresh egg into it. While he stirred
this nourishing concoction, Mother exhibited the page bearing
his younger son's name.

"Fine! Fine!" he said, glancing at the page and then squinting at the raised cup to make sure that the emulsion was complete, without solids of yolk or albumen. Little flecks of tea and
egg, like gilding-fluid, stood on his moustache as he repeated,
"Fine, my son. Stick to it! Stick to it!" and then changed the
subject, to tell us about one of his colleagues and of some
absorbing minor drama in the South-West District Post Office;
a field of endless fascination to him.

The attitude taken by my family thus ensured that I should
not fall into precocious self-congratulation over my first literary
success. Whatever Jack may have believed, as the instigator,
he would never have dreamed of congratulating me. Any
praise from Mother I should have had to regard as partisan.
Father's attitude conveyed no snub; it was merely a symptom
of his complete unconsciousness of any such thing as an art of
letters, or indeed any æsthetic realities. So his "Fine! Fine!"
meant as much as he was capable of meaning.

Gradually I settled down to the routine of home life, attend-
ing more regularly at school and showing perhaps a little
greater moral courage in tackling the tasks of memorising and
thinking over the concerns of arithmetic, grammar, geography,
history and French. The last subject was new to me, introduced
as I entered the Fourth Standard. At first I was puzzled, then
I was dazzled, for I began dimly to recognise that a grammar

meant something constructive; a basic fact which I had not
stumbled upon in my struggles with the theory of my native
language.

This discovery added a new dimension to my reading, for
now words *in themselves* had not only a musical effect upon my
senses; they lured me to the dictionary, like a cat to the larder,
where I feasted my imagination on origins. This was the beginning of the historical approach to all matters, that instinctive
and immediate inquiry, when confronted with a new experience
or idea, which demands 'what started all this?'

It is not easy to describe the happiness, a deep content like
that of the religious initiate who has found a substantial com-
panionship in his God, which now enriched my days. I felt in
myself a distinction, an authority, because the life around me
was now seen to be a reflection from a more serene prototype,
the matrix, the Word. My sense of Christ, whose nature had
already dawned upon my infant consciousness some two years
earlier, now became much more defined: I saw him as Mind
itself, the Me within myself, but a perfected *eidolon* because his
flesh and blood were not this troublesome stuff that moved and
breathed in the Battersea fogs. His body was the Word itself.
My groping after this realisation was suddenly, miraculously
rewarded one morning in school, during the first lesson of the
day, which was always that odd subject called 'Scripture', an
activity to be compared with the scratching given by a dog to
the door-mat before he curls up to sleep on it; a racial act.

We had been set to learn a passage from one of Paul's
Epistles by heart. I had already got this, and I sat turning the
dreary-looking pages of the school edition of the Bible, covered
in shiny black. One hand was thrust into my inside pocket,
clasping the tiny silver watch as a talisman. The other stopped
at the page opening on the Fourth Gospel. I saw the phrase,
"In the beginning was the Word, and the Word was with God,
and the Word was God."

I felt the hair on my head tingling, and a curtain of red blood
appeared to fall before my eyes. I leaned forward, clasping
myself close, while the world rocked around me. And as this
earthquake subsided, I saw a new skyline defined. It was a

landscape in which objects and words were fused. All was one, with the word as the verbal reality brought to material life by Mind, by man. It was therefore the very obvious, tangible presence of the Creator.

Sitting in Surrey Lane School, crouched over my fluttering and burning stomach, with one hand still clasping the silver watch given me by my mother, I received a philosophy which I have never lost, a working faith in the oneness of all life. My fears of evil, the old Satanic dreads due to the division between the flesh and the spirit, vanished in that moment of revelation. Everything was now contained, for me, in the power of the Word.

Such literalness did me no harm, for on this sharp and concise symbolism I was to build a concept of universal singleness that gave me authority over the horrors, the divisions, the guilt complexes, that beset us all as we go through life, in a world supposedly split into two, the flesh and the spirit, where civil war rages eternally, in sombre Miltonic gloom and hopelessness.

That blinding yet revealing experience was too violent to be lived up to. For the rest of that summer term of 1904, I subsided into a quiet mood, wary but confident, looking out from my new citadel like a crusader from the walls of Antioch, over the Holy Land. The presence of a God was constant, and I never again lost the conviction that His authority lay in words, in language, that differentiated man from the rest of creation, making him master of it. The knowledge was a fire within me, lighting my mind, consuming my body.

I was, however, to retreat from the consequences of this profound ascertainment, for more experience now came flooding over me; this time from outside myself.

The term ended; the small garden filled with upstanding balsams and sunflowers, waiting to flower. The jasmine bower once again was white-starred with perfume that set me longing for I knew not what. The July day came when I ran home from school at midday, fished out the back-door key from behind the water-closet pan, let myself into the house, started the midday meal cooking, and realised that for a month the everydayness of life was to be broken.

Mother came in, and I ran to meet her in the shady tunnel of the jasmine. In my sense of freedom, of exaltation, I flung my arms round her and buried my face in her neck. She staggered and protested.

"Oh, don't, dear! I'm so tired!"

My excitement collapsed. I looked at her, as she preceded me into the house. She was bent, and the nut-brown, silky hair hung in wisps. She dropped the great black handbag to the floor and sat down at the table, resting her elbows on it and her head in her hands.

I was frightened. All my new-found armoury was useless. But I knew what to do. I warmed a little milk on the gas-stove, poured it into a breakfast cup, and added a tablespoonful of rum. She sipped this, breathing wheezily; and gradually the dear identity returned. She smiled, and talked to me about the forthcoming holiday and the problems of packing.

We had the afternoon to ourselves, and after dinner we sat in the yard, our backs to the cycle-shed, looking into the forest of annuals contained in the flower-bed beyond the drooping foliage of the sycamore tree. I found a shawl and put it round Mother's shoulders, then set up my fort at her feet, and staged a battle among the lead soldiers, which included a company of the Coldstream Guards, who looked rather incongruous among so many dressed in this drab khaki which had dimmed the British Army since the Boer War. My artillery consisted of one field piece, which fired india-rubber shells a quarter of an inch in length; but they were lethal among the leaden campaigners.

Behind this slaughter, however, and the momentary excitement it engendered, my mind was at work on its own and more unique concerns, chief among them being my sense of foreboding as I watched my mother, furtively, from time to time. She seemed content to sit there doing nothing; and I was startled by so uncharacteristic a mood. But she was cheerful enough, and we filled the afternoon with happiness and anticipation. The heat came down on the concrete at our feet, and the hot air stirred the nasturtiums and jasmine flowers, teasing our instincts with hints of something larger, wilder, more open and free than could be contained in this Battersea environment

M

of suburban backyards, and the tiny continent of our bread-winning days.

The heat-wave deepened during the following few days while Jack and I lazed about in the house and yard, wearing ragged shirts and discarded garments, because the more presentable were being packed by Mother. She was obviously not strong enough to cycle down to Hampshire, where Father and Jack had been one week-end, to see and rent a cottage at Ropley, near Alresford. From this prospecting journey Jack had returned with half a dozen photographs taken with a plate-camera which he had made for himself, the aperture being a pin-hole. This was only one of his many ingenious artifacts. I had studied the pictures, which included a church that leaned backwards, in the hope of finding that perpetually teasing certainty which we look for when about to take some adventurous step into the unknown. But Ropley remained unreal.

The heat became a torture over the river flats. We watered the concrete in the yard, conjuring a temporary purity and freshness into the air. But this had to be repeated again and again to make the hours endurable, as we fretted and gloomed, in the irritation of boyish impatience, while Mother bent over the tin trunk and the smaller boxes and baskets, pausing from time to time to rest, and ease her breathing, so harassed by the oppressive heat.

Father had not been idle meanwhile. Deciding that Mother could not face the journey by road, he found a second-hand trailer, which he fitted to his solo bicycle. It looked like a bath-chair, being made of wickerwork with padded leather upholstery and a small square of oilcloth at the feet. A long iron bar secured it to the saddle-pin of the bicycle. The combination was of vast length and had to be assembled out in the street, the process causing several gangs of boys to gather round, some of them being from Surrey Lane School, and therefore superior in all respects to the rest, the anonymous ones.

Father had rehearsed in the street, for in all matters of this kind he was a good soldier. He left nothing to chance. Every nut, every link in the chain, of his steed was scrutinised, tightened, oiled, tested. By the morning of our departure the junior tandem shone like the accoutrements of a crack regiment.

A luggage carrier was fitted to the tandem, on which we were to carry the food for the journey. The great tin trunk was to go by train, with Mother. Father took all the rest, loading up the trailer and roping all safely under a groundsheet. The trailer was so full that no room could be found in it even for the water-melon which Father had brought home the previous evening on his way from the Post Office. So he carried it in a string bag, slung from the handlebars of his bicycle.

On the eve, we slept but little. The heat held through the night, and Jack and I tossed about under a single sheet whispering to each other incoherently. Dawn came as a relief, with a gesture of coolness, and we tumbled out of bed, almost sick with excitement.

It was raining!

We stood at the scullery door, studying the sky beyond the sycamore tree. The clouds rumbled over, but their ruggedness assured Father that they would break, and he pretended to jeer at us because of our downcast visages. He had the confidence and energy of a god that morning. The trunk was corded and addressed to the Ropley cottage, Father's copperplate calligraphy standing out like a public notice. He dragged the trunk down to the front door, then had to pull it back a little way so that the door could be opened. This waste of power only increased his reserves. He undertook to cook the breakfast, so that Mother could have time to herself, to dress at more leisure and take stock of all the luggage, the locking up of the house, the final arrangements about the cat being left to the care of the next-door neighbour, and a hundred other minor responsibilities any one of which, being neglected, would have lain under her holiday like the rose petal under the mattress of the little princess.

The odour of eggs and bacon filled the house, while Father stood at the gas-stove, squinting up at the clouds with one grey eye, making meteorological pronouncements calculated to re-assure every member of his family.

"Pah! Pride of the morning!" he cried, cracking another

egg into the pan and easing up the others with the flat of a knife. "Rain before seven, fine before eleven!"

So confident was he that we started off before the milk and post arrived. Mother pleaded with him to wait, fearing that her boys would catch chills: but Father brushed her anxiety aside as he brushed away the steady downpour of rain—as though it were morning dew. This was his great day, marred only by the defection of his wife; but he promised himself, and her, that to compensate for this he would take her for rides in the trailer while we were at Ropley.

We put on mackintosh capes over our cycling outfit, the trailer was attached to Father's machine, Mother came to the front door to see us off, receiving a smacking kiss and an admonition to "take it easy, old girl", and then we were off.

The rain beat against us as we pedalled south-west, past the candle factory. Father led the way, steadily chugging along, the trailer with its covered load gliding behind him like a faithful dog. We followed, sometimes dropping back because so long a procession could not be maintained unbroken on the public highway. I was now almost as expert as Jack at pedalling and economising my strength. With our legs hidden by the wide-spread capes, we had the sensation of being propelled by magic.

As we drew out of the inner suburbs towards Kingston the clouds broke and the rain ceased. We stopped on the Portsmouth road to discard our dry mackintoshes and to eat some raisins. But excitement would have carried us on without the help of other nourishment. This was my first great journey by road. I was now deemed to be cured of my stomach trouble, and indeed I believed so too. I needed no urging from Father.

The sun came out. The wet roads steamed, and the beams of golden fire combed the wet grass like hair, raising it up, and raising also a plague of flies that buzzed about our sweating heads, our foreheads granulated with salt as the sun dried the exuding pores.

Steadily round and round moved Father's calves, clad in stockings and spats. No variation in speed broke their rhythm. Jack and I plugged away. The tandem was in fine fettle;

perhaps a few more ounces in weight than when we started an hour and a half earlier.

From time to time Father broke into song: 'Marching with the Deathless Army', 'I'll sing thee Songs of Araby', and the piece that in modern times would have been called his signature tune:

> "Oh merry goes the day
> When the heart is young."

He had been born afresh that morning: not a care in the world. He broke off songs recklessly, like a prince squandering alms, to point out interesting features on the road: pubs where he and his Post Office pals had stopped; corners where on former rides he had hesitated, or had a puncture; places where he and the Boys' Brigade philosopher had taken a photograph.

The traffic thinned out, the suburbs dropped away (for London was smaller fifty years ago), the countryside grew deeper, wider, more lush. We crossed the Surrey commons, and for the first time in my life I heard larks trilling in the sky.

It was impossible to grow weary, or at least to acknowledge it. Jack too was a different person, if it was possible for so pronounced a character to change overnight. He caught some of Father's enthusiasm, and even cracked a laconic joke or two with me, as he pedalled in front, with my legs and feet shadowing his. There were no complaints from him, as yet, that I was not pulling my weight, or dragging on the up-pedal (the great crime).

In 1904, bicycles were the fastest vehicles on the roads. Father and his trailer were eyed suspiciously by policemen when we passed through Guildford, for this long combination of bicycle and demented bath-chair wriggled its way round the sober horse-traffic like a salmon slipping upstream. The roads were plain macadam, an inch deep in dust of many colours, the tints varying with the nature of the road metal used by the local councils. But the over-all hue was cement-grey; a fine, choking powder that gradually settled along the creases of our skin, our garments, and on every plane surface. By the time we reached Guildford we were three millers, and the trailer gave the appearance of a load of limestone.

On we pushed, though by now I was faint with hunger and Jack was beginning to grow irritable. "We'll stop on the Hog's Back," said Father. "A grand view from there over the Devil's Punchbowl."

A minor adventure befell us almost as he spoke. We were bent over our handlebars, at the bottom of a sharp rise. Behind us rode a young man, alone, who had attached himself to us as we left Guildford, using us as pace-makers, perhaps. Jack was annoyed, for he hated collections of people, as being conspicuous demonstrations.

"Can't you let him go, Dad?" he said, urging Father to slow down. But Father had everything timed, and reduced to an economic output. His pace did not vary for some passing flipperdigibert of the road. He replied that we should be stopping soon for our midday meal, and that would enable us to shake off the stranger.

Suddenly we heard a cry of alarm. I raised my bemused head, and saw a stout woman on a tricycle, tearing down the hill with her feet off the pedals, which were flickering up and down, as it seemed, faster than the eye could follow. An instant later there was another cry from the stout woman, and a crash alongside us. The young man had pulled out, intending at last to pass our slow cortège. But he chose the wrong moment, for the tricyclist went slap into him. Machines and human bodies appeared immediately to multiply, and to be scattered all about us, amid a cloud of white dust, and groans and cries.

Jack and Father now both showed a common characteristic, for the bicycle with trailer, and the tandem, calmly slowed and stopped, the drivers dismounting and looking round in mild surprise. I had jumped clear, with a jolt that shook my bones, and I stood trembling, my eyes refusing, for a moment, to focus on the dreadful scene of carnage.

Father strode over to the mound of humanity in the middle of the road, lifted her up as though she were merely an inflated balloon, and assisted her to the side of the road.

"Now stay there!" he said, allowing her to relapse into tears and hysteria, while he returned to pick up the youth, who was kneeling within the frame of his bicycle, while the front wheel spun round, as an afterthought.

The ball of his thumb was grazed and bleeding. That was the only damage, apart from shock. Father whipped the young man's handkerchief out of his pocket, spat on the wound, wiped and bound it. The poor fellow, a weedy creature, sat on the bank, growing paler and paler, his teeth chattering.

"Pull yourself together, lad!" cried Father. "Your machine's not damaged. I've straightened the pedal, so you can push along before there are any questions asked. Wrong of you, y'know, turning out like that!"

His brusque warning acted like a pail of well water on the youth, who was obviously about to faint. Shaking himself, he stood up, took a deep breath, that brought the colour back to his hollow cheek.

"No fault of mine," he muttered ungraciously, and stumbled off, walking his machine up the hill, examining it as he went.

Meanwhile Father was directing the tonic of his personality at the stout woman.

"Now, Ma'am!" he cried. "Is nobody with you?"

She was still incoherent, but we could detect references to her poor husband, and demands for the police, and denunciations of that monster of ungallant depravity who had brought her to this pretty pass. "It's nobody's fault," said Father, brushing away at her garments, and flicking her face and hands with her own handkerchief. "You lost control. Should never do that, you know. Might have ruined your machine."

By this time the poor husband approached down the hill on a bicycle of rare vintage, the back wheel being about two-thirds the size of the front one, and the chain encased in a honey-coloured, transparent gear-case square at both ends. The handlebars towered up, with grips of cork at least six inches long.

He was a small, nervous man, and he looked at my father beseechingly, like a spaniel.

"I will take charge," he said. Though that was unbelievable, we left him and his runaway spouse, remounted and rode on.

I was still shaken when we stopped by the roadside before entering Farnham. But the cool deep grasses of the verge soon persuaded me into a calmness that restored my appetite. I looked about me while I devoured hard-boiled egg and bacon sandwiches. The sun was now beating down from a cloudless sky, over a rain-washed landscape every feature of which stood out in hard outline. The only blurred thing was the film of dust on my eyelashes. I blinked, wiped my eyes, and then all was crystalline.

"Ah," exclaimed Father, "the melon!"

He cut it in halves, scooped out the seeds, divided one of the halves and passed the quarters to his sons. We dipped our sweating faces into the fruit as though we were playing mouth-organs, while Father worked at his half with his clasp-knife, shovelling the dripping flesh into his upturned mouth and mumbling with pleasure. When all the flesh was scooped out, he split the empty gourd almost to a division, and clapped it, like the Tarnhelm, on his head, fixing it there with the huge handkerchief that had recently succoured the stout lady of the tricycle. With his fine Roman nose, his clear grey eyes, black moustache, surmounted by the white-bound helmet of gold, he looked like a Crusader. That is how he rode on, during the fierce afternoon, to the wonder of townsfolk and villagers as we trundled along through Farnham and Alton, past lovely parks, pine woods, farmsteads, over streams and round hillsides, further and further from London, and from our familiar selves, the world growing stranger and wilder, and we with it, until at last, as dusk fell, we stumbled off our machines in the tiny lane before the meadow-fronted cottages, fabulous beings no longer in command of our limbs, or our wits. But we recognised the Mother who awaited us, cool and serene, the last daylight glinting on her gold spectacles, and behind her an interior of candlelight and a huge hearth full of shadows.

CHAPTER SIXTEEN

Further Intimacies with Nature

IT MAY HAVE BEEN MY GREATER PHYSICAL VIGOUR that made me respond to all green things during that holiday. I found myself constantly aware of the fecundity, the lush extravagance, of those Hampshire valleys, in one of which the cottage stood.

The owner lived in one end, and ran a smallholding. She was a widow, with a son younger than me: a tall, handsome woman with black hair coiled on top of her head. She had settled in this isolated place with a sick husband, recently dead. Before marriage she had been lady's maid to Dorothea Baird, the wife of H. B. Irving and famous as the first 'Trilby'.

This woman, with her two cows and her little boy, her hens and geese, attracted me instantly. Her voice drew me like a magnet. It was soft and modulated, full of flute-music. She was kind, too. She took to me, let me carry her empty pail to the cow-shed, where I stood at the door watching the thin streams of milk gushing into the pail through the persuasion of her small, work-moiled fists.

I asked a lot of questions, for all this was new to me. Once or twice she laughed, a low, gurgling chuckle that filled me with mystified pleasure and deeper curiosity.

"You must ask Mother to tell you about that," she replied, to one inquiry about the origin of all this supply of concentrated nourishment. She made me drink many a glass of the milk still warm from the cow.

"Don't spoil that kid," said her neighbour, a man from a neighbouring farmhouse, where he lived with his old parents and an elder married brother. He was a bachelor, and he appeared to be a man of leisure, for he strolled about in his shirt-sleeves, his forearms tanned like bog-oak, a cigarette

177

dangling from his full lips. His strolls always led him into the wake of our landlady, wherever she might be, indoors or out, a shadowing which she accepted without demur.

"Don't spoil that kid," he said, as though my worshipping presence might ruin the prolonged *tête-à-tête*. But she would only smile, and ruffle my hair, and murmur something to tease him.

She was kind to Mother, too. She insisted on doing a bit of cooking so that Mother could make the most of the holiday by resting in a deck-chair under one of the giant elms in the meadow between the cottages and the lane. She found an old woman from up the lane, who came in and tidied up each morning. This crone had a huge goitre that flopped to and fro like a puppy in a sack, as she talked. And she *did* talk! We heard all about her ailments, and her man who suffered from what she called '*in*so-mania'!

Mother spent most of the holiday sitting in front of the cottage, chatting with the landlady and hearing about London theatre-land. She worked at her crochet, turning out yard after yard of it, even though I had long refused to wear blouses decorated with it. Father and Jack went off frequently for whole days' expeditions on the junior tandem—to Southampton, Winchester, Midhurst, and to see the newly-discovered Roman villa at East Meon. Mother and I were left much to ourselves, and I read to her as she crocheted. I read *Esmond* aloud, for it was one of her favourite tales.

Sometimes I went roving with the landlady's son and one or two other children; but after some days I found them too inarticulate for my taste, and they could tell me nothing about the countryside, its geography, its flowers, birds, butterflies. These glories I had to find for myself, though that was no difficulty, for indeed they came and found me, even where I lay supine in the grasses at Mother's feet, staring up vertically along the trunk of an elm, into the retreating heights of foliage, branch beyond branch, fan over fan of ever-folding green, where hover-flies stood in air, a squirrel crouched in a fork, a woodpecker clung, indistinguishable from the brown bark, but drilling with his penetrating thrust until the whole tree-scape seemed to vibrate above him, and even the earth beneath me to catch the last agitation of that needle-like vigour.

These influences were new to the town-born child; new and startling. I was a young Ali Baba in the treasure-cave, and could find no way to grasp the riches. I had, however, brought my paint-box and the collection of pencils in its coffin-like container. I tried to draw trees, but my efforts looked like green bonfires of billowing smoke. I reduced my ambition, and tried to paint single flowers and sprays. This was more encouraging, and Mother praised my work, sometimes taking a hand herself and producing clean stylised studies, as she had been taught in her Victorian girlhood. By comparison, my flower pictures were crude pieces of impressionism lacking both perspective and precision.

That holiday at Ropley was the first of four summer vacations spent there. Mother never was able to go down by road, and each year her movements during the holidays grew more confined to round and about the cottage, or to gentle patrols in the trailer behind Father. She avoided this means of travel as much as she could, without hurting Father's feelings, for she could not trust the bouncing wickerwork to remain upright, especially when turning corners.

Jack or I would stay with her, taking it in turns to ride with Father on the smaller tandem, on expeditions whose outset would find Father somewhat subdued because Mother was not well enough to come. The excitements of the road, however, quickly inspired him, and for the rest of the way he became an animated and musical guide and philosopher. On one journey to Southampton he and I stopped to admire the German liner the *Deutschland*. A steward, standing by the gangway, smiled at my wonder-stricken face, and offered to take us over the ship. This occupied the whole afternoon, and I was so tired after it that I was in danger of falling asleep while riding back to Ropley, which we reached after dark, to find Mother distraught with anxiety, fearing we had come to grief on the road.

The ride home after that first holiday at Ropley was melancholy. I was in love with the kind widow, her dulcet voice, her caressing touch, her cows, and even her jealous follower. I saw

them all, seemingly waist-high in vivid grass, inhabitants of
paradise, a remote tract where the thatched cottage lay hidden.
Beside it ran an ancient turf road, rising over the hill, and
marked by yew bushes of great age. It was part of the Pilgrims'
Way that ran from Winchester to Canterbury; broad, quiet,
haunting.

We rode home, Father, Jack and I, all three subdued to the
spirit of retreat. Gradually the lushness and romantic beauty
subsided, and the solitude was filled with traffic. It is a notable
illusion, that on a return journey the outskirts of Town
appear to have spread further afield. After we had passed
through Guildford I felt no· more interest in the ride. It
became a treadmill boredom, and Jack must have agreed, for
he was morose, and accused me frequently of not doing my
share of the pedalling.

All too soon, yet not soon enough, we were passing the candle
factory, the greasy smell, the menacing half-light, and we
reached home to find Mother already opening up the house; a
house shrunk and shabby, a garden overgrown as though it had
been planted with the magic beanstalks under the shadow of
threats from an upper-storey giant.

I lay in bed that night, brooding over lost delights; sunk in
a vague, desolate misery that robbed me of all particular
recollections. The holidays were over, and Surrey Lane School,
with winter in Battersea, and Mother still unwell: these lay
ahead.

But the desert prospect was soon to be changed, and the
world that seemed to be dead was suddenly to open afresh.
The last months of 1904 were gloomy with Battersea fog and
rain, the air rancid. Mother was so unwell that she stayed
away from school. The doctor was called in, for she had to
submit medical certificates in order to receive her pay. At the
same time Father, setting off for one of his Sunday rides with a
crony or two, skidded while crossing Putney Bridge and hurt
his leg. This injury developed into water on the knee, and thus
both parents were laid up over Christmas, and Jack and I had
to run the house, an improvisation that we took as a matter of
course. But the Christmas was a sombre one, with all of us

confined to the house, under premonitions and forebodings of disaster.

On Christmas night, after dark, Jack and I went for a walk to get some fresh air. Gifts had been few, and the feast perfunctory. The streets were empty and overhung with a frosty fog. Every corner held a threat: under every green-blue lamp-standard in the main road (now a silent canyon) lay a shaft of darkness. A lamp here and there hissed, consuming some dreadful soliloquy, to spit in venom, throwing down hot sticks of carbon that sputtered on the wet pavement, then died. I picked up one or two of these fragments, but they roused no further curiosity in my dulled mind. I dropped them again, and walked on with Jack, who had stopped and waited for me without looking round. We were both afraid of something: of what, we did not know. Life, and the meaning of life, had ebbed. We could expect nothing more.

Within a few weeks this desperate situation found its own cure. Our parents decided that another winter in Battersea might be disastrous for Mother. This resolution cured Father instantly. He was out and awheel within a few days, and Mother too took a new lease of health as the days lengthened and a gleam of greasy sunlight spilled itself from time to time over our yard, and through the lattice-work at the front windows into the aspidistra forest.

Every week-end was now spent house-hunting. We ranged over the southern suburbs of London on our two tandems, exploring the outer parishes such as Wimbledon and Herne Hill, where speculative builders were running up street upon street of jerry-built houses, designed in the Edwardian mode, with curved windows and tulip-patterned inlets of coloured glass.

We found a unique house standing between Herne Hill and Dulwich, at the post-barred end of a lane running up to Denmark Hill to join the main road opposite the house where John Ruskin had spent much of his life. Our lane was therefore called Ruskin Walk.

The house was detached and double-fronted. That was important. It signified social progress. It was a pretty house, somewhat confined in a triangle of ground, occupying the majority of it, and leaving only two tiny triangles at the side and the back of the house, joined by an isthmus six feet wide, between the angle of the house and the boundary fence. A row of aspens ran alongside Ruskin Walk, up to the top of the hill. Beyond the trees, a few acres of meadow land, with a real hedge and derelict farm buildings, stretched as far as Herne Hill station. An old horse brooded by a pond.

There stood a little piece of country, stone-dead, waiting to be buried by the jerry builders. Similar patches of rural survival littered the district, gradually disappearing, with their hedges of hawthorn, their uncut grass, their nettle-beds, as the builders nibbled with teeth of brick and slaver of mortar.

All this would have depressed a sophisticated person. To a boy coming out of Battersea, it was half-way to paradise. I could not believe in our good fortune. Our own small garden had three chestnut trees in it, two double-red hawthorns, two laburnums. It had also a wedge-shaped greenhouse at the acute angle furthest from the house, by the main road called Half Moon Lane, where once an hour a horse-bus jogged along on its way to or from Peckham. And on the other side of Half Moon Lane stood large houses in their own grounds, with great elms towering up, in whose branches I heard, for the first time in my life, blackbirds and thrushes at their spring-time song.

The house, too, changed our whole concept of domestic habits. It had been built by a theatre architect (when he was building the Kennington Theatre) for his own use, and he had been lavish with lincrusta and mirrors. The little drawing-room was lined with lincrusta, of a bold, oriental splendour, in gold.

Each side of the Alma-Tadema fireplace the recesses were filled by mirrors from floor to ceiling, which doubled the size of the room and the identity of its furniture. One could never be alone in that room, for a third mirror cunningly placed threw a series of receding reflections into infinity, so that for as long as I lived in this fairyland houselet I had to sit reading in that drawing-room, in the presence of ten thousand detachments, or *ecstasies*, of myself, all sitting book on lap.

It was sometimes disconcerting. It was always wonderful.

The gold walls, too, were endlessly repeated, diminishing in perspective and darkening as the reflected light, cut off from its source, died a little in each relay, until the furthest recesses of this 'vasty hall' were lost in the final deceits of the whole fantasy.

But in my eagerness I am already trying, though breathlessly, to describe this magic home in a magic land before we have got there. The boyhood excitement revives after half a century and makes my pen trip over itself.

What happened first was that the Battersea home, hitherto the solid axis of the universe, was sold to Father's Post Office colleague who had taught me to row, the hero who walked upon the water. The price was £375; what my parents had paid for it—or rather were paying for it, the building society still having an interest.

This venture into landed property had been bold enough. Mother's ambition had startled Father. Now she was going to a larger commitment, for the price of the Herne Hill oriental palace was £550.

The gap was bridged, and the building society continued to show confidence in my parents' earning capacity. Lady Day of 1905 came, and two moving vans came with it. I can still smell straw, and sacking, and dusty emptiness. I can still see bottled beer and mugs standing on bare boards from which the linoleum has just been wrenched. I can see the two pianos floating out of the house into the street, and resting there on little trolleys while the sweating cyclops take breath, before lifting these uprooted harps into the vans, one into each.

What puzzles me now is that I left that home without a glance backward, or a pang of regret. Maybe the gloom of that preceding Christmas had poisoned my emotions, and detached me from the house and from Battersea, long before I left in the flesh. I was also spellbound by the prospect of the new environment, the house in its own garden, with its own trees, and two little greenhouses (for on a second inspection I had found that a verandah at the back, by a side-entrance from the street with a monastic miniature portcullis, projected into another tiny greenhouse). Both had leaden water-tanks, and heating apparatus of a baroque elaborateness.

We left Battersea on a sunny spring day that made the whole parish a reproach to us, the deserters. I rode on one of the vans with the foreman and his men. We stopped twice at public-houses on the four-mile journey, to rest the horses after the climb over Clapham Common. Our last halt was for lunch at the Half Moon Tavern, near our destination. I sat on the tail-board and the foreman treated me to a ginger-beer and a meat-pie, for, owing to the thousand and one things to be done and thought about, Mother had not supplied me with food for the journey; indeed, I doubt if she knew quite what had happened to me that day, until I turned up with the furniture.

There she was, already at work in our future home (whose name was 'Gardencourt', a most apt and literal description). She had brought with her one of her retinue of Battersea 'mothers', whom she collected in a Sarah Gamp-like disciple-ship at her slum school in the Battersea Park Road, contagiously near Nine Elms. This woman, briefed with pints of porter, had scrubbed down the floors throughout the house with carbolic. She was polishing the rusted kitchen range when the vans rolled up.

Later in the afternoon Father and Jack appeared, and when the moving-men and the charwoman had gone, the family worked on arranging the furniture, laying oilcloth, hanging curtains, unpacking crockery; tasks that forbade daydreaming or any other departure from the task in hand. I found, however, as I was to find for years to come, until the hallucination vanished, that I was aided in these physical and mechanical jobs by my ability to rise from the ground, flitting from point to point like a worker-bee, half-consciously enjoying the privi-leged faculty as I flew. It did not occur to me to remark that nobody showed surprise at my unusual means of passing from pillar to post. The process was so patently valid that I was not concerned to think it could be questioned. The advantage was that my lack of muscle and physical staying power were amply compensated by this birdlike gift.

I could not move swiftly through the air; the progress was

stately rather than adroit, but it was also unerring; I rose as I wished, by a mere pressure of will-power, visually commanding the pull of earth, and I alighted where I wished, cool and precise, wise with what I had seen from my bee's-eye view while in flight. This added power secured me from much distress, the doubts, the shyness that would otherwise have accompanied a boy whose poor health prevented him from a physical equality with his fellow-mortals.

Mother was a swift and dexterous worker, and Jack was like her. Under their direction, Father and I worked with zest, and within a few days the house was set up, the familiar furniture looking rather self-conscious in its new environment. The Broadwood-White, as taciturn as ever, stood in the dining-room on one side of the hall; the Klingmann in the golden drawing-room on the other side. So rivalry between them was much reduced.

Another division marked the new *ménage*. Jack had his own room, and I had mine above his. So much has been said and written about a room of one's own that I need not labour the point. Mine was hardly more than an attic; but its window looked into the aspen trees, over the fields and the pond, and along to Half Moon Lane. From the elm-tops across the road came the morning song of the thrushes, the triple-shouters, and the flute music of blackbirds. I woke to this music, and lay under the small square window in an agony of delight, seasoned only by the expectancy that it would end, or that I was not fully appreciating it. I had spent twelve years on earth and had never heard this morning salutation, nor the persuasive whispering of the aspen leaves, a perpetual sound of rainfall, but on some fabulous soil in a land of sorrows too exquisite for common humanity to experience. My acute response may have been due to the fact that I was still young enough to have these Wordsworthian, subconscious recollections acceptable before

'Shades of the prison-house begin to close
Upon the growing Boy.'

N

These first mornings of awaking in my room to such intoxicants were a foretaste of the over-rich life now about to open before me. The other members of the family took up their regular work. Mother had much further to go to school, but this added fatigue was offset by the healthier situation of our new home, its brightness and lightness. Jack went off with her each morning.

My position, however, was different, for I could not travel to and from Battersea every day. Father quickly solved the problem of my education.

"Come along!" he said, one afternoon when he got home about three o'clock, after an early 'duty'. I had been hanging about for over a week, acclimatising myself like a cat to the new premises.

We got out the junior tandem (now housed in a new and smaller lean-to shed) and set off in the direction of Dulwich, which had not yet been visited.

Over Father's shoulders I observed the increasing density of giant trees, all breaking into bud in the van of that early spring. I saw period houses, but was ignorant then of the cause of my pleasure in seeing shapely windows and porticos. We came to the head of Dulwich Village, with an enclosed green bordered by laurels and posts and chains. The sidewalks were already shadowy under the lattice of boughs, for an avenue of venerable trees stood by the roadside.

"We ought to find a school down there," said Father; and we turned down the village street, moving at walking pace, looking about us. Father was right. The school stood in the middle of the village.

"There we are, you see," said Father, and with that we pulled up, and we went in together to the boys' department. I was not abashed, because the buildings were single-storey, and small, a welcome distinction from the sooty three-decker of Battersea.

The hall too was small, intimate. Sitting at a raised desk was a plump man with full jowls and iron-grey hair. Father put his arm round my shoulders and propelled me forward, saying to the Headmaster that he wanted to enrol his son.

The response was grave, the inquiries and answers passing in an atmosphere of serene quietness. I looked around, but there was no sign of a chest filled with canes. Then I felt two cool blue eyes scrutinising me; and the inquisition was amused, kindly. He asked me if I could read, and I replied yes, I could read and I could also draw.

"Well, we have an art school here," he said, and I was accepted as a pupil in Dulwich Hamlet School, by its Head-master, Charles Thomson Hunt, where for the next three years I was to find an almost impossible happiness, and to be set on the road to the only education that is of any value—self-education.

I left Surrey Lane with relief, and thought about it no more until, forty years later, I met a fellow-clubman at the Athenæum who had also been a pupil there: Albert Mansbridge, founder of the Workers' Education Association, an original character, of healthy religious vigour, who had kept his Cockney accent and perkiness of spirit, with which he tackled the self-imposed tasks of his nation-wide campaign for creating a working-class university in every British community, commanding Church and Parliament as his auxiliaries, and triumphing in his purpose.

My first few months at Dulwich Hamlet were not easy, for though this was not a 'Higher Grade' school, the standard of work there was more advanced than at Surrey Lane. I found myself sadly backward in arithmetic, geometry and algebra, and became so fixed in my despair that I have neglected these subjects all my life, to the detriment of orderliness of mind and economy of reasoning power. I tend to wade through by instinct, and frequently to become bogged, where a little discipline in what Bacon called the 'subtlety' of mathematics would save me from much floundering. I think of the opening words of that poem 'To Number' by the French naturalist J. H. Fabre:

> 'Nombre! Regulateur des effets et des causes,
> Qui donne le comment et le pourquoi des choses,
> Que me veux-tu, Nombre Imposant?'

and I realise sadly that whatever 'Number' has demanded of
me, I have failed to respond, and that in consequence this
Pythagorean divinity has never revealed to me 'the how and
why of things'; an ignorance that has restricted my range in
philosophic speculation, and thrown me into an over-stressed
sympathy with intuitive thinkers, Plato, Plotinus, Spinoza,
Bergson, rather than the precise minds who look to Aristotle,
and the Statisticians.

Maybe the man who constrains himself, or is constrained by
nature, to become an artist in his means of self-expression, and
in comprehension of his environment, is doomed to this
partiality which prevents him from the cool, philosophic command of knowledge, and its mathematical arrangement.

I began to surrender myself to this bias as soon as I found my
deficiency at Dulwich Hamlet School. There were other tempta-
tions to deflect and restrict me. I was put into Standard Four,
and the master was a fierce little man, constantly preoccupied
in arranging exhibitions of work. Half the class-room would
be commandeered for this purpose, blackboards being laid over
whole groups of desks, on which drawings, paintings, woodwork
and other crafts were collected and prepared for display. While
the master was thus engaged, monitors handed round cards of
problems in arithmetic, which the boys had to work out, inter-
changing cards, so that the boring process went on indefinitely,
day after day, the only intermission being when other masters
came to take us for geography, history or French.

Thus there was no effort to introduce us to the *mystery* of
figures, or to show us the integral part it plays in equipping the
mind with conscious method, the keystone to all knowledge and
command of knowledge.

I felt this lack as soon as I had found my way about in the
new school, for Jack, my powerful-minded brother, had already
made me aware of my own intellectual weaknesses. I knew
just where I needed the tonic. I knew too that I should
succumb to any encouragement in the other direction: the
direction of sensibility, of dreaming emotionalism, of indulgence
in idiosyncrasy. And all this I found in my new surroundings.
Dulwich was for me the island of Circe: lovely, but dangerous.

In the first decade of our troubled century, before Arma-
geddon broke over the world, Dulwich Village was still the
rural spot to which Mr. Pickwick had retired nearly a century
earlier. His villa stood just beyond the village, on the road to
Sydenham, opposite a pathway called Lovers' Walk, a retreat
arched by gigantic elms and black poplars, with green fields
beyond.

In the centre of the village, near the Hamlet School, on a
narrow triangle of ground hemmed in by the High Street and
Court Lane, stood a Huguenot cemetery, its headstones and
monuments awry, many of them yawning to show rough brick-
work beneath the sculptured stone. Trees towered over the
neglected tombs, and the annual tides of grasses and wild
flowers rose above them, broke in spray of seeds, and ebbed
again.

It was enclosed by locked gates of hand-wrought iron, over-
arched by an empty lamp-cage. The fine metal calligraphy of
those gates was forged in a language almost as dead as the
inmates. Rust and moss softened the scripture, which nobody
read except a few handicraft enthusiasts who came to photograph and sketch the gates.

This was a spot where Thomas Gray, or William Collins, or
Young of the *Night Thoughts* might have lingered to feed
their melancholy and enrich their verses. Maybe they did,
when visiting the Old College of God's Gift, to hear Handel
play on the organ whose manuals were unique in having the
main keys black and the half-tone keys white.

Eighteenth-century villas abutted on the cemetery, facing
cottages on the opposite side of the High Street that stood back
in long gardens of lawn, hollyhocks, and mulberry trees embraced by roses. Towering over both the tall villas and the
low cottages stood the ancient trees, so close and abundant that
the whole village had the character of being abandoned at the
bottom of a canyon green in summer, and brown in winter.
Such an exuberance of foliage gave the neighbourhood an air
almost of gloom, had it not been so serene; just as the features of
a person lost in deep sleep will counterfeit an expression of
despair, even though the soul behind them is at rest.

All this was in the immediate surroundings of my new school. The contrast with the environment of Surrey Lane could not have been more emphatic. I had been used to a sinister barrack of sooty brick, crowded by a network of monotonous streets. It was a wonderful experience to come out of school into quietude, to be able to walk under trees immediately I left the school gate, and to find among the boys a temper here and there congenial to my own. Within a few weeks of joining the school I made friends with two boys who remained my companions during the three years I spent there, one a tall, quiet fellow named Bryden, grandson of the doctor who behaved heroically at the Khyber Pass; the other an impish midget named Richards, son of an architect, and later to discover a religious vocation.

Childhood friendships are of no general interest, and it is difficult to make them so. Yet to the children they loom as large as later love-affairs, and sometimes have a more lasting effect, because deeper, finer, at a period when the spirit is budding. These two boys, the one so dignified, the other so puckish, served to bring a touch of humanity into the enchantment of my new life, a life so different from that of my first twelve years in Battersea that I had the sensation of being born again.

The chief influence in this second incarnation, at least during schools hours, was the Headmaster. Something I may have said at that first interview gave him an interest in me. He never relinquished it, though my precocity must often have made him suspect that I was angling for his special attention. His calm severity prompted me to this, but I never broke through his reserve, and I never learned why he singled me out, or what he expected of me. I know now, as I knew then, that his personality was a constant force, quietly pressing me to a less self-concerned activity in all things, even in my own development. He made me begin to realise the quality in the books I read, and to drop the rather morbid contemplation of my own response to that quality. This first step toward objective living was what my brother had been urging me to since I first began to read.

CHAPTER SEVENTEEN

The Influence of Joy

ONE IMMEDIATE EFFECT of our removal to Dulwich was a loosening of our close family life. My parents and brother had further to travel each day, and I saw less of them, in point of time. Jack and I were also developing more individually, and instinctively demanding a personal independence. I was growing less timid toward the outside world, and this robust habit was encouraged by the new surroundings. I was no longer molested by fear of gangs of urchins; the aspect of the streets no longer threatened me with a sullen gloom, of poverty, bareness, and the negative picturesqueness of squalor and brutality.

I began to feel more confidence in life. How could I do otherwise, after being transplanted into paradise?

I hardly know how to begin to describe the riches that began to pour over me, and to spring up within me. I became a creature enchanted, singled out for such an endowment of wealth that I craved again for solitude so that I could savour these wonders. But no sooner was I alone than I wanted company, in order to tell of my discoveries and the full drama of new experience that marked my daily life at home and at school.

The internal pains which had made my last year or two at Battersea so restrictive were now almost forgotten, though from time to time a distant rumble threatened me, like departing thunder over woods still dripping when the rain has ceased. I was able to take much more physical pleasure, and I began to make a practice of running instead of walking the half-mile to and from school. And what a glorious half-mile it was, in comparison with that hazardous span of bricks, mortar and kerbstone through which I had been used to creep, my stomach fluttering with dread, to Surrey Lane.

My way now lay down a decline between grassy banks, under an iron railway bridge of delicate tracery. Wild barley grew on those banks, and I frequently had to stop, unable to resist my surprise that wild growth could be so lavish. I delighted to lie there, peering *through* the stalks of grasses, and to lose myself in this recognition of growing vegetation; its vitality, even its fierceness. I had never known it before, because I had never seen nature in spring-time and high summer, except through the medium of one sycamore tree, the tile-bordered flower-bed in our Battersea backyard, and occasional visits to the park.

But now, every morning and afternoon, I ran between green banks, and under an increasing company of trees of all kinds, some of them towering giants whose upper branches and crests swung in the wind and the light, making me crazed so that I would attempt to imitate their huge gestures, flinging up my arms as I ran, and uttering incoherent noises in my efforts to capture their rhythm and their almost monstrous beauty.

One windy day, that first autumn, I had turned by the laurel enclosure at the head of the village street, and saw the sunlight catch the pale-gold foliage of an elm just as the wind tossed its upper fans that towered above the surrounding trees. A whole treasury of leaves was flung out from the swaying head, dancing and spinning in the September air.

I cried out, I leapt up, my limbs mastered me and made boastful passes at the Universe. The great elm responded and tossed more largesse in the air, while the wind laughed and encouraged me to further extravagant conduct on my way to school.

The Headmaster, cycling sedately through the village, saw me. He slowed up, rode alongside me, gave me a shrewd glance yet keeping his eyes on the road ahead.

"My boy," he said, severely, "what are you doing?"

But his personality was such that his severity was an encouragement rather than a terror.

"I am an elm-waif, sir," I said.

He looked at me again, as he had looked during that first interview when I stood with Father before his desk.

"I see," he said slowly. "Well, don't let it make you late."
And he rode on, the shadows of autumn leaves flickering over
his stubborn grey head.

As I recall that picture of him now, after that curious
moment of contact, I realise why, many years later, when I
met the pianist Artur Schnabel, I stood talking with him,
puzzled by a sense of having met him before. He was almost a
double of my headmaster, both in physique and manner.

The elm-waif proceeded a little more soberly to school that
morning, remarking the carpet of coloured leaves on the moist
pavement, the crimson of the creeper overhanging the wall of
Beech House, a Georgian house that stood sideways on to the
road and faced the school-room window where I sat, so that I
could see the shapely façade, its windows staring through a veil
of creepers, across the meadow to the widespread willow
that stood in the centre of our playground, ringed by an iron
railing.

Instead of arriving at school idiotic with depression and un-
controllable fears, as I had formerly done at Battersea, I now
took my place each morning, excited by the adventure of getting
there, eager to communicate, to share it. This put me into a
state of mental alertness, a perpetual hunger of the mind. It
was so acute that it set my nerves working. I could hardly
contain myself within my body. I was tempted again and again
to vaunt myself, and to exhibit my power of command over
gravity by lifting myself and cruising above the school-room
desks.

Happily, some voice within, some eleventh-hour mentor, held
me back from the ultimate indiscretion, warning me that I had
the indulgence from an authority not of the world of common
sense, maybe not even from the moral order which I had found
in the Bible, under the dear personality of Christ, still my
constant companion. No! I was half-ashamed of it, as though
it were something I had stolen, just as later, when I began to
practise verse, and found myself seized by phrases not of my
conscious making, I set the words down in shame. Yet in both
aspects of flight, physical and verbal, I revelled in the wrong-
doing, having a remote conviction of faith that the obligation

was put upon me by a more ancient command, perhaps at the beckoning of the hand that scattered the largesse of autumnal gold from the elm-tops.

This assurance of some directing agent or force at the back of my identity, a more general and yet more intimate Being than any named in the great religions, took a still firmer hold upon my mind during that miraculous year. I was now hardly ever without a quiet consciousness of that power, latent in me as in everything else: the green leaves, the bird-song, the secretive stones and the boastful clouds, all things of nature to which my recognising eye was drawn as part of the joyous drama of my boyhood.

The ever-present problem was—which way to look! The riches were too abundant. The more I explored in and around Dulwich, the wilder became my rapture. No day was long enough, no night sufficiently oblivious in sleep, and I found my way only by a constant reference, a kind of inward thanksgiving, to this anterior genius of life who brooded deep in my nature, below my religious nominations, below my devotion to my parents and my brother, below the wonder and awe with which I was beginning to contemplate the faculty of self-expression, an activity for which I am still unable to account, though I have been its servant for half a century.

For the time being, I gave myself less to reading. Maybe this was due to improved health and physical vitality. Certainly life itself had more to offer me than I could absorb. For that first year at Dulwich, I roamed about the district, between Ruskin's Denmark Hill and the ridge where the Crystal Palace stood. It was only a few square miles, a gentle valley between Herne Hill and Sydenham Hill; but it was the same Garden of Eden which had caused Edward Alleyn, three hundred years before me, to fall on his knees in prayer, thanking God that at last he had found the place where he could build his college, the thank-offering of a successful man of the theatre, colleague of Shakespeare, husband of John Donne's daughter.

It was due to the terms of Alleyn's will that I was able to find Dulwich still in much the same condition of rural serenity as it had been in the beginning of the seventeenth century. He had forbidden the cutting down of trees on the estate which he bought from the heirs of a goldsmith named Galton, who had it in payment of a debt from Henry VIII, who seized it from the Abbey of Bermondsey at the time of the Dissolution of the monasteries, just as today the State is seizing the large private estates and country houses, with their cultural treasures, and dissolving these pearls into the trough of the Exchequer, to feed the jostling proletariat.

I had seen something of that proletariat in Battersea, my birthplace. This may be why Dulwich appeared to me as the Promised Land appeared to Caleb when Moses sent him to "espy it out from Kadesh-barnea". I had come to the Land of Peace, and quiet purposes. I had begun to know the meaning of civilisation, in its strictly social sense; the build-up of a concise community, whose values, customs, ceremonies, and created and natural possessions could enrich the mind of the individual and discipline his emotions into an appreciative sense of historical perspective, through humility to joy.

Such recognitions were still only tentative in my mind, but they were there, and I went about quietly savouring this sense of order and dignity, that characterised and controlled the lush beauty of Dulwich Village and its surrounding slopes.

I surrendered myself completely to the double stream of enrichment, the social and the natural. Their waters mingled and carried me along so rapidly that the experiences of a day made me feel a year or so older when night came. I used to tumble into bed exhausted with experience: things seen, felt; ideas sown, others ripened and seeded.

Jack took less part in all this than he had formerly taken in my life during the years in Battersea. He still had to spend much time in the old parish, by comparison a land of darkness to me. But at week-ends our early intimacy prospered, and we went out together exploring the village, penetrating up College Road, through the toll-gate to the Dulwich woods where Robert Browning, as a boy, also learned much of his nature-lore. We stared through the gates of the public school at the queer terra-cotta buildings, and saw the boys playing Rugby football. They had the appearance of mortals of a different incarnation, for we knew that they would go on to Oxford or Cambridge; and in 1905 that distinction was almost a biological one. It was probable that such creatures had whiter skins than ours and certainly minds of an impressive authority. Many years were to pass before I should discover that this was an illusion due to our timidity, and to the utter lack of training in the social techniques of deportment, rhetoric, debate, and administration in the elementary schools.

That was not quite true of Dulwich Hamlet School, however, for the Headmaster had set up a prefect system, and in the English lessons boys were made to get up and say something instead of being merely receptive of instruction, sitting at their desks as servile members, inwardly rebellious, outwardly indifferent.

It is not easy to recall what I owe to that school. The whole régime there was positive. I found that it took me at my own valuation, enriching my faith in myself, sharing my enthusiasm in the world opening out so extravagantly to me. Yet with all this encouragement, the work was always just ahead of me, especially on the science side.

In the arts and in English, however, I quickly took a lead. The Headmaster invited me several times to his home in East Dulwich, where I looked through portfolios of engravings and prints. He introduced me to the *Liber Studiorum* of J. M. W. Turner, and thus I added a new god to my pantheon. Then I discovered that David Cox had lived at Sydenham and that a delightful woodland walk in Dulwich was named after him.

One day I found myself, half-entranced, copying a print of Turner's colour-crazy picture of Norham Castle. One of those revelations took place, suddenly, while I was plodding away, and a door was flung open in my consciousness, flung open with a bang by the wind that bloweth where it listeth, at no man's bidding. It was certainly not at my command. I was the passive victim of this expansive process; but a willing one, and a joyous one, though the experience was almost painful in its intensity.

From that day I began to draw and paint with all the passion that I had formerly given to reading. The encouragement from the Headmaster was enlarged by the woman artist, Miss McKinlay, who came for two days a week and ran the art school. This was in a separate building on two floors, a fine, light and spacious adjunct to the school. The art-room was on the top floor, and I soon contrived to spend these two days a week there while Miss McKinlay was in attendance. There must have been some favouritism over this; but at the time I took it as a natural right; what the poet Robert Bridges called 'as pleasing to our laurels' when an admirer sent him a jar of honey from Mount Hymettus.

Miss McKinlay, a miniature-painter by profession, was a small, strongly-built woman with jet-black hair, braided luminously on her head, which she carried with grave deliberation. Her face was sculptured, the lips full, pale, heavily moulded. Her eyes were dark, contemplative, reserved. She seemed to think through her hands, which she used in an exploratory way, as it were testing the universe about her. She once or twice put that stubby hand on my shoulder, and I felt my bones and the character in their marrow being sized up.

My days in that light-drenched art-room brought to a focus much of the delirium of emotion in which I lived. Miss McKinlay singled me out and made me work at perspective. I enjoyed this, and mastered it. The following year she brought with her, one spring day round about my thirteenth birthday, some tubes of oil paint, brushes and a palette. She set up a still-life composition of several lustrous sea-shells and showed me how to begin to lay the paint on the canvas.

There I sat, at the easel, with an improvised mahl-stick, quite unconcerned, but concentrated like a diver about to plunge. And I did plunge. I lived in that picture for weeks, supervised by this dear disciplinarian. It is odd to realise now, in recalling the scene, that the other boys took all this specialisation for granted.

From that experience in 1906, I learned enough to make me determine to become a painter by profession. I drew and painted with such devotion that Mother set the second attic, adjoining my bedroom, at my disposal as a studio and there, until I left school two years later, I spent my time in a new

form of solitude, giving to pencil and brush the fervour that I
had formerly given to reading.

My brother would not allow me, however, to become wholly
monomaniac. He obliged me to go with him to enrol at the
East Dulwich library, where I met the chief librarian, a large,
moon-faced man who often went round the shelves, chatting
and pointing out books. He put me on to John Addington
Symonds's *History of the Renaissance*, and Mrs. Adys's book on
the Florentine painters. I found George Eliot's *Romola* and
took it home. I had crossed the Channel!

But my chief discovery was John Ruskin, whose ghost still
walked beneath those aspen trees up to Denmark Hill. He took
me by storm, and I bought my first volume of Everyman's
Library, Ruskin's *Lectures on Architecture and Painting*, on pre-
Raphaelitism, and on Turner's work. This explosive collection
was edited and published that year by Laurence Binyon, whom
I was to meet years later, and work with in affection on the
Directorate of the Oxford Festival of Spoken Poetry.

This meeting, sooner or later, with congenial spirits is a
process which I have experienced all my life, and I have
wondered at it: how it is brought about, whether by telepathy,
trend of personal achievement, or at the will of some Overall
Intelligence, as Thomas Hardy might call such convener. One
thing I am assured of, that birds of a feather certainly do flock
together.

So for the rest of my schooldays I was a slave to the art-room
and the exacting but generous mistress to whom I owed so
much. She often showed me her own work, exquisite miniatures
in which every hair, every vein in the white of an eye, were
faithfully recorded. This technique, and the philosophy of craft
behind it, was the more valuable to me because it was so
different from my own approach. It reined in my wayward-
ness, subdued my self-assertion, at least for the short time that
I was under its influence; too short, alas, for circumstances were
soon to snatch me out of that quiet disciplinary atmosphere and
to fling me into reckless responsibilities that gave me premature
self-confidence.

Though Miss McKinlay played an important part in my life

during those years at Dulwich Hamlet, I did not fail in my
other interests. The Headmaster's character was too strong to
let me escape. There was also the master of the top standard,
where I spent most of my time in the school. He was an open-
hearted man, a keen cricketer, and secretary of the Old Boys'
Football Club (a famous one).

Much of our classwork was interspersed with demonstrations
of batting technique, or how to bowl breaks, so that today I still
recall the Acts of the Apostles as taking place in the neighbourhood of an English cricket field, in perpetual summer weather,
and the signing of Magna Carta being staged between Association goal-posts.

The fact that I was useless at football, and little better as a
batsman, because of my increasingly short sight, did not
prejudice Mr. Wheeler against me. Indeed, he treated me with
a jocular familiarity that warmed my timid nerves and brought
me out as a member of the small community. He soon saw to
it that I was made captain of the school, though no sportsman;
merely a paint-slinger and a bookworm, as he not infrequently
remarked, to the amusement of my school-fellows: but no ill-
feeling on either side. I would sit there, grinning at these almost
affectionate *sorties*, and go my own gait unperturbed.

This application of myself to drawing and painting trained
my eye to a detailed observation of the glorious world around
me. I grew more particular in my pleasure, noting the subtlest
shades and forms in 'rocks and stones and trees' while being
whirled round with them 'in earth's diurnal course'. My
resources were infinite and so was my treasury. I spent much
time out of doors watching pond life, staring into the skeletons
of dead leaves in Dulwich woods, lying silent to study a squirrel's
fur, or the wing of a chaffinch, or the way that great trees
swayed almost down to their boles during a high wind (a fact
I verified by taking time exposures with the box camera which
I had bought for eighteenpence).

Jack shared much of this indulgence, for he too was a painter,
much freer, clearer, more spontaneous in his work than I, and
he kept up this interest to the end of his life, concentrating
upon this, alongside his music, and thus filling his home,

wherever he might be, and the lives of those drawn into it, with beauty for eye and ear.'

I was fortunate in having a second interest also. It was evoked and enlarged by the school and the special associations of the history of Dulwich. Mr. Hunt was a Shakespearean enthusiast, and he made much of the fact that Dulwich College was founded by Edward Alleyn, the boy-actor most renowned on the Elizabethan stage, son-in-law first of Philip Henslowe and secondly of John Donne. The foundation, in 1616, the year of Shakespeare's death, was conventional to those times. It catered for the maintenance of twelve poor boys and twelve old men, allotting for each the income from a parcel of the estate, amounting to three or four shillings a week. In the course of time, these rentals expanded with the value of the land, so that by the mid-nineteenth century each pauper was receiving about two hundred pounds a year. A private bill had to be introduced to Parliament to adjust the matter reasonably.

The old College survives today to speak for itself, more eloquent in its muteness that I can be in my reverence. The chapel is impressive; and the garden behind the College, a setting for the Picture Gallery which was the first public gallery in London and another haunt of Browning during his boyhood, was of an Italian temper because a colonnade ran along the back of the gallery, forming one boundary of the garden, where a baroque leaden tank stood, from which the gardener drew rain-water to nourish his flower-beds.

I became friendly with this gardener because I spent so much time sitting there, either painting in water-colours or reading. I knew the personality of each tree, just as I knew the features of that garrulous man, who was so courteous that he never once examined my handiwork, but spoke to me with his eyes averted, attentive to his own hairy forearm, or riveted upon a distant weed which he had spotted while talking and was recording for later action.

In those days the gallery was sleepy, and overcrowded with pictures on its dull red walls; suffering from an embarrassment of bequests from Chantry and others. During the 1939–45 war both old College and gallery were badly damaged. The reparation of the gallery has made it one that compares in elegance, taste, and wealth of material with the Fitzwilliam at Cambridge and the Ryks Museum at Amsterdam. But the colonnade and the leaden tank have disappeared, so that the garden is now wholly English in character, tended by another gardener.

The provision by Alleyn for poor boys has developed into the foundation of Dulwich College, and a secondary school named after him, Alleyn's School. The only person of repute whom I have known as a scholar of the latter school is my friend V. S. Pritchett, a critic of life and letters who dips his pen in lysol, practising his art rather in the operating theatre than in the study. His surgery is most helpful when applied to reputations suffering from a malignant growth. I have never met a man from Dulwich College, and its scholars still remain as fabulous and remote as they were fifty years ago, when I stared at them through the railings of their football fields.

The spirit of Alleyn, with all its Elizabethan associations, lingered in Dulwich. It touched my imagination with a ghostly hand making the trees more eloquent as they murmured into their own foliage, the grass more artificially green, the flowers more desperate in their beauty. The more I read, the more I listened to the easy discourse of Mr. Hunt, the more I explored and identified myself with the village and its surroundings, the more conscious I became of this eloquent past, where the Elizabethan poets, dramatists, actors and audiences still lived. My days were spent in an atmosphere of Shakespearean survivals, so that I absorbed it through my skin. This sense of close relationship with writers in whom I was interested became habitual, and it has remained with me, so that the reading of a book brings into my field of contemplation a physical presence, the author in the flesh. It would be a strange sensation, were it not so natural and assuring.

Darker Ingredients

I HAVE CALLED THE PREVIOUS CHAPTER 'the influence of joy', and there could be no more accurate description of the full flood that flowed during those three years at Dulwich Hamlet School, carrying me so buoyantly. The keyword to that period of my boyhood is 'recognition'. I moved about in a widening universe and everything I saw, touched, smelled, every idea and mood, was new and burnished in its newness. Yet all was familiar to me. I had the conviction that I had travelled this way before, but on a darker day. Now my recognitions were in a world sun-drenched. I needed more hours than the day contained, to take up this inheritance, to voice (by that inward, silent thankfulness which is the most fecund form of prayer) the joy which now worked in my mind and body, a tangible power adding to my strength.

The drawing, painting, and reading about art and artists occupied most of my time. I spent Saturday mornings in Dulwich Gallery, gazing into canvases by Teniers, the Gainsborough portraits of the Linleys, searching for I knew not what, perhaps the secret of an excellent craftsmanship, which later I was to try to transfer to another art, spend my life at, and still not succeed in mastering.

All this was maintained in a daily life sufficiently full of immediate experience: the friendships at school, the home life still so intimate and tender, the expeditions on the tandems, with two more annual holidays at Ropley.

Our little garden, so oddly shaped, like an exposition by Euclid, had a sub-tropical quality, in comparison with the concreted yard of our Battersea home. Through this jungle, of honeysuckle and rambler roses, Jack built a miniature railway from scale-model parts by Basset-Lowke, laying a tiny permanent way that even had wooden blocks to hold the rails in the shoes. Out of his pocket-money he bought a Great Western Atlantic model locomotive, that would have been gigantic in the land of Lilliput. I made enough money that Christmas by drawing greeting cards to buy a Midland local.

Jack also designed and built a cabinet gramophone. This was pioneer work, for in 1906 gramophones were still of the shape that survives today only in the trade mark of H.M.V. The horn in Jack's cabinet was concealed, and consisted of practically the whole of the cabinet, its mouth throwing the sound upward to the ceiling. Jack painted this instrument in black lacquer, and decorated it with a landscape in the manner of Watteau. He was much under the influence of Claude Debussy at that time. As the years passed, he turned more to the composers who appealed to his odd temperament, that amalgam of sardonic realism and the most elusive and nervous tenderness. Scriabin, MacDowell, Glazounov, Ravel, Arnold Bax, were composers whose pianoforte work he played with an authoritative understanding.

Even Father was impressed. Indeed, he retreated before the advance of so emphatic a talent, and he raised no objection when Jack made another revolutionary proposition about the Broadwood-White instrument.

Like a former proposal, this began with the visit of a tuner. The two professionals, however, were totally unlike. The first had been a long-haired, cadaverous æsthete. The second was a burly fellow who wore a Norfolk jacket and leather leggings, which gave him the appearance of a gamekeeper or farmer. But he had a good ear, and he kept a music shop in Stockwell.

He and Jack became friendly. I had already begun to notice that Jack attracted people of this kind: matter-of-fact, reliable watch-dog kind of folk. They gravitated towards him, and were content to serve him with no reward except his rather shy courtesy, an occasional penetrating remark, and sometimes a flick of his mental whip that only made them the more devoted. He went his own mysterious way, not concerned with ambition or making a career. His power of concentration in a creative mood was intimidating to an onlooker. It terrified me, for at that time I hovered over life with as much certainty as a dragon-fly over a brook on a hot day. Jack had his interests ordered and defined; and they were absolute.

Perhaps there were too many of them. It is hardly possible in one lifetime to be both musician and painter, to invent and make instruments and mechanical objects, to brood and ruminate over ideas, and finally to become a lover and a husband, with just the same intensity of impassioned purpose. It may have been this magnetic force in him which drew the allegiance of the stolid, the inarticulate, the male and female Marthas, so that they served him with a protective devotion.

The new piano-tuner was one such. He fastened on to Jack, who was still only a schoolboy, as to a master. His first act of piety was to suggest that the Broadwood-White took up house-room, and that he knew of a period-piece pipe organ, just removed from Park Walk Chapel, Chelsea, which would take little more floor space than the upright piano.

After some parental deliberation the change was made, and the organ arrived in a van. Jack and I helped to unload it: hundreds of wooden and metal pipes, the eight-foot wooden Stopped Diapason being turned at right-angles six feet from the base. The tuner spent several days assembling the pipes in the five stops. The case was in dark oak, with the conventional imitation pipes as ornamentation. The pedals could be used only if another person were pumping, by a foot-lever at the side. The player could also pump by another lever under the front between the pedals.

When assembled, the organ just missed the ceiling of our little dining-room and stuck out three feet from the wall. The rest of the furniture was dwarfed, but that did not worry Jack. It is a miracle that he did not rupture himself, playing and pumping together, one leg and his body heaving up and down while those expressive hands rattled over the dry old ivories, unravelling the concertos of Vivaldi, transcribed by Bach for the organ, or thundering out (so far as the tiny organ could respond) the massive periods of Handel, that Rubens of music. I was press-ganged into pumping whenever I showed signs of being unoccupied, but I worked this treadmill with reluctance because of the grating and chafing it caused in my unreliable abdominal apparatus.

The tone of the organ was sweet and pure, an eighteenth-century voice that interpreted Bach, Haydn, Handel, Couperin, Rameau, Corelli, Mozart and Vivaldi as contemporary, taking the initiative out of the hands of the young twentieth-century amateur. I should not have been surprised, as I stood beside him to work the ancient bellows, to find his head crowned by a Hanoverian wig, and lace ruffles impeding those lean fingers.

Father was mollified by the change because the organ went happily with his violin and flute. We heard less of his music, however, after the move to Dulwich. Jack's increasing command of the art may have intimidated him. Another cause of his relinquishing both string and reed was Mother's deteriorating health.

Our main purpose in moving to a healthier district was to cure her of the bronchial asthma which she could not shake off in the atmosphere of the Battersea marsh. For a time she appeared to benefit by the change; but gradually the longer daily journey to the slum school, and the heavier burden of the house, began to tell upon her vitality. She was also approaching her climacteric. The cough became chronic, and the effort of breathing scored lines round her mouth and nostrils.

But there was still the house to pay for, and her boys to be launched in the world. She would not give up. But the effort of will made her show signs of eccentricity. She conceived an animus against her own sex, and would not have a woman in the house. This made harder both her own lot and that of her men folk who could not idly look on and see her struggling to keep the house clean, the clothes mended, the cooking and bed-making done. Father, Jack and I became heavily domesticated.

I, being at home more than the other two males, caught the brunt of this ill wind. The need developed a feminine capability in me, but it also interrupted my school work, which was already broken into by my drawing and painting.

From time to time, when Mother was stricken down by winter

fogs, I felt the cold hand of fear clutch me, but for the three years of my school life this shadow remained in the background, to vanish whenever Mother recovered. My confidence in the wonder of the world, and in my secret faculty of being able to appeal to this image of Christ conjured permanently, and maintained by my impassioned reading of the New Testament, gave me a nervous strength and a coherence of purpose. My happiness was an intoxication, overflowing and affecting my family and friends.

Further, I had also the strange and dubious resource of the faculty which I had acquired, or believed myself to have acquired, that frosty winter morning at Broadstairs, when time and space betrayed themselves as fraudulent, and the law of gravity was overthrown by a trick of breathing and a contraction of the muscles. I had indulged less in this winged luxury since my health had improved and my environment had grown so much more acceptable: but on occasions, when some setback made it necessary for me to reassure myself of my unique and unconquerable nature, I would practise the Icarian magic, quite unconsciously, and absolutely convinced that it was actual, a matter of demonstrated fact.

Thus armed severally for the combat against life and the future, I kept up my painting, my reading, my dreaming, while running to and fro between home and school. New enthusiasms unfolded, new sources to feed my joyous confidence were discovered. I was sitting in school one summer day in 1907, beside my friend Richards, the puck-like imp who was later to develop a religious vocation. We were supposed to be working out a number of equations in algebra; but the sun was standing in the blue heavens, and the great willow tree in the playground dreamed in the blue-white heat, its foliage moving as though it were breathing gently.

My friend and I, under cover of Pendlebury's *Algebra*, had been reading the American author Bret Harte, but we tired of this and turned to our work again. My attention soon strayed to the willow, for a waft of midsummer air had set it murmuring, a sound which my acute hearing accepted greedily. I looked out, through the grille of quadratic equations, and saw the old

tree metamorphosed into a fountain of shuddering gold lights
and green shadows. At the back of my mind was the inkling
that somewhere, somehow, this play of sunshine, this lift and
relapse of leaves, was a part of the same conjunction as I was
expected to make in the solving of these equations in algebra.

But my failure to link the evidence of my senses with that of
my reasoning brain baffled and irritated me. In a mood of
rebellion, I turned from the figures and symbols and opened a
concealed copy of Shakespeare's *Tempest*, the play then being
studied during 'English' lesson. It was a casual, almost a
peevish, incursion, as I began to read Scene I in Act III, where
Ferdinand and Miranda meet before Prospero's cell and fall in
love.

Something broke within my mind, some tension, some barrier;
I saw the shape of the verse, its cadence, its opulent flood of
vowels and the meaning it carried. When Miranda said

> ". . . but, by my modesty
> (The jewel in my dower) I would not wish
> Any companion in the world but you;"

I felt that dreadful visitation which had found me years earlier,
on the day I suddenly began to read *The Swiss Family Robinson*.
It was dreadful because it made me so isolated, so egoistic; a
self-centred emphasis which I knew would not be approved by
my family, or by my inward monitor, the Christ whom I had
conjured as my constant companion.

But the twinge of conscience was quickly subdued. I was
master of a new estate, and on the strength of it was ready to
claim a larger authority over my fellow-creatures, over circumstances kind or adverse, over the very laws of right and wrong.

This mephistophelian state of mind was soon to be put to the
test. Urged on by this initiation, I worked at my drawing and
painting, with the result that in my last year at school the Headmaster sent up a selection of my designs, and two canvases, to
the L.C.C. In the spring of 1908 I was awarded a scholarship
in art, to be taken up at Camberwell Art School. I was
instructed to report there, with further examples of my work.

Jack, who was now a pupil-teacher, due to enter the Goldsmith's Training College in the autumn, was free in the evenings. He went with me for the interview. We walked, fatefully, over Denmark Hill, carrying a portfolio (lent by Miss McKinlay). "Don't say too much," counselled my brother. "Your tendency is always to put your foot in it." Under this command, I was demure at the interview. The Principal appeared to be interested more in Jack than in me. He was a quiet, slow-moving figure, and I watched him with awe while he turned over my drawings in the portfolio.

"Yes," he said finally to Jack, "it will do to start with."

Unelated by this crushing triumph, I walked home thoughtfully, while Jack pointed out how lucky I was; for I believe he never was impressed by my efforts in painting. He said they were like my piano-playing, too erratic and uncontrolled. He said something on that walk home which I have always remembered.

"To be really good at any art, you ought to make your living by it."

I can see now the look of clouded melancholy that settled over him as he added, "I doubt if we're the kind of people who can do that."

His words depressed me, after the cold douche I had received at the art school. A sense of fatality in this venture closed about my heart, and drowned my courage. The mood must have been prophetic.

However, my last weeks at Dulwich Hamlet passed happily enough. The Headmaster gave me the three-volume edition of Shakespeare in Everyman's Library (which I still possess) and took me aside to utter a word of parting advice. "Don't let your tongue run away with you. Remember that's your little weakness." Confirming so quickly what my brother had said, these words lodged in my conscience, and all my life I have wished, with remorse, that I had practised this wise precept.

Leaving the school where I had been so happy, and beginning as an unimportant novice at Camberwell, was a humbling experience. It brought me down to earth. Other circumstances also darkened the sky. Mother did not make her seasonal recovery that spring. Her cough still racked her, shaking the flesh from her bones: but she dragged herself to school through the summer term. Her eyes grew strained and alert with fear; her mouth drawn with the lines of asthma. "We *must* keep up the payments on the house," she said, with a finality that dismissed all our efforts to persuade her to stay away from school.

Father meanwhile had been adapting himself to the changes due to Mother's poor health and to the manifestations of growth in his sons. Our junior tandem was sold, and the proceeds put to the purchase of two second-hand bicycles. By 1908 a freewheel was taken for granted, and rim brakes were *de rigueur*. For a while the senior tandem was kept in the shed, but we knew that Mother would not ride it again, and at last, all pretence being relinquished, Father sold the machine and casually proposed that something might be done about one of those motor-bicycles, which were beginning to appear on the changing roads of England.

Mother's rejection of his boyish scheme was so emphatic that he did not push it further. From that time he appeared to accept defeat in this matter of getting Mother to share his wanderlust. He went off more alone, or with cronies from the Post Office, for it was not often possible for Jack and me to accompany him. Nor did we volunteer, for as Mother grew weaker, we agreed in an unfair criticism of his seeming indifference to her illness. We could not realise that he was helpless and frightened, in conflict with her determined character.

Suddenly he took that obstinate decision which is a symptom of timidity. He said that this business of my art scholarship was all nonsense: that I had my living to earn, and the sooner I set about it, the better. Some concentricity inherited on the paternal side made him insist that the only safe means of earning a living was to enter the Post Office; what might be called his own regiment; for he had the character, habits and appearance of a very gallant soldier. He proposed that I should become a telegraph boy.

This suggestion was not altogether new, because it had been mooted some years earlier when Jack was of an age to adopt the leather belt, the armlet and the peaked cap of these latter-day Ganymedes. Jack had rejected the proposal by one sardonic glance, an expression which he must have copied from the Ancient of Days.

Since then, however, Father had developed a more authoritative gesture in the household, encouraged perhaps by Mother's increasingly poor health. His purpose was to take the burden off her shoulders; but in effect he only increased her anxiety, her distrust of the future.

I was therefore not to escape so easily as Jack. I expostulated; but being insulted by the suggestion, and amazed that Father totally disregarded my abilities and aims, I protested too violently. This angered him, and I saw those pale grey eyes grow cold.

We were sitting opposite each other at the meal-table, with Mother and Jack at the other sides. The bread-board, with the knife beside the loaf, lay before me. I looked at Father again, and saw the cold anger still in his eyes; the hostility to all I wanted to do in life, and intended to do.

I stretched out my hand to the knife. But Jack was before me. "More bread?" he asked, taking up the knife and putting his other hand delicately, ritualistically, on the loaf.

I shrank with terror and guilt. I could not look at my father, and I despaired of making him understand, even had I not put myself so wickedly in the wrong by my glance at the bread-board and the movement of my hand, which only Jack had interpreted.

I left the table and crept up to my bedroom, still numbed by what I had almost done. Kneeling by my bed, I buried my face in my arms, burrowing into the darkness of suspended thought, into that cavern of the self where the beast inhabits, and the angel sometimes comes to wrestle with it. Such a struggle took place now, as I lay there apparently inert. This was authentic prayer, that intensity of appeal which frets the flesh away, and either destroys or saves the spirit.

It was so indelible an act that it established a lifelong habit, it might be called of consultation, of abnormal soliloquy, of ruthless stocktaking. Its commoner name is prayer. On that dreadful occasion, and through my youth and early manhood, it was accompanied by a lively image of the personal presence of the Christ whom I had established in my secret life, from my reading of the Bible, and my frequent short sessions in local and village churches, where I loved to retreat for half an hour at a time, either from home, or when on a cycle ride alone or with Jack.

This habit had been encouraged by my school-friend Richards, the puckish imp, who was already showing his sense of religious realism. We went cycling frequently together, and punctuated our exploration of the Kentish lanes with visits to wayside churches.

We had both been confirmed only a few weeks before I was faced by this conflict with my father. Thus I was able to write to my friend and suggest that on the following Sunday we should meet at dawn and cycle down to Westerham, about fifteen miles from my home, to take Holy Communion. I hoped by this extra exertion before breakfast, and the sanctity of the Mass, to expiate my evil temptation.

After I left the table, much family debate must have followed. Jack was indignant on my behalf, and Mother and he joined forces to persuade Father to relent. They only half succeeded, and the outcome of this heavy touch of domestic drama was that I agreed to sit for a Civil Service examination that summer, for a post as boy clerk. This was a Treasury grade, of a temporary standing, during which tenure the boy between the ages of sixteen and eighteen had to pass another examination to become a permanent, pensionable Civil Servant. There were several outlets, the Second Division, the Customs and Excise, the Abstractor Class. The last was the lowest, and I determined to make for it, after becoming a boy clerk, for I was still not reconciled to my father's will, and I hated the prospect of becoming a Civil Servant.

The autumn of 1908 was therefore a dark and confusing period in my life. I was not prepared for such tempestuous moods and circumstances, for hitherto I had dreamed away my childhood years in serenity, and an exaltation from which not even the bouts of pain, the brutality of Surrey Lane School and the cold institutionalism of the convalescent home at

Broadstairs could reduce me. Further, the three years spent at Dulwich Hamlet, learning so rapidly and richly, reading Shakespeare and painting, in the calm and timeless atmosphere of the old village, had so prolonged my innocence that I looked out on the universe, believing it still to be the Garden of Eden.

But now I was shaken. I began to feel that some foreign force had crept into our home, working a various mischief, and enlarging it not only in our circumstances but in our hearts. That dreadful incident of the bread-knife remained to torture me with remorse, weakening my resolution against Father.

I left Camberwell Art School and went back to evening classes at Dulwich Hamlet, where under one of the day-school masters I plodded away at the subjects required for this boy clerks' examination; subjects so repulsive that even now I cannot clearly recall them; vaguely I remember such things as digest of returns, commercial geography, précis writing, book-keeping. Even at that time the term 'book-keeping' had a very different connotation for me. It conjured great libraries in Gothic settings, folios and quartos in leather bindings, alchemists and grammarians scratching away with quill pens on vellum, their brains heavy with imagery and ancient lore, I amongst them sharing and savouring their pedantry. But now I had to learn that book-keeping consisted of something called double entry, and that it was concerned with the manipulation of money, a commodity which, in my oddly-warped young mind, was associated with shopkeepers, sinister figures such as bankers, stockbrokers, race-course touts, and Judas Iscariot.

In those desolate weeks of autumn I went, evening after evening, to my old school, having spent the days rebelliously swotting at these dreary subjects, damping down the fires of my imagination, treading out the sparks of my ambition to be a painter. I succeeded; but I could not wholly subdue my response to the work of other artists, or my delight in form and colour. But at that time, commanded by my remorse and driven by a despairing perverseness, I gave up not only the external form of my art scholarship, but also its deeper significances, the faith, the enthusiasm, in painting. Throughout that autumn and winter I remained with no means of self-

expression, drudging sullenly at subjects I despised, toward a
purpose I dreaded.

Then Mother fell ill again; and this time she was ill not only
bodily but in her spirit. She had the air of having been
destroyed, disillusioned. Something seemed to have come
between her and Father, something other than this contest over
my future. I spoke to Jack about it, but he became evasive and
told me to concern myself with my own affairs or I should fail
in the examination.

The instability of our home life at that time could not be
disguised, however, and I worked away, prepared every hour
for some catastrophe. I walked to the village school as darkness
fell, treading the fallen leaves, smelling the acrid odour of the
dying year, waiting for the next untoward stroke of fate.

The rest at home improved Mother's health, and suddenly
she decided to visit her sister in Wakefield. She said she must
get away for a while. This restlessness was out of character, but
Father raised no objection, and, the decision once taken, Mother
and I quickly found ourselves settled in the sombre, professional
house in the narrow Southgate, in Wakefield, where we stayed
for the whole of October, in a semi-darkness under overhead
fog, listening every hour to the carillon of 'Abide with Me'
sprinkled out from the spire of the cathedral at the top of the
road.

Mother spent her time in the upstairs drawing-room, lovingly
tended by her younger sister, a small and gay-hearted figure,
even more of a hamadryad than my mother, and heightened in
personality by a flirtatious touch and ampler means. I had, of
course, known her all my life, but now I discovered her; and
that is a vastly different relationship. She took an immediate
interest in me, and I made a friend who, until her death in
1921, encouraged me in my ambitions.

During that holiday she talked to me about myself, the family
history, the books and people that interested her, colouring
every theme with the gaiety of her temperament. I fell in love
with her, and courted her, much to the amusement of her
Yorkshire husband, the bearded dentist who treated her as
though she were a Dresden shepherdess—but in *his* cabinet! He

was a formidable man, who always referred to my father as 'Church', which puzzled me. At that time this mode of reference had a singular effect because it brought to a head my misgivings about the absolute solidity of the structure of family life. Here was an uncle speaking of Father as though he were somebody outside the sacred enclave of the family. What did it mean?

I was quite distressed at having to part from my miniature aunt of the Titian hair, mischievous eyes, and wide and generous mouth. Why, I wondered, had Mother ever been estranged from so enchanting and sympathetic a sister, along with the rest of her family. I had yet to learn how limited is the range of a human being's emotions, even after the enlargement through cultural interests, education and that smoky lens of personal philosophy which is often miscalled religious instinct.

While we were in Wakefield, my aunt gave me a copy of Tom Hood's poems; and when we left, she gave me a grandfather clock which had belonged to my grandparents.

The journey down from Yorkshire was an anxious one, for Mother could no longer take the initiative. She was concerned solely with breathing. I had her propped up with two cushions in the compartment; our luggage and the grandfather clock in the guard's van.

That was Mother's last excursion from home. She took to her bed that winter, and it fell to me to nurse her. She persisted in her distrust of her own sex. I suggested that we should ask a cousin of hers, who had been visiting us frequently during the past summer, appearing out of the blue and making herself almost one of the family, to come and do the housekeeping. This young woman was robust, vigorous and possessed a magnificent figure.

Mother repudiated the suggestion with such vehemence that the resultant fit of breathlessness and coughing broke a blood vessel. From that time her struggles for breath and the attacks of bronchial coughing ended in these small discharges of blood.

Father and Jack had their work to go to, and as I remained at home, save for the evening-class attendance, I became

Mother's nurse; washing her, changing her bedclothes and garments after the disasters caused by the body-racking bouts that broke down all muscular control.

It was a strange and even morbid introduction to the intimacies of womanhood. It made my love for Mother increase almost to a fanaticism. It also made me practical. I did not lose my pleasure in life, for the childhood delight in the wonder of things remained with me, and the constant factor of words, like the amber preserving the bee, pervaded my conscious mind with a sense of golden viscosity, just as a shaft of sunlight catches the dust-motes in the air, enhancing it with particles of fire.

I worked in a bored, desultory way at the subjects needed for the Civil Service examination, for which I had to sit in January: but this daily grind was broken by my sick-nursing, that became more exacting as Mother grew weaker and dependent. She could not help being exacting, and fastening upon me emotionally, for Father and Jack appeared to be withdrawn from her; perhaps through self-preservation, or the tyranny of circumstances; or even she may have been deluded in this matter by her illness and its effect upon her over-sensitive imagination.

I could see how helpless my father and brother were. Everything they tried to do for her, in the sick-room, was mistimed or wrong, causing her such irritation that her asthmatic spasms were aggravated by their efforts.

Further, Jack was already in deeper toils, that had begun to draw him out of the home life which we had thought so permanent. He had begun the course at Goldsmith's Training College in that eventful autumn of 1908, and was no sooner enrolled than he met a girl student with whom he fell in love. That process with him was like all his other interests; fierce, absolute, fatal.

I wonder that the object of his concentration was not frightened away, especially as she was an only child in a household seemingly (if that were possible) more immured in ivory than ours. But timidly, shyly, the young woman responded. She came to visit us, and Mother left her bed for the occasion, coming down to the drawing-room and sitting there waiting, after I had lighted the Edwardian gas-fire (a vast, Indian shrine full of miniature skulls through which jets of smelly gas flame trickled furtively upward). I also fumigated the hall of mirrors with Potter's asthma cure, timing the sinister censering so that the atmosphere of the room should be thick with palliative smoke at the moment Jack ushered his dear stranger into Mother's presence.

What the girl of eighteen made of this introduction I cannot even now imagine, nor has she been able to tell me, though we have been intimate friends for the subsequent half-century, sharing many joys of the mind and many of the soul's burdens, those dolours which no human shoulders have been spared, in the trudge from the cradle to the grave.

It was impossible to allow this young stranger to take any part in a household so deranged. The miracle was that Mother accepted her. Jack's courtship from that point proceeded simultaneously with his professional training as a teacher. The combined activities, however, took him out of the home. As for Father at that time, he seemed to be neutralised by the gravity and abnormality of events. I could have said of him then, as Keats said of the nightingale:

"Thou wast not born for death, immortal Bird."

For he seemed ageless too, retaining his magnificent physical stamina, his handsome looks, his genial, boyish impulsiveness, his few but intense enthusiasms for the open road, the company of his Post Office colleagues, the lesser mysteries of freemasonry, a sodality into which he had recently been initiated. "I go," he would say, expansively, "to worship my Maker!" and off he would ride on his bicycle, usually with an office crony, to explore another tangle of the labyrinthine byways of England.

So I remained alone with Mother, fumigating the air which she inhaled with such agony that my body sweated with hers, and my nerves gathered up into knots of resistance as I watched her, or held her in my arms as she coughed and struggled, her features distorted by the convulsions.

I developed a rapid technique in administering oxygen to her. The doctor at first advised that I filled a goldbeater-skin bag

with the gas from the metal cylinder: but this was impracticable
when the paroxysms seized Mother without warning. I learned
to fix the mask and tube direct to the cylinder of compressed
gas, tapping the lever with the ball of my thumb so delicately
that the supply reached Mother's lungs instinctively, my
muscles and intelligence being an involuntary extension of her
need.

It is often assumed by novelists that people on their death-
beds become confiding in the people about them, unburdening
themselves of old secrets, making the world they are about to
leave their confessional. I have not found it so. I watched
Mother during the last eighteen months of her life, and saw her
gradually withdrawing herself from the world, loosening one
by one the bonds that moored her affections to husband and
sons. The process was not an estrangement. It was as though
she were quietly drifting away, in a mist, on some reluctant
tide whose pull was so gentle that she was not aware of any need
to resist it.

I had no means of speaking to her about it; but I knew my
heart was breaking. My love for her had swollen and become
abnormal after such clinical intimacy as had been forced upon
me. I continued to nurse her, with every opportunity for
tenderness and confidence explored, hour by hour; but her
weariness increased and it took the dreadful form· of indifference.

Thus I began to realise that she had lost the savour of life and
must die. Night after night that winter, I went exhausted to
bed, after days committed to uncongenial study and to sick-
nursing. What most disturbed me was the terrifying realisation
that in spite of my fear, my grief, I was still in love with life,
still looking enraptured at the future, still urgently aware of
the myriad small miracles being worked around me, in the air,
on the earth and in the sun-drenched universe of my mind.

I began to think I must be mad, callous, wicked. I knelt at
my bed every night, praying so vehemently that the sweat
soaked my shirt, and the agony closed my throat; praying that
Mother might be restored to me; that I could be made more
fully conscious of what was happening, and that this evil numb-

P

ness, this kind of inattention of the soul, might be dispelled.

During this turmoil of heightened emotions and desperate circumstances, I sat for the boy clerks' examination and passed it. In the April of 1909 I was instructed to report to an office called the Land Registry, of which I had never heard. It was in Lincolns Inn Fields, and at once I thought of the scenes in Dickens's *Bleak House* and the death of the solicitor Mr. Tulkinghorn. I pictured the Land Registry as an establishment similar to that of the sinister lawyer, where I should be employed as a junior at a high desk in a little ante-room.

On the morning of the 21st of April, I set out with deep misgiving, worried about Mother being left alone all day, and afraid of the unknown before me. I entered Herne Hill station, and as I walked through the subway to the up-platform, a spasm of dismay shook me. I saw myself imprisoned for life in a job in which I was likely to have no aptitude and no interest. My heart was still sullen with the mood of renunciation of my drawing and painting: for I had savagely resolved that I would never touch pencil or brush again.

I have kept that perverse resolution; but the obstinacy could not then destroy, and never has since, the abounding joy in life, moment by moment, that has made me so rich.

I saw a Dover boat-train glide through the station, and again a spasm of despair shook me, as I thought of the monotonous future in the Civil Service, with no opportunity for exploring the wonders of the world; no freedom, no solitude. I resolved that as soon as I reached Mr. Tulkinghorn's office I would demand to be allowed to bring my little dog with me; a fox terrier of dubious lineage given us by a woman who had clung to Mother for some years, since meeting her at one of the gatherings of Post Office cronies. This quiet, kind soul lived in a public-house at Penge, over the hill southwards, and came regularly during Mother's last illness, with offerings of eggs, jellies, and other sick-room fare.

To my dismay, I found the Land Registry anything but a Dickensian lawyer's office. It was a red-brick, modern institution, standing at the corner of Lincoln's Inn Fields, just outside the great gateway into Lincoln's Inn proper. I have not yet discovered how I found my way to it, for I knew nothing about London, other than the two suburbs where I had spent my sixteen years.

The idea of taking my dog, Roger, with me vanished abruptly as I inquired of the commissionaire in the entrance hall where I was to report. By that time I was ready to ask him as to my own identity, for in strange places and circumstances I have always found that I dissolve like a lump of sugar in a cup of tea, unaware of what sweetness I may be adding to the situation.

In a dreamlike condition, with distant rumblings of nervous diarrhœa, I was carried to the first floor and deposited in a vast room filled with bound volumes of property titles—the registry; and there, under the direction of a pale little man with a cripple's face and curved spine, I was seated in a bay window overlooking the Gothic gateway of the Inn, my table surrounded by card-index cabinets, which it would be my duty to keep up to date, hour by hour, as the documents of land and house property registration flowed through the department.

Another new boy was installed with me, warm, ruddy-haired and friendly. When the lunch-hour came, he and I went out together to seek a meal. He told me his name was Arthur Sullivan, and that he was named after his second cousin, the composer, his parents having been married from the flat in Victoria Street where an L.C.C. plaque now records that "Sullivan lived there".

My response to this genial companion was instant and we forgot, for an hour, the nervous tension of being new boys in a cold, terrifying institution. We found a little eating-house in Clements Inn, next door to the vicarage of St. Clement Dane's Church. It had back-to-back settles, and the customers had to slide themselves into the cubicles. A small, elderly woman waited on the diners, and appeared to know most of them by their Christian names, greeting them with a fretful cheerfulness, as of a mother of a large and noisy brood.

Seeing two strange and undecided boys peering shyly in, she came to us and beckoned us with a red finger, "Come on, ducks. I'll find a place for yer." And she did. We sat crushed between compositors from the St. Clements Press, devouring steak and kidney puddings, small domes of luscious content, with gravy bursting out over the outbuildings of potato and greens. This was known as a 'baby's head', as our fellow-diners informed us, between their discussions of form and the lunch-time winners. The next course was also sustaining: suet roll and syrup. The meal cost sevenpence, and Sullivan and I decided that out of our salary of fifteen shillings a week this outlay for five days was a possibility.

During the post-prandial confidences, while we walked under the giant plane trees in the Fields, I learned that my colleague was an orphan, and that he lived with distant relatives. This at once moved me to imaginative sympathy, and I drew from him the fact that he loved music, especially that of his famous cousin, whom he had made into a father figure as a prop against the assaults of loneliness. Within a few days we had become friends, and maintained that friendship for many years after the tides of circumstance had separated us. On our first pay day, the following Friday, we went together to Denny's bookshop in the Strand and spent some of our earnings. I I bought Palgrave's *Golden Treasury*, in the World's Classics; my first plunge into book collecting. Back in the registry, I stood at the window, gloating over my purchase, and dividing my attention between that and the gateway that led to the almost forbidding seclusion of Old and New Squares, where the lawyers had their chambers. Many years later I was to live in chambers in Old Square; but that fact would have meant nothing to the boy staring out of the bay window over an eighteenpenny copy of Palgrave, bound in Sultan red leather.

"You must attend to your work in office time," said an acid voice at my elbow. It was that of the tiny invalid with blue, transparent eyelids and thin moustaches that drooped from beneath his nose like two stalactites. That statement was an axiom which I tried bravely to practise during the twenty-four years spent in the Civil Service; bravely, but with sadly inter-mittent success. It had something of the same effect as when a child is told to eat its crusts. The nurse stood throughout those twenty-four years over me, to see that I did so; but a 'most kindly nurse', as I was to discover, even an indulgent one. The multitudes of cultured men whom I met in the Civil Service, friends, advisers, monitors, served me in those first years in lieu of a university, helping me to educate myself, to enlarge my range of mind and experience, and finally supporting me in the heady and dangerous adventure of commencing author.

Sullivan and I clung together, spending our luncheon hours exploring the neighbourhood of the Inns of Court, between the Embankment and High Holborn. Denny's bookshop in the Strand, and Glaisher's in Holborn, became our reading-rooms, where we stood at the tables, or the shelves, imbibing free of charge, frequently guided to the fountain of knowledge by the managers and their assistants, it being understood that once a month we might spend a shilling on some cheap edition of the classics.

Literature was not our only pursuit, free of charge. At St. Clement Dane's Church in the Strand lunch-time organ recitals were weekly events, and we attended them, sitting if possible in Dr. Johnson's pew in the gallery, to enhance our enchantment. These hours offered us manna in the wilderness; for in spite of my vigorous appetite for life, I found the assault of the crowded streets and the inexorable stoicism of the Civil Service life somewhat merciless. I had not been trained for this combination of forces which both aimed at subduing individuality and grinding it small, to make it an ingredient of the vast civic structure. I was not even aware of the existence of that structure, and could not therefore be conscious of its demands upon me, nor its traditions, nor its utter disregard for private emotion and eccentricity, elements upon which at that time I almost wholly subsisted.

One advantage of public school and university is that this necessary conditioning of the individual to the bracing climate of society, with all the disciplines and self-controls involved, begins at an early stage. The day-school boy, and especially the board-school boy in a close, petty family circle of little or no cultural and social contacts, is doomed to late development as an adult with worldly confidence and authority. That is why in his early years he is so often hostile to the man with a public school and university sophistication, thinking him to be cold, brutal, insincere: usually a mistaken conception that leads to all kinds of antagonisms, distrusts and miseries.

CHAPTER NINETEEN

Over the Bridge

NEW EXPERIENCES, new events, began to crowd my days. The mere coming and going between our suburb and the City (the process on which satirists and reformers love to exercise their scorn) widened the world for me. I was still a minor Achilles, sulking in my tent, resentful of this career which had been forced upon me, and wilfully determined on a ca'canny policy, repudiating pencil and brush, and making up my mind to play the part of a 'cowerin' beastie', the unobserved mouse in the Civil Service.

This unhealthy state of mind lasted through that spring and summer of 1909, a year of gloom and frustration. Since relinquishing my scholarship at the art school, I had no means of expressing myself or of responding to the wonders of life, which even in my morbid mood I could not fail to notice.

Alienated from my father (who was wholly unaware of the estrangement, or the cause of it); watching my mother drifting towards death; realising that Jack had, in spirit, already broken away from the close contact of childhood, I faced the future in a mood of rebellious anarchy. Even the Secret Companion, the Christ who was the very soul of love, and my most inward Self, appeared to desert me. My agonised prayers at night, pleading in sweat and tears for Mother's recovery, were unanswered. She was dying; and I knew it, though I would not acknowledge the fact. I continued to nurse her as usefully as I could, but the seven-hour working day, with the time spent in travelling to and from the Land Registry, made our domestic arrangements only more of a nightmare. Mother still refused to have women about her; even her sister from Wakefield. Somehow or other my father, Jack and I contrived to run a rota of sick-room

duties, so that Mother was not left for too long alone. But even
a half-hour was too long, and the doctor urged her to let him
send her to hospital. The suggestion made her hysterical and
desperately ill.

Autumn shrank into winter that year with an added touch of
ominous drama. The leaves were no sooner fallen from the
aspen trees than a gang of men arrived, the jerry-builders'
heralds, with saws and axes. The posts at the bottom of the
lane beside our house were taken down, and the Borough
Council began to widen the road while the trees were being
felled and the fence removed. Almost the first traffic round our
house, out to the main road, was to be the funeral procession
carrying my mother to her parents' grave in Highgate Cemetery.

Before that, however, much suffering and an amazing compensation were to come my way.

I was standing at the end of my brother's bed one morning.
We were both cheered because the late autumn sun shone on
the villas opposite, touching them with chrysanthemum tints
of old gold and umber. Mother had responded to this St.
Martin's weather, and was comparatively at ease. Jack lay in
bed with a cold, but this did not deter him. The quilt was
covered with books. I picked up Keats's poems, a little book
bound in red leather.

What followed is impossible to describe. I may compare the
experience with that which swept over me that morning six
years previously at Broadstairs, when again I was looking out
of a window at veteran sunshine, my mind sunk in a fallow
despondency. In my more immediate awareness, I was concerned because I had never known Jack to be ill before. In
contrast with me, who had taken all the epidemics known to
childhood, he had gone through his school life with hardly a
day's absence. He appeared always to be tireless, his neat,
slow-moving frame carrying him without fail to every purpose
of his mind. And it was a resolute, even a ruthless mind, in its
ardent determinations.

But Jack was not a person who would permit anybody to
worry about him. I saw him at that moment, sitting up behind
the breakfast tray which I had brought. He was at work on

some music manuscript, dotting away with a diligence that
excluded all other observation. Mother, in the sick-room across
the landing, was dozing after I had washed her and adminstered
a few cubic feet of oxygen.

I opened the book of poems, and idly began to read the verses
beginning "I stood tiptoe upon a little hill". What followed is
best described by words which I wrote in an Introduction to
a selection of Keats's poems in 1948, some forty years after the
event.

"I recollect still a physical cataclysm that came upon me. A
great flash of light blinded my eyes; a sense of something opening, as it were a parting of clouds. I found that I too was
standing tiptoe, staring up the hill in a sort of agony of
attention, trying to absorb something that had happened to
me. The sound of the aspens, like surf on shingle, came sighing
into my flung-open soul and it was too much for me. I turned
to my brother in my distress, to find him looking at me
curiously, but with an understanding that made the ordeal
more tolerable. The dreadful loneliness of it was shared.
Neither of us said anything. We even looked away from each
other shyly. After a pause, I asked him if I might borrow the
book, and he agreed almost gruffly. That was for me the
beginning of my life in the world of poetry, the world which is
the sunward side, the very reality of our everyday life."

Re-reading that passage six years after it was written, I find
it accurate, though I had set the scene in summer weather,
deceived in my recollection by that gracious morning of
November sunshine. The visitation came after nearly a year
of spiritual dolour. Giving up my plan to become a painter
had not only shaken my self-confidence; it had also robbed me
of any means of expressing myself, of unloading the wealth of
living that poured into me, moment by waking moment.

Suddenly I was armed. Poetry was to be my weapon. The
revelation brought up all the reading I had done since I was
seven years old. I saw a reason in that odd interest in words,
and the sound of words through the music of speech. I now
understood what had attracted my child-mind to the lips of
those two ladies wheeling their bicycles in Battersea Park; an

incident lost in the past, because children know no past. But now it rose to the surface of my mind. The words of Keats's poem became embodied in lip-shapes. I *heard* them in the silence of Jack's room, their syllables falling and rising into rhythms that clustered round the metrical beat of the axe-strokes being laid to the trunks of the aspen trees which I had loved so dearly. So even in this release and triumph there was a fatality, and a dreadful reminder.

The burst of light was followed by an anti-climax; of tears which I tried to conceal from Jack by advancing to the window and pretending to fix my attention upon the outdoor scene. I had the book still in hand, but it was impossible to read more, for I was trembling, and my eyes were blinded.

A few moments of resolute effort enabled me to regain control, except for the lump in my throat. I could say nothing, for I had not yet fully discovered what had happened. I knew that power had returned, to assure me of that early sense of having been selected for some particular destiny. It was a superb illusion, without which no mortal could dare to undertake any lifelong enterprise likely to single him out through suffering, persistence, unrewarded drudgery, and a self-imposed isolation, from his fellow-creatures.

From that time I began to write verse, pouring it out as a kind of hæmorrhage of the mind, sometimes several poems a day. The first piece was called 'Elm-waif'—embodying perhaps that moment of excitement when I leapt along the village street on my way to school, intoxicated by the vision of the autumnal elms scattering their worthless gold so proudly to the winds. There was no headmaster now to caution me against excess.

I sent one of the verses to a Socialist weekly journal called the *Clarion*, and the editor, Robert Blatchford, printed it with the comment that its young author should 'go far'. He did not prophesy how far, or of what advantage such a peripatetic future might be to me. This, my second appearance in print, was a sufficient confirmation of my assurance that I had found my *métier*. All the anger, the guilt, the frustration of the past year disappeared, and I believed that I had taken the place reserved for me among those 'stars of morning' who sang together, in that song of praise which is overheard in every generation, by seers and innocents who believe they have found the key to the secret of the universe.

That first poem 'Elm-waif', written a day or two after my Pauline encounter in my brother's room, was left by me on the blotting-pad in the desk, opposite the pipe organ. Picking it up later, I noticed a comment pencilled in the margin, and a word underlined in the text. I had mis-spelt the elm-tree bole as 'bowl'. Jack had read the poem, and spotted the mistake. His marginal comment was 'Ugh!' This was the first criticism I ever received, as a poet. It has remained one of the most salutary. I have seen in it an admonition to accuracy, to a reverence for tradition and an avoidance of eccentricity. It has helped me to the belief that poetry, and indeed all art, should in its first purpose be a communication, as direct and simple as possible, while carrying the content of the artist's sincere purpose.

This early definition of my principle as a writer has, perhaps, made my work uninteresting to experimentalists, and those critics who have fostered the fashion for puerilism and obscurity in the arts and literature during the second quarter of the twentieth century. To aim at simplicity and a complete candour in poetry is dangerous because it is so proudly ambitious. It demands that self-confidence shall be justified by results, in verse of an authoritative statement that leaves the critics nothing to say, since idiosyncrasy has been purged from the work, so far as this is possible in any artifact by an individual. Obviously, the more concise and crystalline a poem is, without excrescences due to fashion or wilfulness, the more likely it is to survive the criticism of time, that most abrasive of all monitors.

This sounds solemn. A writer's life is not solemn. It is a release, a gaiety, an extravagant claim, even a wantonness. Its immediate effect was to carry me over the grim circumstances of the next year or two, following my mother's death in the April of 1910, two weeks after my seventeenth birthday. It gave me energy and a most resolute purpose, though I was consumed with grief when I found that my self-concerned prayers for Mother's recovery were disregarded. It enabled me to survive the breaking-up of our home and family unity, with Father's second marriage, and the terrifying adventure when Jack and I left the Dulwich house and took rooms in a little house in a street behind Denmark Hill.

By that time, in 1911, Jack was a school-teacher earning £100 a year, and I had passed an examination which made me a permanently established Civil Servant, commencing at £45 a year and rising by annual increments of £5 to a maximum of £150. This I considered (I was then eighteen) sufficient for my purpose. It would supply, for the rest of my life, bread and butter and shelter, so that I could thenceforth give myself wholly to the divine and prophetic vocation of writing poetry, to join the company of immortals.

My life was quickly to supply other contingents which I had not taken into account. After Mother's death, I believed I had done with emotional ties. Jack made no demands upon me, though for the next two years we lived together. He was concentrated on the relationship that led to his marriage in 1913, by which time I was receiving (though not *earning*) £55 a year, and was able to keep three of the four rooms and set up as hermit.

In this I was helped by the fortunate, though chance, choice of our landlord and his wife. They were deeply religious people, the husband an enthusiastic Thomist and Dante scholar. Jack and I had seen these rooms advertised in *Dalton's Weekly*, and they were the only ones which we inspected. We walked innocently from our home to this rather gloomy, nondescript back-street, to find this kind couple who made no objection when we installed the pipe organ and an eight-foot concert grand Erard piano, which my brother had picked up at white-elephant price in exchange for the Klingmann. The floor of our upstairs front sitting-room became saucer-shaped under the weight, and the power of that mighty Erard dislodged slates and set window-frames yawning from several houses up-street.

Our oddity did not disconcert our landlord and landlady. On the contrary, their interest in us was both humorous and considerate. Within a few weeks of our arrival, I was presented

with a copy of Chapman's *Homer*, and shortly after that a copy
of Sir Thomas Browne's *Religio Medici*. Further, when in 1913
I kept the three rooms, my rent was reduced to eight shillings
a week, and my sitting-room redecorated in a cinnamon-
coloured paper most becoming to my habits, since I was
thus enabled to spend my many hours of solitude in a brown
study!

I was then working in the Government Laboratory, on the
top floor of the Custom House in Billingsgate Market, below
London Bridge. This scene, so picturesque, has been fully
described in the first of a trilogy of novels that portrays, amongst
the individual drama, the workings of the British Civil Service,
showing how it is based on the Stoic philosophy. This intention
gave the title of *The Porch* to the first volume, whose success was
aided by the award of the Femina Vie Heureuse Prize.

Fortunately for me, the function of the laboratory was to test
samples of all kinds of imports and exports for duty and rebate
purposes. The discarded samples included much nourishing
food, such as wines and lager-beers, tinned fruits and milk,
biscuits and chocolates, cocoa, coffee, tea, egg-yolk and malt
extract. With these, and the daily purchase of a large bloater
or kipper for twopence, I was able to feed myself during the
two years that I lived alone. It might have gone on quite
serenely, had I not fallen desperately ill, a misadventure that
led to emotional and domestic commitments carrying me outside the bounds of this present story, and severely affecting my
self-dedication as a poet; retarding, but also feeding it with
reality.

During those two years, I had sufficient margin to be able to
buy a tenth-hand Collard & Collard grand piano for £8, after
Jack had removed his two instruments and allowed the sitting-
room floor to bulge back to the horizontal. My instrument was
only a bi-chord, but its gentle voice carried my favourite
Vivaldi, so far as my stiff fingers were able to interpret what I
heard with that inward ear as I studied the scores of the volumes
of music which Jack had allowed to overflow from his huge
collection, when he left me to face the world alone.

To face the world alone! That is a common statement of a

common condition. I did not find it a strange way of life, for during the working day I was in the company of men, chemists and young Excise officers, all of whom were stimulating to my green mind. I made good friends among them, and as a body, from the Chief to my few fellow-clerks, they encouraged me in my belief that I had a vocation in poetry.

My first book of verse was paid for by an officer in the collector's office below stairs (those grim stone stairs down which I floated by levitation every afternoon, as it were on 'wings of song', a poet being, as my hallucination convinced me, a semi-angelic creature with a body, as well as moral laws, of a privileged specific gravity).

A colleague of my own age, who died through overwork while taking an external degree at London University, gave me on my twenty-first birthday a copy of Marlowe's plays, on the fly-leaf of which he had written the following triolet, intended to be prophetic of my future.

> "Though long be the day in breaking,
>   Assured are the golden skies.
>   Unseen is the Sun ready-making,
>   Though long be the day in breaking,
>   And soon the whole Earth will be waking
>   To see the new Splendour arise.
>   —Though long be the day in breaking,
>   Assured are the golden skies."

I have found that daybreak to be even more tardy than was anticipated by the young Excise officer, though I am still looking eastward toward that assured sunrise.

Every night and morning I used as substitute for those hours when an undergraduate at Oxford or Cambridge is secluded in his room. I set myself a routine, getting up at 5 a.m. and reading until 7. The hours at the laboratory were from 9 to 4, and I was thus able to be back in my rooms by 5. For evening after evening I continued my reading until midnight, sometimes having to prevent myself from falling asleep by standing with my back flat against the wall, or, if this did not avail, by gently crushing my foot or hand in the door until the pain dispelled the somnolence of mind and body.

But all this is part of the later story, a prolegomenon to maturity and a life of heavier responsibilities. Between it and that paradisial decade of innocence which opened the twentieth century to me, I can hear still the crunching and stamping of wheels and horses' hooves, as the hearse bearing my mother's body turned from our front door, to be the first vehicle to cross the loose-metalled, newly-making road beside the house, watched reverently, cap in one hand, an axe in the other, by the workmen who were felling the aspen trees and silencing their music, the very voice of the past.